Creolization and Transatlantic Blackness

Departing from more conscribed definitions, this book argues for an expansion of the concept of 'Creolization' in terms of duration, temporality, population, and importantly, in regional scope, which also impact climate and the practices of slavery that are typically included and excluded from consideration.

Eschewing the normative focus on language and music, the authors instead center art and visual, and material cultures, as both outcomes and practices, in their explorations to consider the ways that cultural production in the period of slavery and its aftermath was irrevocably impacted by the collision of races and cultures in the Americas. The chapters probe how creolization unfolded for differently constituted individuals and populations, as well as how it came to be articulated both in the historical moments of its enactment and in its retroactive cultural representations and production. In so doing, they seek to both expand the terrain (literally and figuratively) of the definition of creolization and to turn towards an examination of its relevance for art and visual, and material cultures of the Transatlantic world.

The chapters in this book were originally published in *African and Black Diaspora: An International Journal*.

Charmaine A. Nelson is a Provost Professor of Art History in the History of Art and Architecture Department at the University of Massachusetts Amherst, USA. She is also the Director of the Slavery North Initiative which focuses on the study of Transatlantic Slavery in Canada and the US North. Nelson has made ground-breaking contributions to the fields of the Visual Culture of Slavery, Race and Representation, and Black Canadian Studies. She has published eight books, including *The Color of Stone: Sculpting the Black Female Subject in Nineteenth-Century America* (2007); *Slavery, Geography, and Empire in Nineteenth-Century Marine Landscapes of Montreal and Jamaica* (2016); and *The Precariousness of Freedom: Slave Resistance as Experience, Process, and Representation* (2024).

Creolization and Transatlantic Blackness

The Visual and Material Cultures of Slavery

**Edited by
Charmaine A. Nelson**

LONDON AND NEW YORK

First published 2025
by Routledge
4 Park Square, Milton Park, Abingdon, Oxon, OX14 4RN

and by Routledge
605 Third Avenue, New York, NY 10158

Routledge is an imprint of the Taylor & Francis Group, an informa business

Introduction, Chapters 1 and 4–7 © 2025 Taylor & Francis.

Acknowledgements and Dedication © 2025 Charmaine A. Nelson.

Chapter 2 © 2025 Rach Klein.

Chapter 3 ©2020 by The Wenner-Gren Foundation for Anthropological Research. Originally published In Current Anthropology, University of Chicago Press.

All rights reserved. No part of this book may be reprinted or reproduced or utilised in any form or by any electronic, mechanical, or other means, now known or hereafter invented, including photocopying and recording, or in any information storage or retrieval system, without permission in writing from the publishers.

Trademark notice: Product or corporate names may be trademarks or registered trademarks, and are used only for identification and explanation without intent to infringe.

British Library Cataloguing in Publication Data
A catalogue record for this book is available from the British Library

ISBN13: 978-1-032-41269-6 (hbk)
ISBN13: 978-1-032-41270-2 (pbk)
ISBN13: 978-1-003-35711-7 (ebk)

DOI: 10.4324/9781003357117

Typeset in Times New Roman
by codeMantra

Publisher's Note
The publisher accepts responsibility for any inconsistencies that may have arisen during the conversion of this book from journal articles to book chapters, namely the inclusion of journal terminology.

Disclaimer
Every effort has been made to contact copyright holders for their permission to reprint material in this book. The publishers would be grateful to hear from any copyright holder who is not acknowledged here and will undertake to rectify any errors or omissions in future editions of this book.

To my love, Ellis Maria Ramirez Ortiz

Contents

Citation Information ... ix
Notes on Contributors ... xi
Acknowledgments ... xiii

Introduction: Expanding and Complicating the Concept of Creolization ... 1
CHARMAINE A. NELSON

1 **Blackness and Lines of Beauty in the Eighteenth-Century Anglophone Atlantic World** ... 19
KRISTINA HUANG

2 **"Concatenation": Syncretism in the Life Cycle of David Drake's Earthenware** ... 34
RACH KLEIN

3 **"[A] tone of voice peculiar to New-England": Fugitive Slave Advertisements and the Heterogeneity of Enslaved People of African Descent in Eighteenth-Century Quebec** ... 53
CHARMAINE A. NELSON

4 **Creolization on Screen: Guy Deslauriers' *The Middle Passage* as Afro-Diasporic Discourse [*Le passage du milieu*]** ... 74
SOPHIE SAINT-JUST

5 **Baskets of Rice: Creolization and Material Culture from West Africa to South Carolina's Lowcountry** ... 90
MATTI TURNER

6 **"Wages of Empire": American Inventions of Mixed-Race Identities and Natasha Trethewey's *Thrall* (2012)** ... 105
ELOISA VALENZUELA-MENDOZA

7 **From Raw to Refined: Edouard Duval-Carrié's *Sugar Conventions* (2013)** ... 121
LESLEY A. WOLFF

Index ... 139

Citation Information

This book has been updated. When citing something from this book, please cite the journal articles followed by the book. When citing the journal articles, please use the original page numbering for each article, as follows:

Introduction
Expanding and Complicating the Concept of Creolization
Charmaine A. Nelson
African and Black Diaspora, volume 12, issue 3 (2019)
pp. 267–270

Chapter 1
Blackness and Lines of Beauty in the Eighteenth-Century Anglophone Atlantic World; insert capital letters
Kristina Huang
African and Black Diaspora, volume 12, issue 3 (2019)
pp. 271–286

Chapter 2
'Concatenation': Syncretism in the Life Cycle of David Drake's Earthenware
Rach Klein
previously unpublished

Chapter 3
'[A] tone of voice peculiar to New-England': Fugitive Slave Advertisements and the Heterogeneity of Enslaved People of African Descent in Eighteenth-Century Quebec
Charmaine A. Nelson
Current Anthropology, volume 61, issue 22 (2020)
pp. S303–S316

Chapter 4
Creolization on Screen: Guy Deslauriers' *The Middle Passage* as Afro-Diasporic Discourse [Le passage du milieu]
Sophie Saint-Just
African and Black Diaspora, volume 12, issue 3 (2019)
pp. 287–303

Chapter 5
Baskets of Rice: Creolization and Material Culture from West Africa to South Carolina's Lowcountry
Matti Turner
African and Black Diaspora, volume 12, issue 3 (2019)
pp. 320–336

Chapter 6
'The wages of empire': American Inventions of Mixed-Race Identities and Natasha Trethewey's *Thrall* (2012)
Eloisa Valenzuela-Mendoza
African and Black Diaspora, volume 12, issue 3 (2019)
pp. 337–354

Chapter 7
From Raw to Refined: Edouard Duval-Carrié's *Sugar Conventions* (2013)
Lesley A. Wolff
African and Black Diaspora, volume 12, issue 3 (2019)
pp. 355–374

For any permission-related enquiries please visit:
http://www.tandfonline.com/page/help/permissions

Notes on Contributors

Kristina Huang is Assistant Professor of English at the University of Wisconsin-Madison. She is currently working on her first book manuscript, which develops methods of reading narratives of fugitivity that circulated through abolitionist movements at the turn of the nineteenth century. She is also co-editor with Nicole Aljoe on *The Cambridge Companion to Ignatius Sancho*. Her writings have appeared across scholarly and public venues, including *African and Black Diaspora: An International Journal*; *Eighteenth-Century Fiction*; *Restoration and 18th Century Theatre Research;* *Studies in Romanticism;* *Small Axe Salon;* and the *LA Review of Books*.

Rach Klein is an art historian and artist based in Tiohtià:ke (Montreal, Quebec). They are presently a PhD candidate at McGill, where they are conducting research on early modern feather art and transatlantic avian archives. Rach's doctoral work focuses on migratory remnants, eco-extractivism, and the nuanced power relationships that unfold among more-than-human multispecies encounters. Rach's creative work is similarly preoccupied with birds and mobility, and traverses various mediums to explore the surreal and the sacred, oftentimes through experimental combinations of image/sound/text.

Charmaine A. Nelson is Provost Professor of Art History in the History of Art and Architecture Department at the University of Massachusetts Amherst, USA. She is also the Director of the Slavery North Initiative which focuses on the study of Transatlantic Slavery in Canada and the US North. Nelson has made ground-breaking contributions to the fields of the Visual Culture of Slavery, Race and Representation, and Black Canadian Studies. She has published eight books, including *The Color of Stone: Sculpting the Black Female Subject in Nineteenth-Century America* (2007); *Slavery, Geography, and Empire in Nineteenth-Century Marine Landscapes of Montreal and Jamaica* (2016); and *The Precariousness of Freedom: Slave Resistance as Experience, Process, and Representation* (2024).

Sophie Saint-Just is Assistant Professor of French at Williams College. Her research looks at the filmmaking practices that emerged from Haiti, Guadeloupe, and Martinique and focuses on the ways in which Haitian and French Caribbean collective and individual identities are reframed by the film medium. She is a co-editor of *Raoul Peck: Power, Politics and the Cinematic Imagination* (2015) and translator of a Peck keynote address and of a master class. She has also published on Marie-Claude Pernelle's (2011) film adaptation of Gisèle Pineau's short story "Fichues racines" (2004), Raoul Peck's early fiction film *L'homme sur les quais* (1993) and an article on *La noiraude* (2005), Fabienne and Véronique Kanor's first short fiction film (forthcoming in 2025 in *YFS*). She recently completed a book manuscript on Euzhan Palcy's film *Rue Cases-Nègres* (1983).

xii *Notes on Contributors*

Matti Turner is an independent scholar living in Merville, British Columbia. His chapter comes from his graduate work in the Communication Studies program at McGill University's Department of Art History and Communication Studies. His research interests include political economy, social and environmental history, and science and technology studies. His current research looks at the relationship between political economy and ecological systems in agriculture by applying theories of social reproduction and primitive accumulation to both industrial agriculture and agro-ecology.

Eloisa Valenzuela-Mendoza works as an Academic Advisor for Doctoral Programs in the College of Nursing at the University of Arizona, USA. Her research explores the historical contexts of various literary works and their place within contemporary frameworks of exile and dispossession. She is currently focused on connecting the historical poetics of Joy Harjo and Natasha Trethewey as works that emphasize the impact of historical legacies on lived experience and public memory; ultimately, Harjo and Trethewey challenge traditional views of the archive while demonstrating the art of resilience within the empire of USA.

Lesley A. Wolff, PhD, is Assistant Professor of Art and Design at The University of Tampa, specializing in modern and contemporary global art history and museum studies. Her interdisciplinary research on foodways, heritage, and the visual cultures of the Americas has appeared in various international journals, including *Gender & History* (2022) and *Humanities* (2020). She is co-editor of "Rethinking Contemporary Latin American Art," a special issue of the journal *Arts* (2023), and co-editor of the volume *Nourish and Resist: Food and Feminisms in Contemporary Global Caribbean Art* (2024). Wolff's single-authored book, *Culinary Palettes: The Visuality of Food in Postrevolutionary Mexican Art* (2025), is forthcoming as part of the new book series *Visualidades: Studies in Latin American Visual History*. Wolff is also an active curator committed to revisionist histories of the art of the Americas. Her past exhibitions include *The Kingdom of This World, Reimagined* (2019–2024), *Layered Voices: Process and Paper in Contemporary Native American Art* (2020), *Decolonizing Refinement: Contemporary Pursuits in the Art of Edouard Duval-Carrié* (2018/19), and *As Cosmopolitans and Strangers: Mexican Art of the Jewish Diaspora* (2014), among others.

Acknowledgments

A book is always the manifestation of many contributions. I would first and foremost like to thank the authors who have contributed their important chapters to this book. I am grateful for your brilliance, dedication, and patience. I extend my deepest gratitude to Dr. Fassil Demissie, Professor Emeritus, DePaul University, mentor and friend, for inviting me to guest edit a special issue of *African and Black Diaspora: An International Journal*, of which this book is an expanded version. I am also grateful for the many museums, art galleries, and academic departments who have invited me to present my research in progress as I explored the Canadian and Jamaican fugitive slave archives which were the starting point of my idea for this book. Special thanks are due to Prof. Robin Bernstein and Dr. Linda Schlossberg of Harvard University who welcomed me (through Studies of Women, Gender and Sexuality and the Weatherhead Center for International Affairs) as the William Lyon Mackenzie King Chair of Canadian Studies (2017–2018). It was during that time that I was able to develop and present several lectures which focussed and accelerated my project. My own Chapter 3 was first published in the *Atlantic Slavery and the Making of the Modern World: Experiences, Representations, and Legacies* issue of the journal *Cultural Anthropology* guest edited by Ibrahim Thiaw and Deborah Mack (vol. 61, no. 22, September 2020). I am grateful that they have allowed me to include the work in this collection. Thanks also to my friends and colleagues Dr. Lisa Merrill and Dr. Sirpa Salenius who are a constant source of inspiration, support, and encouragement. My research would not have been possible without a generous Insight Grant from the Social Sciences and Humanities Research Council of Canada (2014–2019) for which I am deeply thankful. Finally, I am grateful to the editors at Routledge for allowing me to revisit this important research.

Introduction
Expanding and Complicating the Concept of Creolization
Charmaine A. Nelson

On June 10, 1776, an enslaved woman named Florimell, described as a "Negro," fled from her enslaver in Halifax, Nova Scotia. Among the various details designed to describe and recapture her, the advertisement noted that "she commonly wears a Handkerchief round her Head" (*Nova Scotia Gazette and Weekly Chronicle* June 18, 1776). On April 29, 1794, an enslaved "NEGRO MAN" who called himself Charles fled from his owner Azariah Pretchard Senior of New Richmond, Quebec who described him in part as "speaks good English and some broken French and Micmac" (*Quebec Gazette* May 22, 1794).[1] Finally, when a man described as a "Negro" named William Spencer busted out of the local Montreal jail in 1792, the jailer Jacob Kuhn described him as wearing, "a round hat and generally a wig" (*Montreal Gazette* November 22, 1792). All three cases are evidence of the multi-directional processes of creolization in the Transatlantic world. Although an often overlooked region of inquiry, these examples pulled from the fugitive slave archive of Canada, expand the traditional limits of the definition and study of creolization.

Florimell's headwrapping indicates the continuation of the West African dress practice in the maritime province of Nova Scotia (Figure 0.1). Combined with what the anonymous enslaver described as her scarred face and her broken English, the three identifiers seem to indicate an African-born woman. English was the dominant European language in Nova Scotia, the one that enslavers forced the enslaved to speak. As such, other than a disability or a deliberate attempt to hide her fluency from her enslaver, Florimell's lack of English suggests a recent arrival and the lack of time to acquire a new language. Although Canadian enslavers documented the scarring of smallpox and other diseases on the bodies of the enslaved in both slave sale and fugitive slave advertisements (for distinct purposes),[2] when combined with her "broken English" and headwrapping, Florimell's facial scars may have been those of the African community-based ritual marking of scarification.

While the concept of creolization can be used to describe and analyze Florimell's retention of African dress practices, Charles' indigenous knowledge expands Sidney Mintz's bimodal definition of creolization to include a third racial population. Although Charles' acquisition of two European languages – English and French – was normal for the enslaved population of Quebec, his ability to communicate in Mi'kmaq – at the time an indigenous language that had yet to be transcribed – indicates his ongoing contact with this population and raises questions about the interaction and community building between black and indigenous people within Quebec Slavery[3] (Figure 0.2). Lastly, William's wig-wearing reminds us that creolization was not simply about the ways that enslaved black people preserved African cultural, material, social, and spiritual practices, but their ingenious adaptation of the European. David Waldstreicher has explained that enslaved black people in the eighteenth-century mid-Atlantic region of the USA "had already learned the trade of wig-dressing, which they employed on themselves as well as on whites of different classes" (Waldstreicher, 1999, 254).

DOI: 10.4324/9781003357117-1

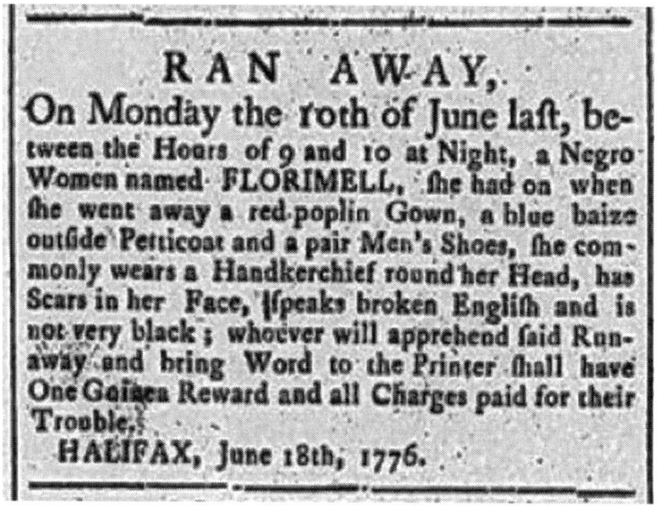

> RAN AWAY,
> On Monday the 10th of June last, between the Hours of 9 and 10 at Night, a Negro Women named FLORIMELL, she had on when she went away a red poplin Gown, a blue baize outside Petticoat and a pair Men's Shoes, she commonly wears a Handkerchief round her Head, has Scars in her Face, speaks broken English and is not very black; whoever will apprehend said Runaway and bring Word to the Printer shall have One Guinea Reward and all Charges paid for their Trouble.
> HALIFAX, June 18th, 1776.

Figure 0.1 Anonymous, "RAN AWAY," *Nova Scotia Gazette and Weekly Chronicle*, June 18, 1776.

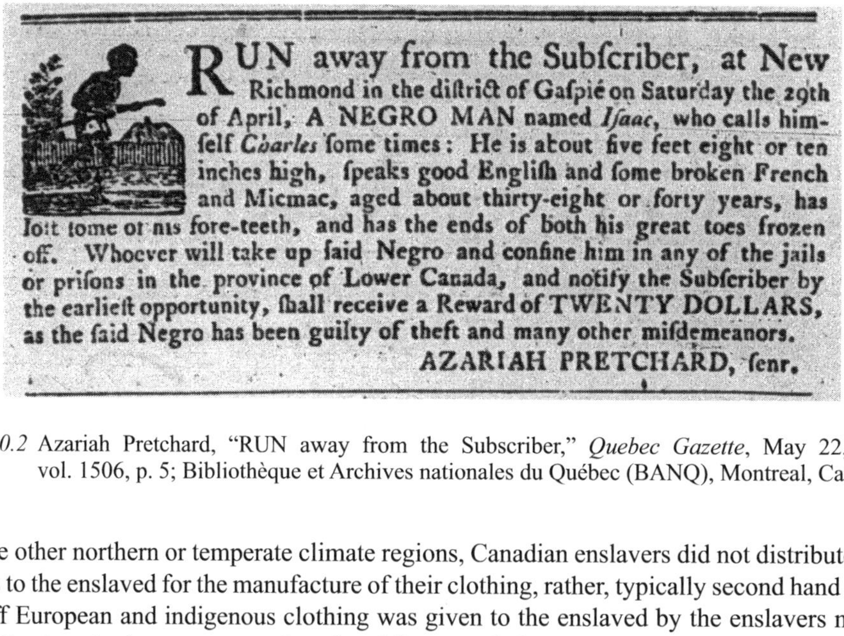

> RUN away from the Subscriber, at New Richmond in the district of Gaspié on Saturday the 29th of April, A NEGRO MAN named *Isaac*, who calls himself *Charles* some times: He is about five feet eight or ten inches high, speaks good English and some broken French and Micmac, aged about thirty-eight or forty years, has lost some of his fore-teeth, and has the ends of both his great toes frozen off. Whoever will take up said Negro and confine him in any of the jails or prisons in the province of Lower Canada, and notify the Subscriber by the earliest opportunity, shall receive a Reward of TWENTY DOLLARS, as the said Negro has been guilty of theft and many other misdemeanors.
> AZARIAH PRETCHARD, senr.

Figure 0.2 Azariah Pretchard, "RUN away from the Subscriber," *Quebec Gazette*, May 22, 1794, vol. 1506, p. 5; Bibliothèque et Archives nationales du Québec (BANQ), Montreal, Canada.

Like other northern or temperate climate regions, Canadian enslavers did not distribute cloth rations to the enslaved for the manufacture of their clothing, rather, typically second hand or old, cast off European and indigenous clothing was given to the enslaved by the enslavers making the distinctions in dress across enslaved and free populations a matter of the condition and not necessarily the type of garments worn. The circulation of wigs, a part of this colonial dress trade, was of importance to the enslaved for their own self-care and adornment practices, and also for their attempts at resistance through flight in a world where enslavers customarily described the hair color, texture, and style of the enslaved fugitive (White and White, 1995, 50; Waldstreicher, 1999, 254).

William's wig-wearing and preferred styling was not necessarily an attempt at cultural accommodation, a valorization of European styles (Figure 0.3). Two key factors must be considered. First, the symbolic power of wigs, their association with middle or upper class manhood,

> Montreal, 20th November 1792.
>
> BROKE Goal and escaped on Sunday the 18th instant, about eight o'Clock in the evening, WILLIAM SPENCER, a Negro, charged with petty larceny; he is about five feet and six inches high, well made, and wore a short blue Jacket, and red waistcoat, black breeches, a round hat and generally a wig.   JACOB KUHN. *Goaler.*
>
> All Officers of Militia in the country, as well as all other H.s Majesty's subjects, are hereby required to use their utmost diligence in apprehending the said criminal and to lodge him in any of the goals of this Province, the respective keepers whereof are hereby required to receive the said WILLIAM SPENCER into their custody and him safely keep until he shall be discharged by due course of law; and as a further encouragement a reward of four dollars and all reasonable charges shall be paid on the criminal being committed to any of the said Goals, by
>
>   EDW. WM: GRAY *Sheriff.*

Figure 0.3 Edw. Wm. Gray and Jacob Kuhn, "BROKE Goal and escaped," *Montreal Gazette,* November 22, 1792, vol. xlviii. p. 3; Bibliothèque et Archives nationales du Québec (BANQ), Montreal, Canada.

made them a vehicle of class mobility. When Devereux Jarratt, an eighteenth-century white Virginian man of humble origins, recalled his attempts at trying to improve his appearance in preparation for an interview for a schoolmaster position, he told of acquiring an old wig so that he could "appear something more than common" (Kasson, 1990, 26–27; cited in White and White, 1995, 61). Significantly, Devereux had purchased the wig from an enslaved man who he assumed had inherited it as a slave owner's hand-me-down (White and White, 1995, 61). But while for Devereux the wig facilitated his attempt to look middle class, was the goal the same for William? Although named as a "Negro" in the Montreal jailer Jacob Kuhn's fugitive notice, Kuhn did not explicitly describe William as a "slave" (*Montreal Gazette* November 22, 1792).

Thus, while free black males in Quebec may have used wigs, like the free white Devereux, to dispel the assumption of their "commonness," enslaved black males likely used them to attempt to free themselves of the social stigma of bondage altogether. But seeking to look above one's station was also dangerous for black people and living in a society where slavery was legal meant that whites felt emboldened to accost and detain black people at will. As Waldstreicher relates, a New Brunswick, New Jersey jailer placed an advertisement in a New York newspaper notifying the public that he had locked up two black men who raised his suspicions because they were wearing "fine clothing." Although the two claimed that their Caribbean enslaver had died, their words were not enough and the jailer appealed for the slave owner, his heirs, or others to come forward with evidence of their status (Waldstreicher, 1999, 253).

Second, William's wig-wearing may have accommodated and/or resisted European and Euro-American styling practices. On a basic level, the hair texture of black Africans – tightly coiled, fine, and dense – created sculptural possibilities in styling that easily allowed black people to mimic and even surpass the design and manipulation of eighteenth-century wigs with their own hair. Indeed, as White and White have explained, "What appears to have happened quite often, however, was that slaves styled their hair to resemble the wigs worn by members of the dominant caste" (White and White, 1995, 62). However, William's hair color (as that of his fellow free and enslaved black community) likely brown or black, was not by European standards, the right color (white or light) to appear wig-like. Therefore, we should contemplate the style, color, and condition of William's wig in relation to his own hair length, style, texture, and color and his personal desire for a specific aesthetic look and even a potential social goal.

Defining Creolization

Often defined as a uniquely American (continental) phenomenon, creolization describes the processes and outcomes of cultural and social contact and transformation that occurred within the overlapping contexts of European imperialism and Transatlantic Slavery. While scholars like Sidney Mintz offered a rather constrained definition, bound by time and location, others like Linda M. Rupert have provided a more expansive description which allows for the possibility of different stages of creolization unfolding over time. For Mintz, creolization was a discrete seventeenth-century phenomenon lasting about a half a century and being characterized by the "plantation thrust" through which the "first large introductions of enslaved Africans were occurring" (2008, 255). Creolization for Mintz then is not merely the meeting of two races or cultures, but a meeting within the context of slavery wherein the majority population was not only African, but also enslaved.[4] His focus on specific Caribbean islands, ones where genocidal practices had led to the extermination of indigenous peoples – also allowed him to overlook their role in what in many regions became a three-way creolization process. Therefore, for Mintz, creolization could only develop from the initial interactions between two *newly introduced* foreign populations – European and African, only take place in tropical plantation regimes, and only involve slave majority populations. Mintz's definition was also logocentric, privileging the emergence of Creole languages – what he called languages of work, trade, or pidgins – as the heart of his investigations. Indeed, he argued that "The sociological importance of these languages is exemplary. I think they are the best example we have of the process of creolization. They were languages of slaves, in some kinds of interaction with non-slaves" (2008, 256).

Although I in no way wish to diminish Mintz's recognition of the central significance of language, overall, delimiting his definition in such a way also imposed boundaries and value judgments on the nature of slave life, social formation, and material culture that was deemed to emerge in his chosen contexts and additionally, his temporal, climatic, social, and durational parameters excluded certain practices, customs, social formations, and cultural outcomes. For instance, since the slave majorities that typically emerged within tropical contexts like the Caribbean were normally rural or plantation based, the type of emerging creole cultural and material forms that were more common in northern/temperate climate, urban-dominated, slave minority societies would fall off the radar of this curtailed definition of creolization. Furthermore, these same sites, like Canada, where groups of enslaved black Creoles typically met and interacted with other black Creoles are also excluded. So what blind spots might such a dedicated focus have produced? What other forms of communal cross-cultural work bear the evidence of creolization and merit our scholarly attention?

Congo Square, New Orleans

I turn to Congo Square, New Orleans, where for decades, white observers and interlopers tried to grasp the extraordinary cultural, economic, musical, and social phenomenon which unfolded between the members of the significant African-born enslaved populations of the city.[5] Originally the site of a French fort constructed in 1758, under the Spanish and Americans, by the end of the eighteenth century and into the nineteenth, the public space had become a place of routine large social and cultural gatherings where hundreds of enslaved blacks congregated on Sundays to engage in singing, dancing, instrumentation, and economic exchanges, all under the invasive gaze of white locals and tourists. In the latter category, the English architect Benjamin Latrobe took detailed and meticulous notes about what he witnessed. A British transplant to the American North, Latrobe's subsequent experience in a slave-dominated southern society must have been, at least initially, disconcerting, especially in terms of the sheer number of enslaved people that he encountered. For my purposes, among his most compelling insights was Latrobe's recounting of witnessing a gathering of five to six hundred darked skinned or unmixed black people ("I did not observe a dozen yellow faces") in Congo Square dancing in circular rings which they defined by "African nationalities or cultural groups" (Donaldson, 1984, 65). As another observer recalled, writing nostalgically decades after the events,

> [O]n a Sunday afternoon ... not less than two or three thousand people would congregate there to see the dusky dancers. About three o'clock the negroes began to gather; each nation taking their places in different parts of the square. The Minahs would not dance near the Congos, nor the Mandringos near the Gangas (sic).
> (*Daily Picayune*, October 12, 1879, cited in Donaldson, 1984, 66)

Taken together these observations are profound. In the less socially restrictive atmosphere of New Orleans, the enslaved, mainly it would appear (by complexion and cultural knowledge) African-born, were allowed to gather in large numbers, a permission they seized upon to create a vibrant social and cultural force through which they remembered, practiced, and ethnically-demarcated their music, dance, singing, and food cultures. If those assembled still recalled who was Mandringo and who Gangas, and even remembered their ethnic animosities, then of course, language too as well as the visual assessment of the corporeal (biological and cultural) symbols of their ethnicities was a part of these interactions and perceptions. But astoundingly what becomes clear as well is that the size of the African-born, unmixed enslaved population and their ability to congregate across households and plantations allowed them to slow the process of their creolization even as their retention of African culture was actualized under the invasive gaze of the white audience. It was the ability, for example, of the individual Gangas enslaved person to leave their specific household in New Orleans, and in Congo Square, to know that they would encounter a Gangas community that also allowed them to preserve their Gangas linguistic and cultural practices on Sundays even if their enslaver's household was bereft of other Gangas. Therefore, the pidgin that emerged within these slave owning households – Mintz's work languages – did not necessarily overcome and replace (at least not immediately) the fully formed ancient languages of Africa which the African-born had brought with them on the slave ships to New Orleans. Or rather, the work languages that the enslaved *had to use* within the enslaver's household or plantation precisely because they were surrounded by people from other ethnicities, could be dispensed with on Sundays at Congo Square. But the implications of Congo Square of course transcend language and enter the realm of the material and the visual, the focus of this book.

The memory of ethnic specificity, and animosity (who would they not dance near), may also reveal a delay in the production of enslaved solidarity in terms of resistance across ethnicity within and across enslaver households and plantations. But it also signals the ways that the actual cultural practices of lyric creation and singing, instrumental music, and dancing were being preserved as ethnically-specific. The permissiveness of New Orleans meant that the gathered hundreds or thousands laid claim to an active public memory of cultural practice and performance that was, in the late eighteenth and early nineteenth centuries, not yet creolized. Instrument-making was also a part of this preservation. Latrobe noted the attention to detail of a carving on a finger board of an African instrument, "the rude figure of a man in a sitting posture" (1984, 65). What is astounding is that in the physically and mentally brutal and exhausting world of the enslaved, the presumed owner of the instrument, the person Latrobe described as "a very little old man, apparently eighty or ninety years old," (1984, 65) had at some time in his life expended the extra mental and physical energy not merely to make the instrument from

6 *Charmaine A. Nelson*

a calabash, *but to adorn it*. What did that figure look like? What symbolic meanings did it bear? What knowledge of the man's specific African ethnicity was inscribed onto what appears to have been his prized possession?

Joe: Quebec City

Just as sites like Congo Square seemed to extend and slow the process of creolization, places where enslavers prohibited opportunity for enslaved congregation and where the enslaved were in the minority seemed to have accelerated it. The life and experience of the enslaved man known as Joe in Quebec City serve to highlight this point. Joe's life was documented far beyond the norm for an enslaved person, in an extraordinary set of six fugitive slave advertisement for five flights across nine years, from 1777 to 1786 (Mackey, 2010, 319, 320, 321, 322, 328, 329). Although owned by the business partners, co-owners, and co-founders of the *Quebec Gazette*, William Brown and Thomas Gilmore, it was Brown (five advertisements) and the local sheriff, James Shepherd (one advertisement) who advertised for Joe's return, in the wake of Gilmore's premature death in 1773. Brown's rather meticulous notation of Joe's age, height, health, dress, language acquisition, and labor offer an assessment of Joe's adaptation to life in the British colony after his forced arrival. Profoundly too, all of Brown's advertisements for Joe proclaim his African birth.

African-born people in Quebec and the rest of Canada were a minority within a minority. Data collected from Quebec fugitive slave advertisements that routinely included a place of birth or previous residence indicate that the enslaved black community was mainly comprised of Creoles (people born in the Americas) including African Canadian, African American, African Caribbean (mainly Anglo- and Franco-), and others (see Nelson Chapter 3). Therefore, Joe's forced migration to Quebec City – one of at least two migrations away from Africa – placed him at an extreme disadvantage to be able to remember, preserve, and practice his ethnically-specific African cultures, languages, and spirituality.[6] There was no Congo Square equivalent in Canada, both in terms of the sheer size of the enslaved populations and in terms of the potential for congregation across distinct African nationalities.[7]

What Brown's fugitive advertisements instead document is Joe's forcible movement toward European cultural acquisition, in dress, language, and labor (Figure 0.4). As Joe aged, the Gazette's readers were witness to his transformation. In the first notice, Joe was described by Brown as "a Negro Lad ... about twenty years of age, about five feet and an half high," who spoke "English and French tolerably" (*Quebec Gazette* November 27, 1777) and in the last notice as a "NEGRO MAN SLAVE ... twenty-six years of age, about five feet seven inches high ... speaks English and French fluently" (*Quebec Gazette* May 4, 1786) (Figure 0.5). Every notice placed by Brown described Joe as "born in Africa," and while the first notice gave no indication of the labor that Brown and Gilmore stole from Joe who repeatedly fled from the printing office, in the last notice astoundingly, Brown claimed that Joe was "by trade a Pressman." Brown, therefore, not only documented Joe's transition from early adulthood to manhood, his aging and physical growth of almost seven inches, but his forced language acquisition and literacy in not one but two European languages and his journey from beginner to fluency.

In a world where enslavers spent considerable energy ensuring that enslaved people were barred from access to literacy, Joe's forced literacy was extraordinary. What is more, Joe's literacy as a vehicle for his labor in the printing office had always been a calculation of Brown and Gilmore. A letter dated April 29, 1768 from the pair to their mentor and former employer William Dunlap explained, "we are at last come to a resolution of trying to get a Negro Boy, wherefore we beg you will endeavour to purchase one for us ... between 15 and 20 years of age, fit to put each other in the public declarations of their loyalty.

ADVERTISEMENTS.

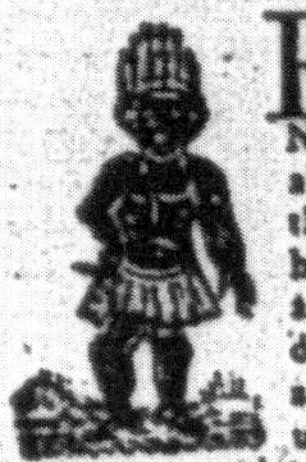

RANAWAY from the Printing-office in QUEBEC, on Saturday evening the twenty-ſecond inſtant, A Negro Lad named JOE, born in Africa, about twenty years of age, about five feet and an half high, full round fac'd, a little marked with the ſmall-pox, ſpeaks Engliſh and French tolerably; he had on when he went away an old green fur-cap, an old ſky-blue broad-cloth coat, an old grey ratteen jacket, leather breeches, brown leggings and Canadian macaſſins. All perſons are hereby forewarned from harbouring or aiding him to eſcape, as they may depend on being proſecuted to the utmoſt rigour of the Law, and whoever will give information where he is harboured, or bring him back, ſhall have FOUR DOLLARS Reward from THE PRINTER.

IL s'eſt évadé de l'Imprimerie à Québec; Samedi 22 du courant au ſoir, un Garçon Negre nommé JOE, né en Afrique, agé d'environ vingt ans, de la taille d'environ cinq pieds et demi, le viſage rond et plein, un peu marqué de la petite verole, il parle paſſablement Anglois et François; il portoit quand il s'eſt évadé un Caſque vert, un vieux Habit de drap fin bleu-céleste, une vieille Veſte de ratine griſe, des Culottes de cuir, des Mitaſſes vinées et des Souliers Sauvages. Il eſt défendu à toutes perſonnes de le retirer ou de l'aider à s'évader, vû qu'elles ſeront pourſuivies ſelon toute la rigueur des Loix, et quiconque l'arrêtera et le ramenera, recevera QUATRE PIASTRES de recompenſe de L'IMPRIMEUR.

ALL Perſons indebted to the Eſtate of *William*

Figure 0.4 William Brown (THE PRINTER), "RANAWAY from the Printing-office," *Quebec Gazette*, November 27, 1777, vol. 639, p. 3; Bibliothèque et Archives nationales du Québec (BANQ), Montreal, Canada.

ADVERTISEMENTS.

PRINTING-OFFICE, *Quebec*, 1ſt *May*, 1786.

BROKE out of His Majeſty's Gaol in Quebec, on Saturday morning the 18th of February laſt, A NEGRO MAN SLAVE named JOE, born in Africa, twenty-ſix years of age, about five feet ſeven inches high, a little pitted with the ſmall-pox, has ſeveral ſcars on his legs, ſpeaks Engliſh and French fluently, and is by trade a Preſſman; he had on him when he broke out a blue great coat, a red out-ſide jacket, a white under jacket, and round hat. He was ſeen ſome time ago in the pariſh of l'Ange Gardien below the falls of Montmorency. All perſons are hereby forewarned from harbouring or aiding him to eſcape, as they may depend on being proſecuted to the utmoſt rigor of the Law; and whoever will give information where he is harboured, ſo as that he may be had again, ſhall receive THREE GUINEAS Reward from the PRINTER of this GAZETTE.

Figure 0.5 William Brown (PRINTER of this GAZETTE), "BROKE out of His Majesty's Gaol." *Quebec Gazette*. May 4, 1786, vol. 1081. p. 3; Bibliothèque et Archives nationales du Québec (BANQ), Montreal, Canada.

to press" (Brown and Gilmore, 1768). Although the fugitive slave advertisements printed for Joe clearly declared his African birth, it would appear that this was never the pair's intention. Indeed, their letter specified their desire for Dunlap to send them a "County born" or Creole enslaved male who had survived the smallpox and "can be recommended for his Honesty" (Brown and Gilmore, 1768). The bluntness of their letter positions the prospective enslaved

8 *Charmaine A. Nelson*

black male as a product they were ordering for which they could define *its* specification according to *their* needs. Their desire that this "Negro Boy" be Creole speaks to their alignment with other enslavers across the Americas who assumed that African-born people – who often had a memory of freedom – would be more resistant. But for my purposes, Joe's African-ness was at least initially at cross-purposes to their intended exploitation of him in their printing office and necessitated what was most likely a very deliberate and aggressive technical and linguistic training to make him "fit to put to press," one that likely subsumed him in various forms of European and Euro-Canadian culture and society. As an African-born male whose linguistic journey presumably initially included no European languages, this could not have been easy. Compared to the African-born enslaved people at Congo Square, Joe's life demonstrates an accelerated creolization under the pressure of Brown's and Gilmore's economic and cultural imperatives, a creolization that we can literally trace in the advertisements that Brown placed to recapture him. To my earlier point about Charles, Joe's creolization in Quebec also included his contact with indigenous people and culture since Brown recalled that Joe fled wearing indigenous footwear, "Canadian macassins" (sic) (*Quebec Gazette* November 27, 1777).[8]

Expanding the Terrain of Creolization

Due to their climates, the practices of slavery, the makeup of their enslaved populations, and the ratio of the enslaved to enslavers, Canada, the American North, and Argentina (among other places) would not fit Mintz's definition of creolization. What is more, for Mintz, once one or more generations of these newcomers had already experienced this "cultural blending and biological blending," the term creolization no longer applied (2008, 254). To be clear, Mintz plainly stated that his interest was in understanding "what the *original* process of creolization was" (emphasis added, 2008, 254). But if the heart of his definition is drawn out – the cross-cultural and cross-racial interaction between enslavers and the enslaved which resulted both in new institutions and new cultural forms – creolization could indeed be said to have transpired in both non-tropical and non-plantation contexts, some of which were home to slave minority populations. An expanded notion of creolization must also contend with the presence – as ghosts, or as colonized or enslaved people – of indigenous peoples, who, in sites like British Quebec, were enslaved alongside people of African descent (hence Charles' knowledge of the Mi'kmaq language). It is this expansion and rethinking of creolization that the assembled chapters undertake, not only in the realms of location, population, and climate but also in notions of duration, speed, process, and outcomes across the visual and material cultures to which each chapter turns. I begin a consideration of some of these elements in this introduction.

Regarding duration and speed, the nature of enslavement for the enslaved African-born man Joe led to a compressed period of creolization documented in William Brown's fugitive slave advertisements, which demonstrate Joe's accelerated European language acquisition, underpinned by his exploitation as a laborer in Brown's printing office. The language skills that were typically attained by enslaved people across generations – or not at all given that Joe's linguistic abilities transcended the realm of everyday spoken English or French in Quebec and also that he was, unlike most enslaved people, most likely literate – were forced upon Joe within a restricted timeframe starting in 1768. Location too needs to be further complicated. As my discussion of Joe's enslavement in Quebec and the congregation of enslaved people in New Orleans' Congo Square reveals, enslaved majorities typically enslaved in semi-tropical or tropical plantation contexts, contained more African-born people and accessed greater opportunities to assemble with people from their own ethnic or national origins either on or off the plantation. Comparatively, the largely urban enslavement of enslaved black minorities in places like Quebec was dominated by black

Figure 0.6 J.C.Stadler after George Heriot, "Minuets of the Canadians," from travels through the Canadas, containing a description of the Picturesque Scenery on some of the rivers and lakes; with an account of the Productions, Commerce, and Inhabitants of those Provinces. To which is subjoined a comparative view of the manners and customs of several of the Indian Nations of North and South America. London: Printed for Richard Phillips, No. 6, Bridge-Street, Blackfriars. 1807. Engraving, 23 × 36.7 cm, M19871, McCord Museum, Montreal.

Creoles who, typically forced to live within the homes or in a lesser building on the properties of their enslavers (like a cabin or barn), suffered under the weight of a heightened enslaver and white community surveillance and were faced with far fewer opportunities to congregate away from white surveillance. As regards population and process, if allowed to congregate, the numbers of enslaved people in Quebec could never have matched that of New Orleans' Congo Square, and the process of creolization would have been severely transformed since any congregations in Quebec would have been dominated by black Creoles and could not have centered to the same extent ethnically-specific African practices, since African-born people like Joe were a minority within the slave minority. Of course, the location and the climate had much to do with why such dramatic differences occurred across these sites.

The Scottish itinerant artist George Heriot's print *Minuets of the Canadians* (1807)[9] – one of twenty-eight published in his book entitled *Travels through the Canadas ...* (1807)[10] – is suggestive of the nature of black congregation and cultural creolization in the province of Quebec (Figure 0.6). As the title indicates, Heriot's print depicts a gathering of white men, women, and children at a dance where the minuet was being performed. The gathering also included at least three musicians at the left side: a standing white male in a coat and plumed hat shakes a tambourine above his head, a seated white male in a coat plays a fiddle, and a standing black male in a rather busy-looking horizontally striped jacket and vertically striped pants plays another tambourine, but with his foot. Two other black men are also depicted at either side of the tambourine-playing black man, but they are seen only from the shoulders or head upward, also on the left side of the print. Given that slavery was not abolished in Quebec until 1834 (alongside the other regions which were to become Canada) through an act of the British parliament in London, UK, the date of the print and the historical enslavement of people of African descent in Quebec (which dates back to the early seventeenth century), it is not inappropriate to assume that the trio of black men was enslaved, or perhaps formerly so. The racially diverse band of musicians which included the black tambourine player who Heriot alone raised above the crowd of revelers hints at the creolization of black slave music in Quebec which likely included both European and indigenous influences, since, although not pictured in Heriot's rendering, the latter group were the fellow bondspeople of enslaved blacks in Quebec.

The tambourine, also known as a toombah or tabor,[11] was a staple instrument in the African musical cultures of enslaved blacks in the Caribbean. In the gatherings of enslaved blacks in slave majority sites, whites often watched but did not customarily, as seen in Heriot's Quebec print, participate with enslaved black musicians.[12] Therefore, although much more evidence needs yet to be discovered, we can surmise that the African musical cultures of the enslaved in Quebec experienced an accelerated creolization due to the small size of the enslaved population, the difficulties in congregation free from white surveillance, and the need for cultural cooperation across multiple racial and ethnic groups that resulted in distinct outcomes which demonstrate my conceptualization of the tripartite nature of creolization – black, indigenous, and white – under Quebec Slavery. The climate with its dramatic seasonal changes and the nature of enslavement in Quebec also meant that opportunities to gather to play music, dance, and sing would also have been driven indoors (as Heriot's gathering represents) for much of the year. Thus, since the opportunity to gather in the fall and winter was limited to places which could provide protection from cold, ice, and snow, and such places would typically be residences of which enslaved and many free blacks were not proprietors, the opportunity for independent black congregation was severely diminished.

I would like to advance a definition of creolization that accommodates the interaction between different groups of enslaved people of African descent – the newly arriving African-born and the Creole or American-born (continental) populations. In places like Canada where slave ships did not arrive directly from Africa, African-born people like Joe were a minority within a minority. In Quebec City, Joe was forced to live within an urban environment where the dominant population of enslaved people was indigenous. Of the black people held in bondage, the majority were Creole, African American, African Canadian, African Caribbean, and others. In such a context, the cultural contact and transformation took place not between whites and newly arriving African-born people disembarking from slave ships that had been loaded with enslaved "cargo" on the west coast of Africa, but instead with enslaved black Creoles who arrived at Canadian ports predominantly through overland travel from the USA and on merchant ships from the Caribbean. The processes of intra-community creolization would also have differed. Whereas the continuing arrival of slave ships in a place like Jamaica meant that people of various African ethnicities routinely mixed with Jamaican and other Caribbean-born blacks, in Canada, this mixing was predominantly between different black Creole populations. What did slave culture as dress, music, singing, dance, economy, food, language, and spirituality become when these various populations met and interacted across the waves of newly arriving enslaved people and the generations of newly-born enslaved children? How was memory activated to preserve specific ethnic or national African practices when the majority of enslaved people were not themselves African-born and those who were, were largely outnumbered?

Creolization impacted the white colonialist and enslaver, as well as the colonized and enslaved. However, the why's and how's are critical. Whereas most whites, especially the elite, had the ability and power to decide which aspects of African and indigenous cultures they

Introduction: Expanding and Complicating the Concept 11

wished to appropriate or adopt, enslaved blacks did not.[13] Popular class whites like indentured servants, also experienced creolization, but with less choice than wealthy whites. Hilary McD. Beckles explains how Irish women in Barbados took to carrying loads on their heads and strapping their children to their backs in the African tradition (Beckles, 2000, 737). This cultural transfer was in part consolidated through the initial presence of Irish indentured servants alongside Africans in the sugar cane fields and the Irish female participation in the African-dominated practice of economic market practices called huckstering (Beckles, 2000).

In comparison, for the enslaved, creolization happened under duress, through the prohibitions placed on expressive cultures like music, song, and dance, through the illegality of literacy, through strategic deprivations like food rations and through impositions like the widespread distribution of osnaburgh fabric for clothing.[14] Therefore, for the enslaved, any discussion of creolization must necessarily engage with ideals of cultural preservation as much as transformation and loss; the loss of the actual African practices as well as the loss of the knowledge of how or why a practice was undertaken in the first place (Mintz 2008, 258).

Building upon Rupert's and Mintz's definitions, I would like to consider creolization as a layered process that unfolded across time and that changed, perhaps drastically, from its first to its latter incarnations. While the earliest forms of creolization entailed so-called pure Europeans and Africans, later cycles would have seen the interaction of Creoles and already creolized local populations with multiple streams of new arrivals; again Europeans and Africans from their respective continents as well as European Americans and African Americans (continental); those whites and blacks who were Creoles from other places. As Rupert has argued,

> As to the question of African retentions versus new cultural creations, I am most persuaded by the interpretations that present both as occurring along a continuum, as well as being time and place specific, dichotomies rather than absolutes. In many places, cultural practices from across the Atlantic (European as well as African) were retained as well as adapted, even while new ones were being created. A broad definition of creolization allows for all these possibilities.
>
> (2012, 6)

Indeed, once an already creolized society or population had developed in a given region, the slave ships did not stop coming. In British Jamaica for instance, the slave ships kept arriving well after the seventeenth century with newly enslaved Africans until the abolition of the slave trade in 1807. After 1807, enslavers came to rely increasingly upon practices of "breeding" and an inter-island slave trade (Richardson 1983, 76) to furnish new enslaved laborers. Meanwhile, as I explore in Chapter 3, in the parts of British North America that would become Canada, one hallmark of the enslaved population may be its extraordinary heterogeneity, especially in British Quebec. Quebec's post-conquest enslaved black community (1760–1834) included, at least, African Canadian, African American, African Caribbean (mainly from French *and* British colonized islands) and African-born people who, besides English and French, spoke at a minimum, Dutch, Earse, German, Spanish, and Mi'kmaq (Mackey 2010, 307–340). This expanded definition also allows for the push and pull and back and forth of creolization, while enfolding Creoles of various races into the process. As such, Florimell's headwrap, Charles' acquisition of Mi'kmaq and William's wig-wearing – the retention of African dress practices, the acquisition of indigenous languages, and the adoption and adaptation of European self-care practices, *in Canada* – would all be considered examples of creolization.

Throughout this introduction, my choice of cultural examples of creolization within the context of slave advertisements was deliberate. Particularly, Florimell and William are reflective of my intentions for this book. In my readings of the literature of creolization, I have been struck by the over-emphasis on certain forms of culture as the measure of this process, mainly language and music. This focus on certain forms of culture has led to an under-examination of the role of creolization in the Transatlantic art and visual and material cultures of people of African descent. This book seeks to help fill that gap. The assembled chapters span centuries, regions, and materials, but coalesce in their concentration on the role of creolization as process and outcome in the art and visual and material cultures of the Black Diaspora. Diversity of media is also represented in explorations of creolization in letter-writing, pottery-making, cinema, rice culture, poetry, and casta painting, the print culture of fugitive slave advertisements, and contemporary art. Together the authors also address the concept of creolization in various regions of the Transatlantic world, some through more typical and well-studied sites like Lesley A. Wolff's exploration of the Haitian contemporary artist Edouard Duval-Carrié's *Sugar Conventions* (2013) or the South Carolinian earthenware of enslaved potter Dave, and others less well known like my own excavation of fugitive slave advertisements in Quebec for signs of enslaved ethnicity and birth origin or siteless contexts like Sophie Saint-Just's analysis of Guy Deslauriers' film *The Middle Passage* as African Diasporic Discourse [*Le passage du milieu*] (2001/1999) that takes us back to the slave trade and the Atlantic Ocean as terrifying conduit and graveyard. But even the seemingly normal regional choices of sites of tropical or semi-tropical slavery are undone by the nature of the art and cultural objects that the collected chapters center in our shared contemplation of the processes and outcomes of creolization.

The Chapters

In Chapter 1, "Blackness and Lines of Beauty in the Eighteenth-Century Anglophone Atlantic World," Kristina Huang examines the cultural and economic activities of Ignatius Sancho. Initially enslaved in his native Africa, Sancho was transported to Greenwich, UK where he escaped his first enslavers and joined the Montagu household, atypically a place in which he was encouraged and supported in his education.[15] In this instance, creolization can be interpreted as both the terrain of Sancho's life as an enslaved black man in London, UK and as the process, practice, and art of his writing. Instead of Mintz's "plantation thrust," unlike the majority of his fellow enslaved Africans, Sancho was forced into contact with whites *in* Europe, and not in the mutually foreign territory of the Caribbean. Like Joe in Quebec City, Sancho was utterly outnumbered, an eighteenth-century African man who, born free, was enslaved and eventually became, against the odds, literate in a European language. But unlike Joe, the leniency and encouragement of the Montagus provided him with the space, means, and time to leave traces of his own life. Juxtaposing Sancho's personal correspondence – in an age where private letters were publicly consumed – with his work as a London grocer, Huang positions both activities within an eighteenth-century society in which an imperial archive of stereotypical representations of blackness proliferated alongside an emerging counter-archive of black writing in the British metropole. How did Sancho's literary (self)representation resist the early modern visual climate of blackness produced in the slave-majority, plantation contexts of the Anglophone Caribbean? By centering the chapter in eighteenth-century London, Huang challenges the *where* of creolization for an African-born, formerly enslaved man whose writing "amplified literary production as a mode for shifting the optics of blackness in the eighteenth century."

In Chapter 2, we travel from Britain to the USA where Rach Klein explores the cultural production of the enslaved master potter David Drake. Nineteenth-century Edgefield, South Carolina came to be informally known as Pottersville, due to the staggering output of thousands of earthenware vessels that were produced in the region. Among the local potters were enslaved people of African descent like Dave who created functional vessels which were mainly created for use on local and regional plantations. Extraordinarily again Dave, like Joe and Sancho, was literate and took to inscribing his pottery with poetic couplets. Why his white enslavers allowed him to do so in a world where the illiteracy of the enslaved was typically violently enforced is not known. Regardless, the result is that unlike most of the pottery produced by enslaved laborers in the region, Dave's signed and engraved work has escaped anonymity. Klein's chapter explores the earthenware pottery of Edgefield as "material manifestations of the complex labour, creativity, craftsmanship and resilience of dozens of enslaved people." Also pushing against the bimodal delineation of creolization, Klein argues that Dave's pottery sits at the intersection of European, Asian, and African traditions and cultural practices; the first dimension defined as the slave owning, Scottish American Landrums, the second as the Chinese dragon kiln technologies in which skilled potters like Dave were trained, and the third as the labor and creativity of the enslaved African and African Creole potters. Klein contends that the earthenware objects of Edgefield were a creolized product of these interconnected systems of labor, technology, and artisanship produced by the enslaved artists who worked under duress as the "property" owned by the Landrum family. Drawing upon Édouard Glissant's *Poetics of Relation* (1993), Klein uses his concept of relation through which identities in contact are not diluted, but extended with often unpredictable results.

Chapter 3 moves from pottery to print culture as I explore the understudied archive of Canadian fugitive slave advertisement in "'[A] tone of voice peculiar to New-England': Fugitive Slave Advertisements and the Heterogeneity of Enslaved People of African Descent in Eighteenth-Century Quebec." That fugitive slave notices proliferated across the Americas everywhere that slavery met the printing press is a demonstration of the ubiquity of African resistance to slavery. As objects, they are complex; simultaneously hopeful in their documentation of black resistance and resilience in the face of pervasive brutality, surveillance, and immobilization, but also sinister in their documentation of far-reaching slave owner power and determination to recapture and reenslave the valiant people who risked life and limb to secure their freedom. My chapter engages in deep analysis of Quebec fugitive slave advertisements to understand how and to what ends slave ethnicity and birth origin were documented in fugitive slave advertisements in the British colony. Mindful of the tactics of escape and examples of slave dress as African cultural retention, I conclude that one incalculable aspect of the enslaved black community in Quebec was its extraordinary heterogeneity which included, African Canadian, African American, African Anglophone and Francophone Caribbeans, African-born people like Joe, and others. In the end, I pose currently unanswerable questions about the temporality of Canadian blackness as the outcome of creolization and the complex intra-group dynamics of this understudied and often overlooked diasporic population.

In Chapter 4, Sophie Saint-Just brings the discussion of creolization into the present through an analysis of Guy Deslauriers' *Le passage du milieu* (France, 1999) or *The Middle Passage* (US version, 2001). Set almost entirely onboard a slave ship, the film represents the harrowing process of the mass removal of Africans during the course of a single slave ship voyage, the visual and sonic landscape evoking the irrecuperable traumas of what Marcus Rediker has called the factory, prison, and dungeon of the slave ship. After being marched or shipped to the West African coast, enslaved Africans were housed in European forts before being packed into the cargo holds of slave ships bound for various ports in the Americas (Rediker, 2007, 41, 44, 45; Jacobovici, 2020). The African people who shared these voyages were often from distinct ethnic or national groups, speaking various languages, and having distinct cultural, spiritual, and social customs. In their struggles to communicate and commiserate within the catastrophic circumstances in which they found themselves, we recover the beginning of the creolization process.

My earlier remark that creolization for the enslaved African was always a process experienced under duress can find no greater example than the floating, nightmarish geography of the slave ship in which the dominantly white crew members were effectively prison guards surveilling, policing, brutalizing, raping, and often murdering their immobilized enslaved "cargo." How quickly were long-held African ethnic animosities dispensed with in such a context? What types of emergent and transferable practices of proto-black solidarity were born onboard? In "Creolization on Screen: Guy Deslauriers' *The Middle Passage* as Afro-Diasporic Discourse *[Le passage du milieu]*," Saint-Just argues that the film's subversive disruption of narrative is enabled by the anonymous, unseen, and yet all-knowing African male narrator who undertakes a visual rewriting of the germinal moments of proto-creolization that was the Middle Passage.

Matti Turner's "Baskets of Rice: Creolization and Material Culture from West Africa to South Carolina's Lowcountry" returns to the southern USA in the period of slavery. Like Klein's discussion of the enslaved potters of Edgefield in Chapter 2, Turner also analyzes a type of material production that is far less understood and acknowledged as the outcome of enslaved labor. In the Lowcountry rice plantations of South Carolina, displaced West Africans transplanted their "rice culture," both knowledge and technological expertise, that included basket sewing. Turner extends and complicates Mintz's definition of creolization positing that various elements of the rice history of the Lowcountry were creolized objects created through creolized processes that at once encapsulate continuity, transformation, and loss, accelerated through the violence of white enslaver control and extended and preserved through black resilience and the cultural continuity made possible by creative resistance.

In Chapter 6, Eloisa Valenzuela-Mendoza examines Natasha Trethewey's literary exploration of the imperial drive to hierarchize racial types in the historical Mexican genre of casta painting. Seemingly unique to the Spanish Empire, that a peculiar art form like casta paintings emerged as a new genre in the eighteenth century within the context of the "peculiar institution" of slavery should not be surprising given the intention behind the didactic and narrative-driven work. Part figure painting, part genre study, most casta paintings were composed with three human figures comprised of a man, woman, and their offspring, typically a young child.[16] As such, the paintings implied the heterosexual union of the couple whose child stood as a sign of their fertility as well as the mixing of their blood across supposedly discrete racial groups. The point of the art was to visualize the emergent racial types that resulted from the creolization of people of African, indigenous, and European descent in the Americas; types that the Spanish and other European empires deemed to be essentially inferior to Europeans at the levels of biology and culture. The web of racial terminology that casta paintings sought to visualize and helped to produce positioned the mixed-race offspring of black, indigenous, and white people as both knowable and exotic colonial types within a racial order with Europeans always the assumed ideal. Valenzuela-Mendoza argues that Trethewey's poem "Thrall" (2012), interrogates the imperial drive to name and define racial difference as a shared preoccupation of colonial New Spain and modern-day US race relations alike.

Lesley A. Wolff's "From Raw to Refined: Edouard Duval-Carrié's *Sugar Conventions* (2013)" brings us back to the twenty-first century through a careful contemplation of contemporary visual art. In Chapter 7, Wolff takes up the mixed media work of the Haitian-born artist Duval-Carrié to explore the entanglement of creolization with canonical Western image production in the nine-part series. Sugar cane and its transformation into the widely traded byproducts rum, sugar, and molasses was arguably, more than any other crop or mined resource, at the heart of competing European imperial projects especially in the Caribbean and rendered colonies like the French-held Saint Domingue (later Haiti) and British Jamaica sites of obscene wealth production for the often absentee white planter class and their surrogates. The three tiered materiality of Duval-Carrié works, Wolf suggests, structurally and figuratively illuminates the complexities of creolization. By sampling and repossessing Western art, *Sugar Conventions* harnesses and subverts European canonical visual languages to expose and interrogate processes of creolization using the very materiality and content by which it was manifest. Wolff then contends that the power structures inherent in European canonical art *and* slavery were both produced by the imperial project of sugar cultivation in the Americas, articulating the role of art-making in the "production and obfuscation of colonial dynamics."

The assembled chapters probe how creolization unfolded for differently constituted individuals and populations, as well as how it came to be articulated both in the historical moments of its enactment and its retroactive cultural representations and production. In so doing, the authors seek both to expand the terrain (literally and figuratively) of the definition of creolization and to turn toward an examination of its relevance for art and visual and material cultures of the Transatlantic world.

Notes

1 The Micmac are today referred to as Mi'kmaq and are among the original indigenous inhabitants of what are today known as Nova Scotia, New Brunswick, Quebec, Prince Edward Island, Newfoundland, Maine, and Boston. Harold Franklin McGee Jr. 2008. "Mi'kmaq." *Canadian Encyclopedia* (Last accessed May 13, 2021). https://www.thecanadianencyclopedia.ca/en/article/micmac-mikmaq

2 While slave sale advertisements typically named smallpox to assure the potential buyers that the enslaved person was inoculated and would be spared in the next epidemic, fugitive slave advertisements exploited the routine scarring of the disease to provide another corporeal identifier through which the public could identify and recapture the freedom-seeker. See *Quebec Gazette* September 1, 1766; *Quebec Gazette* April 13, 1769.

3 Two of the earliest attempts to transcribe and translate the Mi'kmaq language would appear to be: Reverend Silas Tertius Rand. 1875. *A First Reading Book in the Micmac Language: Comprising the Micmac Numerals, and the Names of the Different Kinds of Beasts, Birds, Fishes, Trees, &c. of the Maritime Provinces of Canada. Also, Some of the Indian Names of Places, and Many Familiar Words and Phrases, Translated Literally into English*. Halifax, N.S.: Halifax Printing Company and Reverend Silas Tertius Rand. 1888. *Dictionary of the Language of the Micmac Indians, Who Reside in Nova Scotia, New Brunswick, Prince Edward Island, Cape Breton and Newfoundland*. Halifax, N.S.: Halifax Printing Company.

4 Mintz argued that a lack of royal support led to the uneven growth of the Spanish colonies like Santo Domingo, Cuba, and Puerto Rico and concomitantly the freeing of significant numbers of enslaved people, common interracial mixing, and the growth of the mixed-race free population. Therefore, these Caribbean islands were not centrally characterized by the contact of enslaved black Africans and Europeans. Mintz (2008, 253).

5 The economic activity at Congo Square involved the sale of a variety of food products created by the enslaved including cakes, pies, spruce beer, pop beer, pralines of peanuts, coconuts, popcorn, and tafia (a type of Louisiana rum). Donaldson (1984, 66–67).

6 We know that African-born enslaved people in Canada survived at least two transits because slave ships did not arrive directly to Canada from Africa. Therefore, Joe would have survived the Middle Passage and disembarked in a southern Atlantic region like the Caribbean, the American South or a northern port like New York City, and subsequently would have been forced northward through inland travel, or in Joe's case, most likely on another ship (Brown and Gilmore, 1768).

7 Since Canadian enslavers only seem to have documented African-born enslaved people by language or accent as opposed to place of birth or ethnicity, scholars have yet to determine the ethnic makeup of this community. The absence of stated ethnicity seems to be a product of Canadian enslavers' lack of familiarity with continental African identity. See Nelson, Chapter 3.

8 In a later fugitive notice for Joe, Brown described his footwear as "Indian Macassins" (*Quebec Gazette* December 24, 1778).

9 Heriot's drawing was engraved by J. C. Stadler and "printed for" Richard Phillips of 6 New Bridge Street, London. Based upon an original watercolor, which dates from 1801, the print had significant differences from the earlier work.

10 George Heriot Esq. Deputy Post Master General of British North America. 1807. *Travels through the Canadas, Containing a Description of the Picturesque Scenery on Some of the Rivers and Lakes; with an Account of the Productions, Commerce, and Inhabitants of Those Provinces. To Which Is Subjoined a Comparative View of the Manners and Customs of Several of the Indian Nations of North and South America.* London: Printed for Richard Phillips, No. 6, Bridge-Street, Blackfriars.

11 John Luffman. 1789. *A Brief Account of the Island of Antigua Together with the Customs and Manners of Its Inhabitants, as Well White as Black: As Also an Accurate Statement of the Food, Cloathing, Labor, and Punishment, of the Slaves: In Letters to a Friend Written in the Years 1786, 1787, 1788.* London: Cadel, pp. 135–136; cited in Michael J. Morgan. 1994. "Rock and Roll Unplugged: African-American Music in Eighteenth-Century America." *Eighteenth-Century Studies.* Summer. vol. 27, no. 4. p. 652.

12 On white surveillance of and participation in the musical cultures of enslaved blacks, see Charmaine A. Nelson. 2016. "Representing the Enslaved African in Montreal." Chap. 3 in *Slavery, Geography and Empire in Nineteenth-Century Marine Landscapes of Montreal and Jamaica.* London: Routledge, Taylor and Francis: 133–144.

13 Hilary McD. Beckles early noted that creolization happened in both directions between whites and blacks. For instance, in the case of eighteenth-century Barbados, lower class Irish women who worked as hucksters (market vendors) were seen carrying baskets on their heads and strapping children to their hips in a manner, which Beckles described as "typically African." In another example relevant to the choices of elite whites, Maria Nugent, the white New Jersey-born wife of the lieutenant-governor and commander-in-chief of Jamaica, George Nugent (1801–1806) recalled eating a black crab pepper pot for dinner when dining at the Golden Grove plantation. Beckles (2000, 737), Nugent (1907, 95).

14 Known by various spellings like ozcabrig, oznaburgh or osnaburgs, this type of cheap, coarse cloth was imported to various colonies and provided as cloth rations or clothing to enslaved people. In colonies like Jamaica, oznaburgh fabric was a common cloth ration of the planters. Steeve O. Buckridge argues that Jamaican enslavers, who were required by law to provide sufficient clothing for the enslaved, resorted to the importation of cheap, coarse European fabrics and some Indian cotton. In his testimony to the Lords of Trade in 1745, William Mathew Esq., governor of the Leeward Charibbee Islands, explained that the trade in Antigua was chiefly carried out with Great Britain an included the importation of "Oznabriggs." Mary Prince, an enslaved woman born in Bermuda, recalled how she and her siblings were dressed by their mother in "the new osnaburgs in which we were to be sold" prior to their public auction in the market place at Hamble Town. Oznaburgh was also among the 41 different fabrics that Hunt-Hurst found in the fugitive slave notices of Georgia newspapers (1800–1865). Buckridge (2003, 62, 65); *Copy of the Answers of William Mathew Esquire Governor of the Leeward Charibbee Islands to the Queries Proposed by the Lords of Trade 1745.* Kings MS 205: 855. British Library, London, UK; Prince (1997, 61–62); Hunt-Hurst (1999, 731).

15 *British Library.* 2021. "Ignatius Sancho." People. Accessed 23 May. https://www.bl.uk/people/ignatius-sancho#
Celebrated as a man of letters, the Africa-born Sancho was also a composer, abolitionist, and social reformer. Although brought to England as an enslaved captive, John Montagu, the 2nd Duke of Montagu, provided Sancho with books and encouraged his education. After the Duke's death, Sancho served his widow Mary as her butler for two decades until her death in 1751, and then continued as the valet of George Montagu, 1st Duke of Montagu until 1773.

16 Genre studies or genre are images of human activity. Unlike portraits, they are not intended to represent historically specific human beings.

References

Anonymous. 1745. *Copy of the Answers of William Mathew Esquire Governor of the Leeward Charibbee Islands to the Queries Proposed by the Lords of Trade 1745.* Kings MS 205: 855. London: British Library.

Anonymous. 1776. "RAN AWAY." *Nova Scotia Gazette and Weekly Chronicle.* June 18.

Anonymous. *British Library.* 2021. "Ignatius Sancho." People. Accessed 23 May. https://www.bl.uk/people/ignatius-sancho#

Beckles, Hilary McD. 2000. "An Economic Life of Their Own: Slaves as Commodity Producers and Distributors in Barbados." Chap. 54 in *Caribbean Slavery in the Atlantic World*, edited by Hilary McD. Beckles and Verene Shepherd, 732–742. Kingston: Ian Randle Publishers Limited.

Brown, William and Thomas Gilmore (Quebec City). 1768. Letter to William Dunlap, Esq. (Philadelphia), April 29, National Library and Archives Canada, Ottawa.

Brown, William (THE PRINTER). 1777. "RANAWAY from the Printing-office." *Quebec Gazette*. 27 November. vol. 639. p. 3.

Brown, William. 1778. "RAN AWAY from the Printing-Office." *Quebec Gazette*. 24 December. vol. 695. p. 3.

Brown, William. 1786. "BROKE out of His Majesty's Gaol." *Quebec Gazette*. May 4. vol. 1081. p. 3.

Buckridge, Steeve O. 2003. "The Role of Plant Substances in Jamaican Slave Dress." *Caribbean Quarterly*. vol. 49, no. 3. pp. 61–73.

Donaldson, Gary A. 1984. "A Window on Slave Culture: Dances at Congo Square in New Orleans, 1800–1862." *The Journal of Negro History*. Spring. vol. 69, no. 2. pp. 63–72.

Ferguson, John. 1769. "WHEREAS John Ferguson." *Quebec Gazette*. April 13. vol. 224. p. 3.

Gray, Edw. Wm. and Jacob Kuhn. 1792. "BROKE Goal and escaped." *Montreal Gazette*. November 22. vol. xlviii. p. 3.

Hunt-Hurst, Patricia. 1999. "'Round Homespun Coat & Pantaloons of the Same': Slave Clothing as Reflected in Fugitive Slave Advertisements in Antebellum Georgia." *The Georgia Historical Quarterly*. vol. 83, no. 4. pp. 727–740.

Jacobovici, Simcha. 2020. *Enslaved*. Associate Producers and Cornelia Street Productions. Toronto and London. six-part documentary series.

Kasson, John F. 1990. *Rudeness and Civility: Manners in Nineteenth-Century Urban America*. New York: Hill and Wang.

Mackey, Frank. 2010. *Done with Slavery: The Black Fact in Montreal, 1760–1840*. Montreal: McGill-Queen's University Press.

McGee Jr., Harold Franklin. 2008. "Mi'kmaq." *Canadian Encyclopedia*. Last accessed May 13, 2021. https://www.thecanadianencyclopedia.ca/en/article/micmac-mikmaq

Mintz, Sidney. 2008. "Creolization and Hispanic Exceptionalism." *Review (Fernand Braudel Center) 31 (3) The Second Slavery: Mass Slavery, World-Economy, and Comparative Microhistories* Part II: 251–265.

Morgan, Michael J. 1994. "Rock and Roll Unplugged: African-American Music in Eighteenth-Century America." *Eighteenth-Century Studies*. Summer. vol. 27, no. 4. pp. 649–662.

Nelson, Charmaine A. 2016. "Representing the Enslaved African in Montreal." Chap. 3 in *Slavery, Geography and Empire in Nineteenth-Century Marine Landscapes of Montreal and Jamaica*. pp. 111–156. London: Routledge, Taylor and Francis.

Nugent, Maria. 1907. *Lady Nugent's Journal: Jamaica One Hundred Years Ago*. Edited by Frank Cundall. London: Published for the Institute of Jamaica by Adam and Charles Black.

Pretchard, Azariah. 1794. "RUN away from the Subscriber." *Quebec Gazette*. May 22. vol. 1506. p. 5.

Prince, Mary. 1997. *The History of Mary Prince: A West Indian Slave Related by Herself*. Edited by Moira Ferguson. Ann Arbor: The University of Michigan Press.

Rand, Reverend Silas Tertius. 1875. *A First Reading Book in the Micmac Language: Comprising the Micmac Numerals, and the Names of the Different Kinds of Beasts, Birds, Fishes, Trees, &c. of the Maritime Provinces of Canada. Also, Some of the Indian Names of Places, and Many Familiar Words and Phrases, Translated Literally into English*. Halifax, N.S.: Halifax Printing Company.

Rand, Reverend Silas Tertius. 1888. *Dictionary of the Language of the Micmac Indians, Who Reside in Nova Scotia, New Brunswick, Prince Edward Island, Cape Breton and Newfoundland*. Halifax, N.S.: Halifax Printing Company.

Rediker, Marcus. 2007. "The Evolution of the Slave Ship." *The Slave Ship: A Human History*. pp. 41–72. New York: Penguin Books.

Richardson, Bonham C. 1983. *Caribbean Migrants: Environment and Human Survival on St. Kitts and Nevis*. Knoxville: University of Tennessee Press.

Rupert, Linda M. 2012. *Creolization and Contraband: Curacao in the Early Modern Atlantic World*. Athens: University of Georgia Press.

Waldstreicher, David. 1999. "Reading the Runaways: Self-Fashioning, Print Culture, and Confidence in Slavery in the 18th c. Mid-Atlantic." *The William and Mary Quarterly*. April. vol. 56, no. 2. pp. 243–272.

Werden, Isaac. 1766, "RUN-AWAY, *on Saturday the 22nd of August, 1766*." *Quebec Gazette*. September 1. vol. 87. p. 3.

White Shane and Graham White. 1995. Slave Hair and African American Culture in the Eighteenth and Nineteenth Centuries. *The Journal of Southern History*. February. vol. 61, no. 1. pp. 45–76.

1 Blackness and Lines of Beauty in the Eighteenth-Century Anglophone Atlantic World

Kristina Huang

Lines Between the City and Plantation

London-based artist and grocer Ignatius Sancho (1729–1780) is best known for his epistolary exchange with novelist Laurence Sterne. Sancho's letters appeared in *Letters of the Late Rev. Mr. Laurence Sterne to his Most Intimate Friends* (1775), and the Sancho-Sterne exchange was printed as a model of elegant letters in the popular writing manual, *The Complete Letter-Writer: or, Polite English Secretary* (1778). Given that letters during the eighteenth century were privately and publically consumed, read by and to audiences beyond a letter's addressee, Sancho's fame from his connection to Sterne was extended further through subsequent reprintings and rereadings of his letters (Ellis 2001, 201–206). Not only did Sancho gain notoriety during his lifetime as a man of letters, his presence as a grocer on Charles Street in Westminster ignited the imagination of his contemporaries. For instance, Thomas Gainsborough painted a portrait of him and, according to his first biographer, Sancho was considered to be a biographical subject of the famed lexicographer and writer Samuel Johnson.[1] How do Sancho's interactions—through letter-writing and selling everyday goods—and his contemporaries' reception of his presence in London offer new avenues for understanding the presence of black subjects in the arts during the eighteenth century?

Visual representations of black figures in eighteenth-century London's cultural landscape—from shop signs to elite portraits, from stage performances to character types in novels—outweigh the documents produced by African diasporic subjects themselves. This is, in part, an issue of limited literacy during the eighteenth century. Gretchen Gerzina has noted, "at a time when literacy was low but advancing among the rank-and-file, it is no surprise that a population newly escaped from slavery would leave little written record" (1995, 24). On the other hand, the unevenness between works by Anglophone African diasporic writers and the representations that play with blackness as a perceived signifier of racial difference is exacerbated by literary concerns around textuality. In particular, focus on textuality often leads to an overwhelming archive produced around imperial othering through Britain's cultural fascination with blackness. Catherine Molineux examines the popularization of black figures in British print and material culture, arguing that "colonial reports, pamphlets, travelogues, and sketches provide[d] sources of iconography and ideology for shop signs, prints, textiles, ceramics, playing cards, board games, and other forms of material culture" (2012, 6). This uneven imperial archive asks us to toggle between, at least, two aesthetic modalities: written works produced by black subjects and the visual representations of blackness that circulated within the metropole through popular works of art.

Since the early modern period, blackness as a visual signifier accrued commercial meanings as colonialism and the slave trade and plantation trafficked racial ideology. As Peter

Fryer has observed: "racism crystallized in print in Britain in the eighteenth century, as the ideology of plantocracy, the class of sugar-planters and slave merchants dominated England's Caribbean colonies" (1984, 134). At the same time, as they crystallized in print, racial tropes were simultaneously disarticulated by the growing communities of African diasporic subjects in the metropole whose experiences varied across the spectrum of freedom and enslavement: servants, military men, ex-slaves, and musicians were among the masses inhabiting the metropole. Various migrations, forced and otherwise, transformed the social space of London and, by extension, literally and figuratively reshaped the visual semiotics of the city. As the textual and visual representations testify, contemporaries of Sancho were patronizingly preoccupied with the artist as an emblem of black humanity.[2] Yet, while his presence in London interlocked with and disarticulated racial tropes networked through London's commercial and material culture, Sancho's writings invited his readers to see movement, depth, and variance in black representation. In particular, lines in Sancho's letter-writing—his selected genre of self-representation—functioned as both punctuation and visual remark.

Sancho's sowing of lines and dashes in his letters offer new terms for rereading eighteenth-century representations of blackness that circulated through London and the wider Anglophone Atlantic world. As punctuation and visual remarks, the lines in Sancho's writings amplified literary production as a mode for shifting the optics of blackness in the eighteenth century. Michel-Rolph Trouillot's definition of creolization is instructive here: "Cultural ideals and power relations, including actors' understandings and interpretations of the stakes and forces available to reach their self-defined goals, fundamentally shape the context of creolization" (2002, 196). While channeling the kinetic energy of London, Sancho's lines direct our attention to the social space of literary production as a context for creolization. Given the low literacy rates among ordinary Londoners, Sancho's position as a metropolitan shopkeeper, one who was known and involved in the literary arts, interlocked two critical perspectives—that of the worker and free black subject in the eighteenth century. By calibrating attention to how Sancho's writings visually played with the image of the artist at work, I want to suggest how the visibility of blackness in Britain's uneven imperial archive (between black writing and representations of black figures, real and imagined) can be redefined through eighteenth-century aesthetic understandings of the line. In contrast to how his white contemporaries received and managed his image as an exemplary black subject, Sancho fashioned himself through the everyday environment of city life. I will first close-read the visual aesthetics of Sancho's lines, arguing how he portrayed himself as an artist interacting with his material surroundings. Building from Sancho's remaking of blackness through the visual signifier of the line, I then turn to David Dabydeen's ekphrastic 2013 novel *Johnson's Dictionary*, which connects eighteenth-century artist William Hogarth's line of beauty to the growing visibility and movements of black subjects between the metropole and colonial plantation. Like the grammatical use of hyphens, drawing lines can visually conjoin and combine ideas and, as a result, underscore relationships that would otherwise appear opaque or remain submerged. Eighteenth-century lines not only mediated representations of blackness in the Anglophone Atlantic world: they also make visible literary production in the eighteenth century as an extension of black labor.

Black Subjects and Everyday Life in Eighteenth-Century London

Prior to becoming a member of London's literati, a cultural icon, and a grocer, Sancho was enslaved, eventually freed, and later became a servant in the Duke of Montagu's home. According to his first biographer, Joseph Jekyll, Sancho was born in 1729, on a slave ship sailing toward the Spanish West Indies. The Montagus helped Sancho set up a grocery shop on Charles

Street in Westminster, where Sancho, his West Indian wife Anne Osborne, and their children resided until the artist's death in 1780. By the standards of the eighteenth century, his life was an exceptional one, not least because of his experience with relative stability and social mobility which few African diasporic subjects in the eighteenth-century Anglophone Atlantic world claimed. What distinguished Sancho from his fellow black Londoners was his celebrity status, stemming from his letter-writing, most notably through his correspondence with novelist Sterne. Sancho's letters were posthumously collected and published under the universalizing pretensions to show "before the publick [sic] … that an untutored African may possess abilities equal to an European" (editorial note to *Letters of the Late Ignatius Sancho* [1782] 1998, 4). While living most of his life as a free black Londoner, Sancho was interpreted by his cosmopolitan contemporaries as a moral symbol uplifting Britain from their involvement in trafficking and enslaving Africans and their descendants.[3] By the end of the eighteenth century, Sancho and his letters were conscripted into the debates around slavery in Britain and the nascent United States.

Given his experiences as a free black Londoner and the subsequent framing of these experiences within British narratives of moral achievement, it may seem counterintuitive to read Sancho and his letters within the context of the Caribbean plantation. But, as Sylvia Wynter has argued, the market forces that produced plantation societies are the very same forces that birthed the novel form (1971, 95). Situating the literary form of the novel as a twin phenomenon to the plot of land that planters conferred to slaves so that they could "grow food to feed themselves in order to maximize profits" (1971, 99), Wynter gestures to the ways that ideas and spaces can be both, at once, products and critiques of the very market system and values that produced them. The city is "the commercial expression of the plantation" and built into this space is a confrontation with its marginal masses, disrupted from the plot" (1971, 102). While the known texts written by Anglophone black subjects are relatively small in comparison to the popular, visual representations, the physical presence of African diasporic populations was nonetheless felt and documented. "Over the course of the eighteenth century," Molineux observes, "artists increasingly incorporated blacks into the metropolitan social scene. This critical shift, which accompanied rising numbers of blacks in mid-eighteenth-century London and other port cities, signaled a significant change in the site of imagined British encounters" (Molineux 2012, 201). Although he would be received as a black exemplar by his contemporaries, Sancho was in many ways part and parcel of the marginal masses in the city: his presence as both worker and free black subject was constitutive of London's visual semiotics (from literal shop signs to the growing visibility of African diasporic communities in the city) around blackness.

Literary scholars have observed Sancho's lines, dashes, and full stops are in keeping with the general punctuation style of the period; they have also been largely viewed as Sancho's revelatory, even imitative nods to Sterne's literary stylings. But Sancho's lines and dashes should not be read as mere reflections of literary trends of the eighteenth century—they are also materialized and metaphorical placeholders that accentuate Sancho's letters as partial and elliptical self-portraits of an artist at work. That is, through the visual signifier of the line, Sancho spotlights how his art interlocks with his labor. As seen in the portion of his 3 September 1777 letter featured below, Sancho had a predilection for sowing his writing with full stops, parentheticals, and dashes. It is notable that the first edition of Sancho's collected letters reproduces a blot of ink in the following sentences:

> —I hope [blot] confound the ink! what a blot! Now don't you dare suppose I was in fault—no, Sir, the pen was diabled—the paper worse, there was concatenation of ill-sorted chances—all—all—coincided to contribute to that fatal blot—which has so disarranged my ideas—that I must perforce finish before I had half disburthened my head

> and heart:—but is N[ancy] a good girl?—And how does my honest George do? Tell Mrs. H—what you please in the handsome way of me.—Farewell, I will write no more nonsense this night—that's flat. IGN. SANCHO.
>
> (Sancho 1782, 142–143)

In this letter to John Meheux, an amateur artist who created designs for prints to be etched or engraved by others, Sancho opens with a comment about not having heard from the artist in a while, and gives some general remarks about contemporary events. The letter then detours into a playful reflection on the visual representation of his letter. The blot calls attention to Sancho's materials, ink and paper, and the writer teases out the conceit that mistakes in his letters are connected to the limits of his materials, and that his materials have a life of their own. The "diabled," or bedeviled pen could also be read as a hastily written "disabled." Sancho exaggerates the multiple meanings of "diabled": the "s" is missing perhaps because of the pen's bewitchment, possessed by another force. The disturbance that the ink blot causes in the letter's musings is followed by the staccato-like sputter ("confound the ink! what a blot!"), and the confounding "fatal blot" is highlighted by the alliterative words "concatenation," "coincided," and "contribute." The simple confluence of the blot in the middle of the letter's reflections—an accident—becomes a visual and textual gamboling across the page (Figure 1.1).

As the reader is drawn to the visual effects of the blot, the dashes become more apparent as Sancho attempts to settle back into the conversational matters of the letter. The lines appear,

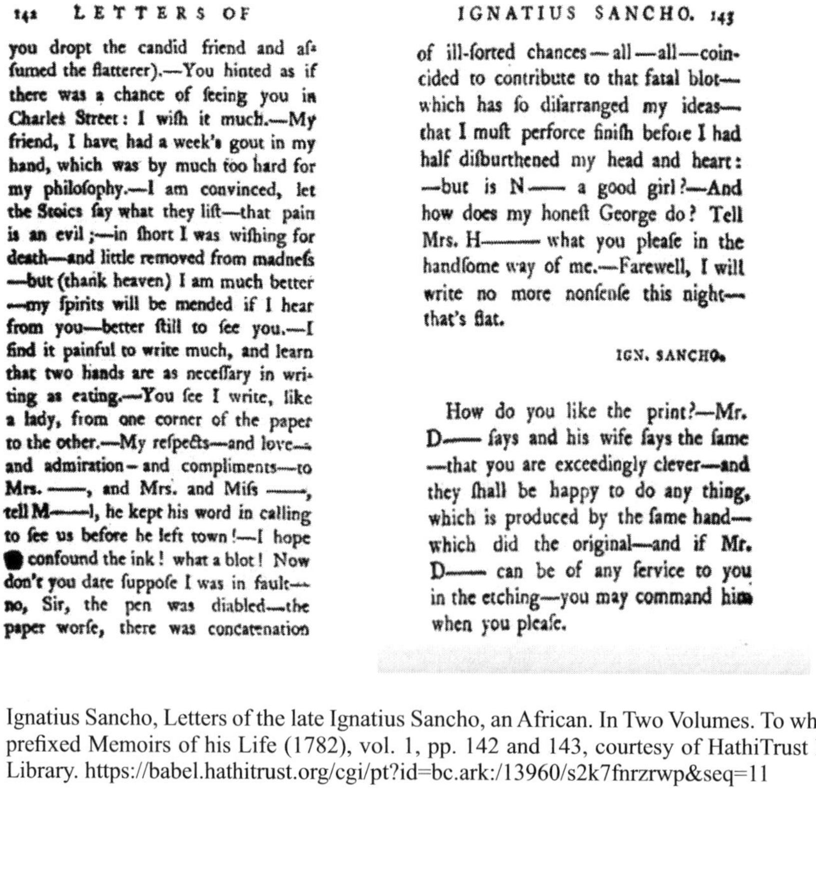

142 LETTERS OF

you dropt the candid friend and affumed the flatterer).—You hinted as if there was a chance of feeing you in Charles Street: I wifh it much.—My friend, I have had a week's gout in my hand, which was by much too hard for my philofophy.—I am convinced, let the Stoics fay what they lift—that pain is an evil;—in fhort I was wifhing for death—and little removed from madnefs—but (thank heaven) I am much better—my fpirits will be mended if I hear from you—better ftill to fee you.—I find it painful to write much, and learn that two hands are as neceffary in writing as eating.—You fee I write, like a lady, from one corner of the paper to the other.—My refpects—and love—and admiration—and compliments—to Mrs. ——, and Mrs. and Mifs ——, tell M——l, he kept his word in calling to fee us before he left town!—I hope ● confound the ink! what a blot! Now don't you dare fuppofe I was in fault—no, Sir, the pen was diabled—the paper worfe, there was concatenation

IGNATIUS SANCHO. 143

of ill-forted chances—all—all—coincided to contribute to that fatal blot—which has fo difarranged my ideas—that I muft perforce finifh before I had half difburthened my head and heart:—but is N—— a good girl?—And how does my honeft George do? Tell Mrs. H—— what you pleafe in the handfome way of me.—Farewell, I will write no more nonfenfe this night—that's flat.

IGN. SANCHO.

How do you like the print?—Mr. D—— fays and his wife fays the fame—that you are exceedingly clever—and they fhall be happy to do any thing, which is produced by the fame hand—which did the original—and if Mr. D—— can be of any fervice to you in the etching—you may command him when you pleafe.

Figure 1.1 Ignatius Sancho, Letters of the late Ignatius Sancho, an African. In Two Volumes. To which are prefixed Memoirs of his Life (1782), vol. 1, pp. 142 and 143, courtesy of HathiTrust Digital Library. https://babel.hathitrust.org/cgi/pt?id=bc.ark:/13960/s2k7fnrzrwp&seq=11

as they do elsewhere in his letters, to break up and fragment thoughts. However, in his letter to Meheux, the flatness of the lines is emphasized by Sancho's signoff, where he puns on the visual appearance of the dashes and their association with the mundane: "I will write no more nonsense this night—that's flat." The blot on the page provides him a playful excursion from work; Sancho half-heartedly returns from it, leaving with the sense that whatever else he had left to say is just flat (dull) by comparison.

Lines, in terms of the literal images of the dash and the letter's written content, materialize as marks of Sancho's mind and movement. Elsewhere in his letters, Sancho alludes to the interruptions his store imposes on his writing: "I write to the ringing of the shop-door bell—I write—betwixt serving—gossiping—and lying. Alas! What cramps to poor genius!" (Sancho [1782] 1998, 81). The lines fragment and break up actions, indexing the presence of interruptions and customers that are part of the social space of Sancho's artistic production.[4] The lines here accumulate another quality: like musical notations, the dashes may harmonize with "the ringing of the shop-door bell." Using the letter, a sociable genre, Sancho draws attention to his materials, paper and ink, while recording his interactions with his surroundings, from people moving in and out of his store, to syncing his thoughts to the sounds of the shop-door bell. The visual interplay between the lines and the written content spotlight the image of an artist in the middle of his composition. As they accumulate and signal various meanings, the lines operate in concert with Sancho's selected genre of self-portraiture: the epistolary form. The characteristics of the epistolary form's "juxtaposition of contrasting discrete units," along with the "very fragmentation inherent in the letter," manifest in the visual aesthetics of Sancho's use of punctuation (Altman 1982, 187).

Figure 1.2 William Hogarth, *A Taste of the High Life* (1746), Etching ink on paper, 20.5 × 26.3 cm, © Victoria and Albert Museum, London, UK.

Sancho's self-portraits of himself as an artist in the midst of creating and interacting with his surroundings run along and, at times, against an archive of representations—from Thomas Gainsborough's portrait of 1768 to the 1789 novel *Fortescue; or, the soldier's reward: a characteristic novel*. In the novel, a character encounters the fictional Sancho "employed at his desk, while his wife, a neat mulatto woman, attended to the concerns of a small retail shop in Westminster" (42–43). The fictional Sancho entrusts this character with an orientalist, picaresque tale "The History of Otang, An Indostan Slave," which is inserted into *Fortescue* (44–46). Illustrator and painter Hogarth was allegedly inspired by Sancho and written commentary about his illustration "Taste of High Life" suggests that Sancho was Hogarth's source of inspiration for the black character (see Figure 1.2). The commentary states that

> the young [lady] is fondling a little black boy, who on his part is playing with a petite pagoda. This miniature Othello has been said to be intended for the late Ignatius Sancho, whose talents and virtues were an honour to his colour. At the time the picture was painted he would have been rather older than the figure, but as he was then honoured by the partiality and protection of a noble family, the painter might possibly mean to delineate what his figure had been a few years before.
>
> (Ireland 1793, 244)

His life and art sparked the imagination of his white contemporaries and this led to an archive of visual and textual genres that domesticated Sancho around a character type, as evidenced in the reference "miniature Othello." A number of textual and visual genres constructed "a fact of blackness" around Sancho. If the city is "the commercial expression of the plantation"—and the printed racist ideologies of sugar planters, and slave merchants migrated from the Caribbean colonies into London—then it appears that some of Sancho's contemporaries trafficked images of him as exotic curiosity and exemplary African. This is to suggest that Sancho's jocular representations of himself as an artist and grocer participated in the mutually-constitutive discourse around the growing visibility of black populations, free and enslaved, within the British empire. Here I follow Katherine McKittrick's reading of Wynter's essay. McKittrick argues that "the plantation town draws attention to a narrative of blackness that is implicit to modernity and indigenous to the Americas—thus a conception of the city that is imbued with [a] version of black history that is neither celebratory nor dissident" (2013, 12). While Sancho's epistolary illustrations of himself, fashioned out of textual and literal lines, unsettle the aforementioned novelistic and pictorial representations, they also became products replotted along the metropolitan narratives around British imperial achievement. Significant here is that Sancho's writings offer routes inside and outside the imperial networks structuring meanings around blackness. This movement of images inside and outside visual representations and documents indexing the palpable presence of black subjects in the eighteenth-century Atlantic world is implemented in *Johnson's Dictionary* through David Dabydeen's reimagining of the eighteenth-century theory of the line of beauty.

Visualizing Blackness as Lines of Beauty

But what of the fact that Sancho was also among London's "marginal masses, disrupted from the plot"—masses that grew out of but remained submerged in the metropolitan narrative around slavery and abolition? By marginal masses, I refer to other eighteenth-century laborers and free black subjects who traversed the metropole-colony circuit and did not necessarily leave a large body of written record because of the low literacy rates among ordinary people.

Among London's workers and migrants were musicians and artists, some of whom Sancho wrote letters to and thus documented their presence. There were Sancho's correspondences, a few of which were reprinted in the posthumous collection of letters, with equestrian, musician, and fencer Julius Soubise, who was born in St. Kitts and brought to England at the age of ten to be the servant of the Duchess of Queensberry. Sancho also wrote letters about and to Charles Lincoln, a West Indian musician. As Sancho's epistolary self-portraitures situate the image of the artist in the kinetic energy of his urban surroundings, readers of his letters are invited into the social world of Sancho's literary production. Sancho's letters give us fragments of his conversations with other Londoners, through which the artist nods to his various lines, as it were, of influence.

In his 2013 novel *Johnson's Dictionary*, Dabydeen also directs our attention to the eighteenth-century social space of literary production and, in doing so, he casts light on the African and Caribbean diasporic subjects who came into contact and shaped cultural ideas and products that are putatively claimed as British. Almost a decade prior to the publication of *Johnson's Dictionary* Dabydeen argued: "Africa and India altered the European psyche profoundly" and the interactions that derived from these diasporic contacts creolized, excited, and remade the European psyche through language and aesthetics (Hand 1995, 80). While accentuating how the cultures of the Caribbean Isles and the British Isles mutually constitute one another, *Johnson's Dictionary* presents its readers with a cast of characters who are inspired by African diasporic subjects who lived in eighteenth-century London. For instance, the novel's title alludes to the famed eighteenth-century writer and lexicographer Samuel Johnson who maintained a well-known friendship with his Jamaican-born servant and apprentice, Francis Barber (c.1735–1801). Francis Barber spent almost thirty-four years of his life with Johnson, and both shared an unusual relationship that could not be simply characterized as one between a master and servant (Gerzina 1995, 44). As someone who participated in the space of Johnson's literary production, Barber appears the primary inspiration for one of the central characters of the novel, Dabydeen's fictional Francis who is given a dictionary by his master in Demerara (British Guiana).

Through the layering of references to historical figures, Dabydeen deepens meaning while creating the conditions for initiating a chain of interpretations through the character of Francis. For instance, Dabydeen may have been alluding to Francis Williams (c. 1697–1762) who was a free black Jamaican who wrote Latin verse poetry and studied mathematics at Cambridge University; the name is associated, as we will see, with Francis Bacon (1561–1626) too. This layering and, in effect, creation of an intellectual lineage representative of colonial and metropolitan enlightenment gives depth and shape to Dabydeen's historical reimagining of Barber. Although engaging the social scenes of artistic production, Barber and Sancho are often trivialized in contrast to their more well-known eighteenth-century literary counterparts, Johnson and Sterne, respectively. In *Johnson's Dictionary,* the fictional Francis is entangled in a web of meanings and definitions, and is thus fleshed out of a footnote in eighteenth-century literary history. The character is fashioned out of a line of influence; Bacon among this lineage, and a crew from the margins, Barber and Williams.

In order to define and renew meanings of the marginal masses of black characters documented in and through eighteenth-century visual and literary arts, Dabydeen implements Hogarthian aesthetics.[5] Hogarth was known to bring a "mode of interpretation to the viewer's awareness by employing meandering lines of sight, odd juxtapositions, and multiple layers of bodies and objects" (Molineux 2012, 181). While Hogarth deployed these strategies through his eighteenth-century visual illustration, Dabydeen redeploys these techniques in his novel, a character-filled, ekphrastic narrative that is interspersed with a number of images associated with European art; many of the images are reprints of Hogarth's illustrations.

In the novel, when Francis first receives a copy of *Johnson's Dictionary* in Demerara, we see how Francis is not only a composite of allusions to Barber, Williams, and Bacon, he is also an embodiment of a mode of interpretation associated with Hogarthian aesthetics. The object and text of the *Dictionary* are additional elements juxtaposed with Francis. As his master, Dr. Gladstone read aloud definitions, Francis' mind meanders between the definition presented to him and the apparent invisibility of his personal past. Between the written word and an unrepresented past, Francis actively interprets:

> I became alert when [Dr. Gladstone] arrived at beauty and declaimed from the book— "'*the best part of beauty is that which a picture cannot express.*' That's Dr [sic] Johnson quoting Bacon, a notable philosopher and logician." I immediately recalled in all its minute details the painting in my past massa's sitting room, of his father, mother and aunt in their opulent setting. I had searched the painting for my mother, as I had latterly searched the sky for utterance, but found nothing. Now Dr Gladstone was telling me that my mother's very invisibility held meaning. That she was absent from memory and from record was a measure of her beauty. And there another word which found my mother in the sightless spaces of a painting, at the very corners and sides where the frame covered over the canvas; or at the back, where the canvas was blank and therefore unexamined by human eyes. "*Imagination: the power of forming ideal pictures; the power of representing things absent to one's self*," it said in the *Dictionary*.
>
> (Dabydeen 2013, 67)

Francis sees that absence is meaningful (and meaning-full), and what is invisible exceeds capture through ordinary optics. Together beauty and imagination are metaphorical, transient placeholders: rather than operating as fixed (holding in place) categories for an artist to aspire toward, beauty and imagination extend from what is inexpressible. In the passage, words are present (and therefore temporary) signposts whose meanings are remade as the interpreter actively attempts to make legible (visible) the lines (drawn connections) between ideas and their referent. Here, Dabydeen recasts Hogarthian aesthetics to play with definition and warps linearity. Time spirals back and forth from past to present as Francis thinks about the dictionary definitions through his personal history. As the passage progresses, dimension is added to the space of interpretation. While Francis attempts to search for his mother in the sky, his mind "latterly" moves; perhaps Dabydeen drags the meaning of the word to resonate with "laterally" and "literally." The word invokes a sense of flatness. As Francis learns more from the dictionary, specifically the word imagination, flat space becomes a surface with more symbolic dimension—the surface of words is in fact the ground for metaphor. His mind wanders as it searches through the margins, "at the very corners and sides where the frame covered" and the "unexamined" space behind the canvas.

Readers of Dabydeen's novel are invited to follow Francis' cue to move between two interpretive modalities, between textual and visual reading. To see the marginal masses, disrupted from the plot of Anglophone Atlantic cultural development, Dabydeen's novel embraces Hogarthian aesthetics of wandering lines—these lines bring into view the interconnectedness of actions, people, material objects, and ideas. Thus, the artist at work as a solitary figure, isolated from society, is a fiction, and readers of *Johnson's Dictionary* confront this image at the novel's opening. Hogarth is reimagined as a drunk painter living in Demerara, situated in a colonial scene of material and ideological production. But it is not Hogarth's perspective that we get; instead, the painter is described through Cato, his slave. Reversing the gaze and offering a narration through the optics of Britain's perceived racial other, a black slave, the novel renders a critique of how an artist from the metropole may, as Cato phrases it, "look but not see, see but not look, for he gazing inward" (Dabydeen 2013, 27).

In his aesthetic treatise, *The Analysis of Beauty* (1753), Hogarth compares the serpentine line to the rigid lines associated with classical traditions, arguing that the waving, undulating line is visually more pleasurable and effective in depicting beauty:

> The eye hath this sort of enjoyment in winding walks, and serpentine lines, and all sorts of objects, whose forms … are composed principally of what, I call, the waving and serpentine lines … Intricacy in form, therefore, I shall define to be that peculiarity in the lines, which compose it, that leads the eye a wanton kind of chace [sic], and from the pleasure that gives the mind, intitles [sic] it to the name of beautiful.
>
> (Hogarth 1753, 25)

Like Francis, Cato embodies Hogarthian aesthetics, but what distinguishes Cato's characterization is that his status as an enslaved black person him as more intimately connected to the line of beauty. The conditions that make it possible for the fictional Hogarth (and, by implication, other metropolitan eighteenth-century artists) to paint are the ones produced by slave labor. Dabydeen underscores this by pointing out Cato's familiarity with the tools and materials for artistic production. In effect, Cato embodies the serpentine line:

> I make pigments of every colour you can dream. Don't ask how many hours or days I spend, for when the paint lap and flow time don't be. Paint stop time, paint stop fear of time, because when my hand twirl and dance on the canvas, and rainbows tangle like hoops in my thoughts, and I have to study hard to separate them out, the last thing in my mind become the first, and the first thing become the past and future thing. Time spin and muddle up and then stop altogether. Then there is only beauty left, beauty which is in the colours of the canvas and is forever—mind you, is only forever when you make sure the paint reach the right point of dryness and you apply the proper glaze, for beauty is also technique.
>
> (Dabydeen 2013, 26)

The verbs in this passage—"twirl," "dance," "tangle," "spin"—coil around the sinuous imagery of arcs and circles. The repetition of words "paint," "stop," and "time" throughout the passage twist the syntax and the chronological direction of meaning in each sentence; "the first" merges with "the last" becoming "the past and future thing." The movement of material paint, facilitated by Cato's hand, bears vivid resemblance to lines that curve and allow the eye to wander. While Hogarth's line of beauty manifests through the characterization of Francis and his interpretative juxtapositions between words and their referents, Cato's labor in stirring and painting interlocks with the beauty that manifests on the canvas. His thoughts and actions are "hard to separate," thus making the border between self and the material world dissolve.

Both Cato and Francis are two variations of Dabydeen's effort to recast the real and imagined representations of black subjects in eighteenth-century art through a reimagining of the line of beauty. As suggested with the circulation of Sancho as exemplary black artist, Dabydeen similarly points to how Britain's artistic networks that created the conditions for certain black representations to surface are deeply intertwined with the system of power and violence undergirding the plantation system. With Cato's narration of his work for and with Hogarth in Demerara, the novel foregrounds the line of beauty as technique and material produced by the eighteenth-century plantation system. When considering the plantation context, we must think too about

28 *Kristina Huang*

the plot: given to slaves as a means to maximize profits, the plot harbors creative practices and narratives of survival and resistance to the very system that centered its logics on (and optics of) violence and dehumanization. Building from McKittrick's reading of Wynter, we are asked to "seek out secretive histories that are not invested in rehearsing lifelessness, the violated black body, and practices of resistance rooted in authenticity" (2013, 12). Moving between eighteenth-century visual and textual lines would enable us, readers of the present, to recalibrate the visual signifier of blackness as a feature interconnected with growth, survival, and social life. We would be retracing these lines as extensions of plot and, in doing so, reread the uneven imperial archive of representations as rooted in and routed through partially-hidden histories of human life.

Following the chapter comprised of Cato's first-person narration of his relationship to Hogarth, *Johnson's Dictionary* shifts our attention from the British Caribbean to London. With the plantation context in mind, and perhaps with Cato's line "wait, wait, plot, persist!" echoing (Dabydeen 2013, 27), readers are asked to conceptually follow the line of beauty connecting Demerara and London. When readers of the novel first step into London, they encounter one of historical Hogarth's images "The Times of the Day, Noon" (1738). The illustration below not only documents the proximity and visibility of black subjects participating in an eighteenth-century city scene, its appearance highlights the novel's interplay between image and text (Figure 1.3).

The reader's line of vision may meander back and forth between Hogarth's illustration (as the marginal mass extending from the narrative) and the central text. In the image, there is an energy and plurality of activities depicted in this street scene. The black man on the left, on the edge where a frame might cover, partakes in the social space of London. Under the suggestive

Figure 1.3 William Hogarth (1697–1764), *Noon*, plate II from *Times of Day* (1738), Engraving, 49 × 41 cm, Guildhall Art Gallery, Photo Credit: HIP/Art Resource, New York City, USA.

sign "good eating," he's a figure who enjoys, consumes, and contributes to the city's vitality. Dabydeen has written about this illustration in *Hogarth's Blacks*, describing the black man and the white woman as figures cast in positive terms in comparison to the aristocratic couple on the right. The two have a "shared animal energy," emphasized by the shop sign above them, and the couple represents mutual love and passion in contrast to the narcissism and ostentation of the aristocrats (Dabydeen 1987, 64). The street is not a static space, for viewers are invited to chase the various lines of action unwinding in the scene. As a reader's eyes may meander back and forth, the illustration not only comprises unwinding interactions: it interacts with the textual narrative that also unbinds and reconstitute the "shared animal energy" of the city street.

Indeed, for its eighteenth-century viewers, the image of the black man and white woman carried with it a mixed charge of eroticism and horror. As defined in *The Analysis of Beauty*, Hogarth describes the line of beauty as a visual form that "leads the eye a wanton kind of chace." If the word wanton alludes to a kind of violent spontaneity and lustful pursuit of the eye, then the sexualized interaction along the left margin of "The Times of Day, Noon" simultaneously lures and brings into sharp focus the dynamics between the black man and white woman. The lines of action drawn around their interaction unwinds and flows into the textual narrative: when the image appears, it is at the moment when readers are introduced to the character Elizabeth, a young white woman involved in selling sexual favors in London. The narrative invites readers to draw a comparison between Elizabeth and the young white woman in Hogarth's illustration. The readers' gaze, then, swivels away from the black figure. By focusing on Elizabeth, a character that symbolizes imperial England, the narrative begins to describe how she is affected and moved by the street signs that bore racialized images. Elizabeth is titillated, momentarily shocked, by the signs. Her fear is sparked only when she associates the signs with Francis (a slave she will inherit later in the novel), a black figure with his own voice with the capacity to respond.

When readers of the novel meet Francis, he is situated in contradistinction to the commercial images displayed on London's shops signs. In the passage below, Dabydeen spotlights how visual signifiers associated with racial difference intersect with (the so-called) New World commodities ready for consumption, tobacco and sugar in particular. These shop images, signs of blackness, showcase goods associated with racial slavery; the painted images equate blackness with material goods (Molineux 2012, O'Connell 2003). Francis disrupts Elizabeth's gaze by magically unbinding himself from the shop images' signification of blackness as inert. The static signs, ordinary and redundant within London's landscape, are juxtaposed with Francis' physical movement and ability to speak.

Many shop-signs in London bore images of Negroes:

> 'The Moor's Tobacco Shop,' 'The Moor's Head,' 'The Blackamoor's Brandy Shop.' The painted Negroes held up sheaves of tobacco, bottles of liquor, sugar loaves and other goods shipped from across the seas. They grinned stupidly; most were half-naked ... She [Elizabeth knew] that the figures were of mere paint and fixed securely to the signposts which bore them. Francis, though, by some pact of the Devil, had freed himself from paint, stepped off the signpost, taking flesh onto himself, and speech.
>
> (Dabydeen 2013, 40–41)

In this ekphrastic moment, one of many in *Johnson's Dictionary*, the narrative imagery continues to unfurl from the left margin of "The Times of Day, Noon." Turning away from Elizabeth's perspective that skims the surface of the street scene, the narrative pivots on blackness, its signification, and significance to the city. If we pause on the multiple meanings of "bore" in the passage, then the word gestures to the fact that London not only contained and tediously reproduced these images of black figures but also interpolated the images into a visual vocabulary of everyday consumption and taste. "Bore" furthermore connotes the act of etching or engraving onto a surface. London's visual signification of blackness (or the "signposting" of blackness) is the result of the repeated drawing (boring) of racial, metaphorical meaning through a material association with color. The moment also interacts with the Hogarth illustration inserted in the narrative, for it compounds how blackness becomes associated with the city's "good eating"; that is, London's consumption and circulation of goods and labor. In other words, through the interplay of textual narrative and visual illustration, the street scene of "The Times of Day, Noon" is imbued with a new context: that London is, indeed, the commercial expression of the eighteenth-century plantation.

In contrast to the overwhelmingly redundant representations of blackness as static feature, Francis unsettles signifiers through embodiment and speech. It is through speech in conjunction with the unsettling visual signifier of blackness ("stepp[ing] off the signpost, taking flesh onto himself") that Francis signals new optics for envisioning the presence of black subjects in the eighteenth century. Through the poetics of voice—embodied, written, and otherwise—Francis highlights how drawn lines (demarcations, definitions, borders) are not static; in fact, they are sites of porosity and dynamic interpretive activity. Words can hobble in and through the uneven imperial archive of representations, renewing and illuminating black subjects in the social space of Anglophone Atlantic life and its artistic production. Turning to Sancho's play with the visual signifier of the line is instructive: his lines are products of art interlocking with labor; it documents a subject involved in a social activity. Following Sancho's written cues, I read *Johnson's Dictionary*, then, as reworking lines—specifically lines of beauty—as material and technique to read for survival, growth, and the social life of black subjects from the plantation to its commercial expression, the city.

Thus, rather than seeing blackness as an ostensive visual signifier of imperial power and consumption, the novel returns to the British Caribbean and its future. Francis muses:

> I will prepare them for freedom by teaching them the *Dictionary*, starting with A for abacus to encourage counting and calculated thrift, and by year-end they will get to Z for zeugma, so that they will encounter the mystery of language, how conjunctive does work and what is the intransitive. They will realise how language stay, how it does congeal then suddenly conjugate, how it turvy and yet straight, true and seeming, yeaing and naying in one breath.
>
> (Dabydeen 2013, 205)

Language is a means to actively and dynamically remake the visual signifier of blackness. The grammar of blackness, as offered and theorized in *Johnson's Dictionary*, attends to the plurality of meanings made possible through the visual and textual forms circulating throughout the Atlantic world. By recasting the line of beauty and the object of the *Dictionary* in the British Caribbean—through the linking of London to Demerara—Dabydeen seems to suggest that the visual signifier of blackness in the past need not simply be an emblem reflecting the power of the plantation system and empire. Rather, new structures and forms of black life can be created through an analysis of the convergences and redirection of meaning (as suggested in the references to conjunctive and zeugma), and in the active reimagining of blackness without a specific object (which is gestured at through the reference to the intransitive).

As we move between, at least, two aesthetic modalities of interpreting the uneven eighteenth-century archive of representations—between image and text—Sancho's lines and the line of beauty offer new terms for reading the presence of blackness across the Anglophone Atlantic world. Although the set of written Anglophone texts produced by black subjects (beyond Sancho, Olaudah Equiano, Phillis Wheatley, Ukawsaw Gronniosaw, and more) are relegated to a minor position in the uneven, eighteenth-century imperial archive, we could attend to the interrelatedness of products (i.e., the novel) and the actions that conditions of production make possible (i.e., racialized slave labor). Given the interconnectedness between the rise of the novel and the rise of the plantation system, eighteenth-century texts and image index the social space of production, artistic and otherwise. By recalibrating the presence of blackness in the eighteenth century—both the popularization of images and works produced by black subjects—to the period's adjoining theories of visual lines, we refresh our optics toward not just the rootedness and mutually-constitutive terrain of slavery and modernity—we might also see the tremors of secretive histories harboring narratives and visions of life that extend beyond the plantation context.

Acknowledgments

This was written with the intellectual support of the Institute for Research on the African Diaspora in the Americas and the Caribbean at CUNY. I am especially grateful to Robert Reid-Pharr, Herman Bennett, Carrie Hintz, Duncan Faherty, Joseph Bowling, Kristin Moriah, Michael Shelichach, Charmaine A. Nelson, and the anonymous referee for all their comments on various versions of this chapter.

Notes

1 There is contention around the prefatory biography that frames the posthumous publication of Sancho's *Letters*. See Brycchan Carey 2003, "'The Extraordinary Negro': Ignatius Sancho, Joseph Jekyll, and the Problem of Biography," *Journal for Eighteenth-Century Studies*, 26, 1–13.
2 As Henry Louis Gates observes in *Figures in Black: Words, Signs, and the 'Racial' Self* (New York: Oxford University Press, 1989), the publication and discourse around Sancho as a public character (which relegated his work to the background) were largely premised upon racist debates about African intellect (8). See also James Sidbury, *Becoming African in America: Race and Nation in the Early Black Atlantic* (New York: Oxford University Press, 2007).
3 I build this assertion from my reading of Christopher Leslie Brown, *Moral Capital: Foundations of British Abolitionism* (Chapel Hill: University of North Carolina Press, 2006). Brown examines the sudden visibility of antislavery as an imperial issue toward the end of the eighteenth century. The American Revolution played a significant role: the loss of the thirteen colonies led to Britain's restructuring of its imperial economy. The consolidation of antislavery movement and its adjoining rhetoric in Britain at the end of the eighteenth century was, in part, a political tool of imperial self-aggrandizement.
4 Sukhdev Sandhu has observed that "Sancho's playful approach was confined not just to language but to the very grammar and appearance of his letters" (1997, 54). In particular, Sandhu has written about Sancho's use of dashes, and he attributes the frequency of their appearance in the letters to four central reasons. First, the punctuation style of the dashes are reverent nods to Sancho's favorite author, Laurence Sterne. Second, the dashes are deployed to swerve the reader in different narrative directions, and they fragment thoughts allowing for multiple detours. The dashes, in combination with Sancho's frequent punning, mock assumptions about "the elegant measured unity of Enlightened discourse." (Sandhu 2003, 42). Third, Sandhu illustrates effectively how the dashes also mime the flurry, bustle, and interruptions that an urban grocer might experience. Lastly, Sandhu suggests that Sancho's use of the dash critiques the racial theory circulated through Edward Long's 1774 *History of Jamaica*, where Long argues that Africans were unable to produce linear and rational thought.
5 Daybdeen has had a career-long scholarly and creative engagement with Hogarth. He wrote his dissertation on Hogarth in 1982, and wrote two studies on Hogarth, *Hogarth's Blacks: Images of Blacks in 18th-Century Art* (Manchester University Press, 1987) and *Hogarth, Walpole and Commercial Britain* (Hansib, 1987). In his 1982 monograph on Hogarth, Dabydeen studies the artist's 1753

aesthetic treatise *The Analysis of Beauty* by tracing "the references to blacks in Hogarth's writings" to demonstrate that the artist was "surprisingly knowledgeable about the philosophical (aesthetic) and scientific issues pertaining to blacks, as well as being aware of the black presence on the English stage" (1987, 51). Hogarth's illustrations and aesthetic theories also appear in a number of Dabydeen's essays and creative work, including *A Harlot's Progress* (Jonathan Cape, 1999) and "Hogarth and the Canecutter" in *'The Tempest' and Its Travels*, eds. Peter Hulme and William H. Sherman, [London: Reaktion Books, 2000]).

References

Anonymous, Fortescue. *Or, the Soldier's Reward: A Characteristic Novel. In One Volume*, Dublin: printed for Mess. P. Byrne, P. Wogan, J. Moore, and B. Dornin, M,DCC,LXXXIX. [1789]. *Eighteenth Century Collections Online*. Web. 14 April 2016.

Altman, Jane Gurkin. 1982. *Epistolarity: Approaches to a Form*. Columbus: Ohio State University Press.

Anderson, Howard and Ehrenpreis, Irvin. 1991. "The Familiar Letter in the Eighteenth Century: Some Generalizations," *The Familiar Letter in the Eighteenth Century*, edited by Howard Anderson, Philip B. Daghlian, and Irvin Ehrenpries. Lawrence: University Press of Kansas, 269–282.

Bundock, Michael. 2015. *The Fortunes of Francis Barber: The True Story of the Jamaican Slave Who Became Samuel Johnson's Heir*. New Haven, CT: Yale University Press.

Carey, Brycchan. 2003. "'The Extraordinary Negro': Ignatius Sancho, Joseph Jekyll, and the Problem of Biography," *Journal for Eighteenth-Century Studies*, 26, 1–13.

Carretta, Vincent. 2004. *Unchained Voices: An Anthology of Black Authors in the English-Speaking World of the 18th Century*. Lexington: The University Press of Kentucky.

Dabydeen, David. 1987. *Hogarth's Blacks: Images of Blacks in Eighteenth Century English Art*. Manchester: Manchester University Press.

Dabydeen, David. 2013. *Johnson's Dictionary*. Leeds: Peepal Tree.

Earle, T. F. and Lowe, K.J.P. 2005. *Black Africans in Renaissance Europe*. New York, NY: Cambridge University Press.

Ellis, Markman. 2001. "Ignatius Sancho's *Letters*: Sentimental Libertinism and the Politics of Form." In *Genius in Bondage: Literature of the Black Atlantic*, edited by Vincent Carretta and Philip Gould. Lexington: University Press of Kentucky, 199–217.

Fryer, Peter. 1984. *Staying Power: The History of Black People in Britain*. London: Pluto Press.

Gates Jr., Henry Louis. 1989. *Figures in Black: Words, Signs, and the 'Racial' Self*. New York, NY: Oxford University Press.

Gerzina, Gretchen. 1995. *Black London: Life before Emancipation*. New Brunswick, NJ: Rutgers University Press.

Gikandi, Simon. 2014. *Slavery and the Culture of Taste*. Princeton, NJ: Princeton University Press.

Gilroy, Paul. 1993. *The Black Atlantic: Modernity and Double Consciousness*. Cambridge, MA: Harvard University Press.

Hall, Kim F. 1995. *Things of Darkness: Economies of Race and Gender in Early Modern England*. Ithaca, NY: Cornell University Press.

Hand, Felicity. 1995. "A Talk with David Dabydeen," *Links and Letters 2*, 79–86.

Hine, Darlene Clark; Keaton, Trica Danielle; and Small, Stephen 2009. *Black Europe and the African Diaspora*. Urbana and Chicago: University of Illinois Press.

Hogarth, William. 1753. *The Analysis of Beauty. Written with a View of Fixing the Fluctuating Ideas of Taste. By William Hogarth*. London: printed by J. Reeves for the author, and sold by him at his house in Leicester-Fields. *Eighteenth Century Collections Online*. Web. 29 April 2016.

Ireland, John. 1793. *Hogarth Illustrated. By John Ireland*. 2nd ed. Vol. 3. London: [from the press of W. Bulmer & Co.] published, August, 1793, for J. and J. Boydell, Cheapside; and at the Shakespeare Gallery, Pall-Mall, [1793]. *Eighteenth Century Collections Online*. Web. 14 April 2016, page 244.

McKittrick, Katherine. 2013. "Plantation Futures," *Small Axe*, 42, 1–15.

Molineux, Catherine. 2012. *Faces of Perfect Ebony: Encountering Atlantic Slavery in Imperial Britain*. Cambridge, MA: Harvard University Press.

Nussbaum, Felicity A. 2001. "Being a Man: Olaudah Equiano and Ignatius Sancho." In *Genius in Bondage: Literature of the Black Atlantic*, edited by Vincent Carretta and Philip Gould. Lexington: University Press of Kentucky, 54–71.

O'Connell, Sheila. 2003. *London 1753*. Boston, MA: David R. Godine Publisher.

Sancho, Ignatius. [1782] 1998. *Letters of the Late Ignatius Sancho, An African*. New York, NY: Penguin Books.

Sandhu, Sukhdev. 1997. "Ignatius Sancho: An African Man of Letters." In *Ignatius Sancho: An African Man of Letters*, edited by Charles Saumarez Smith. London: National Portrait Gallery Publications, 45–73.

Sandhu, Sukhdev. 2003. *London Calling: How Black and Asian Writers Imagined a City*. London: Harper Perennial.

Smith, Charles Saumarez, 1997, Ed. *Ignatius Sancho: An African Man of Letters*. London: National Portrait Gallery Publications.

Trouillot, Michel-Rolph. 2002. "Culture on the Edges: Caribbean Creolization in Historical Context." In *From the Margins: Historical Anthropology and Its Futures*, edited by Brian Keith Axel. Durham, NC: Duke University Press, 189–210.

Wheeler, Roxann. 2000. *The Complexion of Race: Categories of Difference in Eighteenth-Century British Culture*. Philadelphia: University of Pennsylvania Press.

Wynter, Sylvia. 1971. "Novel and History, Plot and Plantation," *Savacou*, 5(1), 95–102.

2 "Concatenation"

Syncretism in the Life Cycle of David Drake's Earthenware

Rach Klein

Introduction

Between 1820 and 1890, the Edgefield region of South Carolina, known informally as "Pottersville" or "Landrumsville," produced thousands of earthenware pots, jugs, and tankards (Figure 2.1). Ranging in size from a few ounces to forty gallons, these highly functional vessels were created largely for use on plantations across the Southern States to store salted meat, syrups, and other preserves (Fennell 2017). This ceramic epicentre was inaugurated by the white Landrum family, who established a number of pottery factories which were "facilitated through kinship and close social networks, capital crucial for the growth and success of the industry, in the form of kilns, clay sources, pine tracts, and most importantly enslaved Africans and African Americans" (Kenline-Nyman 2017). Among the thousands of vessels created by enslaved artisans and labourers, very few can be linked to individual people with the notable exception of pieces created by the prolific master potter and poet David Drake who made extraordinary earthenware which he signed and engraved. In addition to Dave's exceptional creations, other unnamed enslaved African-born people and their Creole descendants produced earthenware in the nineteenth century. From the gathering of clay in South Carolina's mineral-rich riverbeds to the transport of heavy jugs to marketplace, their filling with preserved food, and inevitably, the sweeping of broken shards, Edgefield pottery is inextricable from the system of slavery within which it was created.

Hence, to look at a single work of earthenware created in Pottersville is to gaze upon a material manifestation of the complex labour, creativity, craftsmanship, and resilience of dozens of enslaved people. As stated by archaeologists Mary Beaudry, Lauren Cook, and Stephen A. Mrozowski, historical objects such as these are not merely "a passive product of economic behavior, but an instrumental component of symbolic actions" (1996, 272). In addition to being "symbolic actions," objects created in Pottersville also represent what John Michael Vlach calls "a crossroads of clay where the influences of three continents – Europe, Asia and Africa – were blended to create a distinct pottery tradition" (1979, 17). White families such as the Scottish-descendent Landrums made use of technology developed in China (the "Dragon Kiln"), the labour and creations of enslaved African-born people and their descendants, and the land of Indigenous Americans to create a pottery economy (De Groft, 1998). Sarat Maharaj's essay "Perfidious Fidelity: The Unstranslatability of the Other" echoes Vlach's geographic insights:

> Africa, Asia, Australia, Europe – no position permits a viewing without itself turning into the viewed. What prevails is the sense of watching as we are being watched, of someone looking over our shoulder as we look *l'autre l'ailleurs* – the Other, elsewhere, everywhere

"Concatenation": Syncretism in the Life Cycle 35

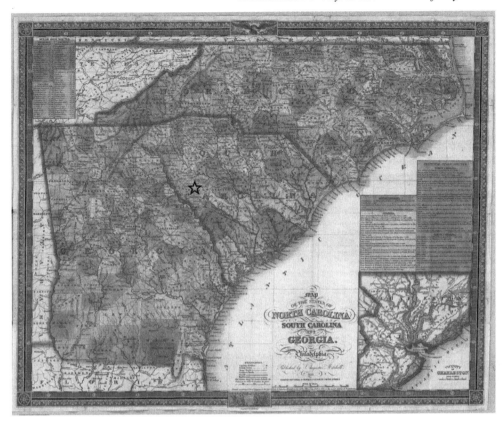

Figure 2.1 Mitchell, Samuel Augustus, *North Carolina South Carolina and Georgia (1835)*, pocket map, 18 × 22, David Rumsey Map Collection, David Rumsey Map Center, Stanford Librarie," Philadelphia, United States. Edgefield region marked by star.

and besides. The very transparency blocks off and shutters, occludes. We are unable to totalise this mapping of the world, each time something slips out of our grip. We grapple with the leftovers, the remainder of the untranslatable.

(1994, np)

The "remainder of the untranslatable" is manifested tangibly in Edgefield earthenware, which resists a single point of view. In particular, Dave's works invite questions about authorial presence and necessitate engagement between viewer and viewed, subject and object, maker and user.

Such questions of authorial presence illuminate the distinct context under which Dave worked, and the intricacies of creolization as it unfolded in Edgefield. While the term "creolization" has been aptly used to discuss the Gullah people in South Carolina, who developed a distinct creole language and culture in Lowcountry regions, it has not been so readily used to refer to the history of Edgefield. My use of the term "creolization" throughout this chapter names the interconnected system of labour, technology, and artisanship that earthenware production in Edgefield relied on throughout the nineteenth century, and locates the vessels produced under such systems as being material manifestations of this interconnectivity. In short, the vessels that came out of kilns in Pottersville fired into material solidification the particular cultural and geographic conditions that allowed for their creation. I additionally consider the presence of Asian kilns in Edgefield to be a facet of the creolization of the region that showcases an intercontinental connexion additional to that of Africa and America. As emphasized in an analysis of authorial presence and coded communication, I also distinguish between individualized creolization – as seen in the particularities of Drake's writing – and a collective creolization of Edgefield's pottery region.

My contemplation of Dave's pottery is situated through three distinct yet intersecting fields of analysis. Firstly, in the signed earthenware work and poetry of David Drake. His couplets, embedded in slanted text upon the surface of large-scale jugs, are a precious source of firsthand reflections written by an enslaved artisan. Dave's writing explored many themes, among them romance, faith, and commerce. Throughout this chapter, I turn back continually to Dave's own words in order to best situate the vessels within the context of his own life, living, and working within a system of enslavement.

This chapter will unfold chronologically, following the physical transformation of pottery from earth and sand to structured objects. Moving through the many labour-intensive and collaborative facets of earthenware production helps to shed light on the number of unattributed labourers who were necessary for the creation of a single vessel. The 2011 archaeological excavation conducted by the Edgefield Field School of the University of Illinois, the University of South Carolina, and the Diachronic Research Foundation provides invaluable insight into the material remnants of the pottery site, as well as the architecture of the spaces of production found on the Landrum potter site. George Calfas's essay, "Shifted Perspectives on Dave: Implications of Archaeological Excavation at the Pottersville Kiln Site" (2018), which initially directed me to the 2011 excavation report, was extremely helpful in translating the excavation's data into accessible terms.

I root this analysis in Édouard Glissant's *Poetics of Relation* (1993) and have adopted his framework for an analysis of the nature of creolized cultures. Glissant, like Umberto Eco, Derek Walcott, and other contemporary scholars of creolization, expands his definition of creolization beyond the first encounter of Europeans and Africans on American (continental) soil, offered by anthropologist Sidney Mintz (2008). Influenced by his own upbringing in Martinique and the cultural collisions and expansions he witnessed there, Glissant's *Poetics of Relation* (1993) includes a globalizing approach that moves towards "tout-monde," the whole world; everyone, everywhere. This is not to suggest that creolized cultures are homogenous, but rather that "Creolization carries along then into the adventure of multilingualism and into the incredible explosion of culture. But the explosion of cultures does not mean they are scattered or mutually diluted." (34). A philosopher, anthropologist, and poet, Glissant heralds a framework of "Relation" that allows for diasporic complexities of identity based on the varying and specific cultural, political, and geographic settings wherein, "each and every identity is extended through relationship with the Other" (11). The physical, cultural, spiritual, and linguistic results of these relationships are unpredictable and are formed through and around the power dynamics between identity and Other. Such power balances and imbalances are pertinent to his study, in which he asserts (agreeing with Mintz and others) that creolization begins "in the womb of the plantation," beginning his *Poetics of Relation* by setting the grotesque and unsettling scene of a transatlantic slave ship for his readers:

> Imagine two hundred human beings crammed into a space barely capable of containing a third of them. Imagine vomit, naked flesh, swarming lice, the dead slumped, the dying crouched. Imagine, if you can, the swirling red of mounting to the deck, the ramp they

climbed, the black sun on the horizon, vertigo, this dizzying sky plastered to the waves. Over the course of more than two centuries, twenty, thirty million people deported. Worn down, in a debasement more eternal than apocalypse. But that is nothing.

(6)

Yet despite this horrific entry point into the Americas, or perhaps because of it, Glissant is able to convincingly and poetically call on his readers to move within studies of creolized culture with a curiosity and compassion towards "both the beauty and multiplicity of both diasporic and African culture" (Mulira 2015, 119). It is Glissant's approach that I find most useful for this particular material analysis.

In addition to his astute observations on the politics, philosophy, and potentialities of forced collaboration, Glissant's own emphasis on language and the significance of poetry make his work especially relevant to examining David Drake's remarkable words. Glissant writes, "Poetry is not an amusement nor a display of sentiments or beautiful things. It also imparts form to a knowledge that could never be stricken by obsolescence" (81). Indeed, Dave's words and work have circulated among the literate and illiterate, have been touched by countless enslaved worker's hands, and have been gathered in museums, continuing to bring themselves into an unwavering relevance to history, to poetry, and to art.

Section One recounts the historical conditions that led to the creation of Pottersville and to the distribution of Dave Drake's work, while also recognizing how records of industrialization and expansion in nineteenth-century South Carolina are incomplete, intentionally hiding and suppressing voices of enslaved artisans and labourers in the region. Drawing on Glissant's theories of fragmentation, Relation, and resistance, Section One makes use of Dave's poetic insights in order to identify the complexities of authorial presence within documentation of Transatlantic Slavery. Section Two begins with a close examination of glazing and firing techniques used in Edgefield, and their connections to Chinese pottery production. An analysis of earthenware's many stages of creation reveals how enslaved labourers may have resisted reduction from personhood to production. Section Three will discuss uses of earthenware after creation, once again referring to Dave's writing on such topics. Lastly, Section Four examines the potential uses of potteries' afterlives – how fragments may have been used and reused once vessels were broken or discarded.

Section One

In the first two decades of the nineteenth century, the white population in the Edgefield district decreased from 13,063 to 12,864 while simultaneously, the enslaved Black population increased dramatically from 5,006 to nearly 20,000 people (Burton, 1985). This rapid increase was due to the use of nearby Charleston as a slave port as well as the accelerated expansion of cotton production occurring across the Southern United States (Greene 2008). Although Edgefield's dominant commercial enterprise became pottery rather than agriculture, these industries are intimately intertwined with the vessels that were created in Pottersville in demand from plantation owners in the Carolinas, Georgia, Alabama, and Texas, among other southern regions (Baldwin 2014). As recorded by George Calfas (2013), evidence suggests that Pottersville was founded between 1809 and 1817, was fully functional by 1817, and continued to produce large quantities of pottery well into the late twentieth century. At the helm of this expansion of enslavement and industry was the Landrum family, who developed the first Pottersville factory and subsequently controlled numerous pottery enterprises throughout the region. While there were several other notable facilities held by other families, the

Landrums, and their merging with the wealthy Miles family through marriage, have a large legacy in the history of American ceramics.

Local newspapers in the early nineteenth century, such as the *Edgefield Hive* and *Edgefield Advertiser*, list enslaved artisans with skills in pottery production for sale. While "turner" is the most common occupation listed, as Cinda K. Baldwin has argued "slaves were undoubtedly involved in every aspect of stoneware production, from digging, hauling, and preparing the clay to turning and firing the ware and wagoning it to market" (Baldwin 2014, 74). Indeed, the very basis of Edgefield's success in pottery production – the region's "naturally occurring deposits of high-quality stoneware and kaolin clays, which have fewer impurities to the clay matrix" – relied on enslaved labour to gather the clay and haul it to the pottery sites. As stated by Christopher Fennell, "The African-American workers at each of these antebellum potteries sites would have included clay mining as part of their regular tasks" (Fennel 2017, 57).

Once at the pottery complex, the raw clay would be mixed with water and sand using an ingenious device called a "pug mill." Although mules and horses would turn the mill by walking in a circular path around the central axis, there would certainly be labourers overseeing the animals and checking on the mixture. After the clay was gathered, mixed and left to set, it could be cut into different sized pieces and transported to the turners who would transform the mess of sand and wet clay into vessels. Using kickwheels, the process of turning clay was labour intensive and required immense strength, particularly for the large-scale vessels created for food storage (Niculescu 2017, 204).

Among the "turners" owned by the Landrum family was David Drake, who is generally referred to in scholarship, censuses, and historical archives as simply "Dave" or "Dave the Potter."[1] After substantial consideration, this chapter will exclusively use the name Dave, in order to refer to him in the name he used to sign his work – although sources referenced may use different nominal variations. The most documented of Dave's pieces are, unsurprisingly, the ones onto which he engraved poetic couplets and musings ranging from the religious to the romantic. To the modern viewer, these writings create dynamic works of art that seem to transcend the utilitarian food-storage purpose for which the vessels were initially built and bought (Fennell 2017). To various scholars of Transatlantic Slavery, accustomed to parsing the words of white slave owners in search of the identities and experiences of the enslaved, Dave's literacy presents a rare and precious opportunity to learn about life for an enslaved nineteenth-century artisan through his own words and in his own handwriting. Dave's writing reveals how his creations were bought, sold, and used; they offer glimpses into what occupied his mind as he turned endless clay and sweated over the scorching kilns of Pottersville, and they indicate how he communicated with the world. Writes Michael Chaney,

> Repeated on one jar after another, the name swells nearly to an imperative: Dave! In the inscriptions above, Dave is an exclamation of identity, personhood interjected. Dave is also a maker and a lyric speaker. He is a busy "I" who sees, shoots, sees more, feels, and belongs.
>
> (2018, 5)

Although these records are incomplete, limited by the censorship of white owners and literacy laws, the cruel industry of Transatlantic Slavery, and the delicate and breakable nature of the material itself, they nonetheless comprise small but important pieces of a life. Like the earthenware fragments excavated in 2011 at the Landrum pottery production site on which he worked, Dave's life and art must be recounted through close examination of many small pieces.[2]

Yet, as Glissant writes, to study through fragments does not necessarily mean limitation, but in many ways, expansion. He states,

> Let us, nonetheless, consult these ruins with their uncertain evidence, their extremely fragile monuments, their frequently incomplete, obliterated, or ambiguous archives. You can guess already what we are to discover: that the Plantation is one of the focal points for the development of present-day modes of Relation.
>
> (1993, 65)

Certainly fragmentation, whether culturally, poetically, or archaeologically readily opens questions of Relation. What is the relationship of a jagged shard to the absent space in the body of the vessel that it once occupied? What are the interactions of the material incomplete to the complete, and the space between the intention of the artisan and the reality of the object's use? Glissant goes on to define his key term in a later section of the *Poetics of Relation*, writing: "Relation: The position of each part within this whole: that is, the acknowledged validity of each specific Plantation yet at the same time the urgent need to understand the hidden order of the whole-so as to wander there without becoming lost" (131). Dave's writing reveals small pieces of a whole that are perhaps best approached as signposts towards decoding the systems that hold up each single creation. Through this outlook, the viewer can attempt (as Glissant cautions) to wander without getting lost. As Robert Baron and Ana C. Cara offer in the introduction to their anthology, *Creolization as Cultural Creativity* (2011):

> Creole expressions have been viewed as manifestations of fragmentation and degeneration, thereby suffering in comparison to supposedly fully formed, reified, and historically sanctioned expressions of a colonial or "Westernized" elite. In sharp contrast, creolists see creolization as creative disorder, as a poetic chaos, thereby challenging simplistic and static notions of center and periphery.
>
> (2011, 5)

This approach is not intended to minimize the extraordinary trauma caused by forced fragmentation but rather to acknowledge that resilience, creativity, and connection can be found even among ruins.

Finding the "I" within enslaved people's labour is difficult because their individuality was intentionally suppressed. By this, I mean that the individuality of the enslaved was carefully stripped away, dehumanizing the individuals while simultaneously scrubbing evidence of their forced labour from its results – the production of cotton, tobacco, steel, and pottery, for example. In the work of artisans, this suppression and lack of accreditation acts as its own form of creative disorder, manifesting objects estranged from makers, art with unidentifiable artists. In *Eloquent Vessels/Poetics of Power: The Heroic Stoneware of 'Dave the Potter'* (1998), Aaron de Groft writes of the deep importance of authorial and personal power:

> The idea of authorship, or presence (I was here, or I am here) is a predominant concept that runs throughout the history of man ... since earliest man, the need for authorship, acknowledgment, and remembrance has been a pervasive human concern.
>
> (1998, 225)

This idea of authorship is a vexed web for many objects, materials, and structures made by enslaved workers. Often, no creator is identified, yet even when they can be – as in the case of Dave Drake – so too can the overseeing presence of their owners be found.

Several of Dave's vessels provide insight into the complexities of authorial presence under enslavement, as well as to the physical processes of creating the earthenware that he wrote on. For example, on July 31, 1840, Dave writes:

Dave belongs to Mr. Miles | Where the oven bakes & the pot biles

Engraved beneath the lip and stretching horizontally towards the two embedded handles of a large, alkaline-glazed jug – a placement that is typical of Dave's signatures – this text denotes ownership and location, while also positioning the self, "Dave," as a tool of production. Not only does he "belong" to Miles but he also belongs specifically to the pottery mill, "where the oven bakes." The vessel onto which Dave is writing conceptually collapses with the person who made it; both Dave and the jug can be bought and sold, are owned by others, and exist exclusively where "the pot biles." Did Lewis Miles, who owned Dave for a number of years, also own the jug on which Dave placed this engraving? Or did it pass hands, as Dave later would, sold to the highest bidder? The materiality at work in this piece includes not only the earthenware vessel and the gentle ridges of the text but also of Dave himself, as he documents his positionality in the clay itself.

Dave's poetry was not the only thing that was engraved upon the earthenware of Pottersville, with many vessels bearing small decorative or functional markings. In 2017, J.W. Joseph produced an extensive study of the many marks found in Edgefield Pottery, "Crosses, Crescents, Slashes, Stars: African-American Potters and Edgefield District Pottery Marks" which presented this intriguing possibility:

> I believe enslaved African-American potters working in the Edgefield District used slash and punctate marks as a type of "coded recognizability." These marks would have been recognizable to fellow African Americans as marks used in scarification to express social and cultural identity. At the same time these inscriptions likely appeared to white pottery owners as innocuous marks used by illiterate potters to indicate capacity, with minor decorative flourishes in the form of additional punctate marks and slashes. The fact that this style of capacity marking and decoration was found in Edgefield, but not in other districts, further indicates that it was a product of the district's African-American potters.
> (2017, 128)

Here, Joseph summarizes some of his study's findings that suggest that various markings on the earthenware vessels "served to signify to other African Americans on southern farms and plantations that these vessels were African made" (119). The marked vessels created by potters in Edgefield would have passed through dozens of hands, being transported to markets and carried on ferries before reaching the homes of enslaved workers on plantations. Therefore, throwers could mark their works knowing that there was a large network of people who may have been able to decode them or, at the very least, been able to recognize that the vessel was created by a fellow African or African American person.

Can these markings then be approached as a form of creole poetics? Glissant, it seems, would support such a claim. As Lincoln Z. Shlensky interprets:

> Creole poetics, he suggests in *Poetique*, are the radically unexpected yet prosaically evental "moyens a chaque fois hasardes" 'risky everyday retorts' (83; 69, translation modified) of the slaves and their immediate descendants.
> (2013, 363)

Figure 2.2 David Drake, *Storage Jar* (1857), alkaline-glazed earthenware, height: 19 in.; diameter: 17 3/4 in., Museum of Fine Arts, Boston, Massachusetts. Engraved with "Aug. 22, 1857," and "I made this jar for cash / though it is called lucre trash."

Certainly, Dave's writing is easily recognizable as consisting of "risky everyday retorts." A fascinating example of this boldness and risk is another poem that considers authorial presence, engraved on a large, glazed two-handed vessel dated August 22, 1857. On it he writes:

I made this jar for cash / Though it is called lucre trash (Figure. 2.2)

In contrast to the earlier piece discussed, here Dave uses the personal pronoun "I," and in doing so takes linguistic ownership of the vessel. The following words, "for cash," are a curious indicator of the financial and personal mobility that Dave may have had. Indeed, South Carolina had a robust "for-hire" system for enslaved black artisans, wherein they would rent out their labour in numerous industries to white owners and overseers (Greene, 2008).[3]

The region's slave-majority demographics also meant that enslaved workers participated in their own labour economy and may have had access to making wages. Says J.W. Joseph,

> In response to a society in which they were heavily outnumbered, planters employed a labor system, referred to as task labor, that provided their African American laborers with time of their own. African Americans, in turn, hunted, fished, grew crops, and made crafts, and marketed the products of their own time in Charleston, as well as other locations.
>
> (2016, 96)

Among African Americans in South Carolina who developed an independent market economy are the Gullah, who produced their own robust Creole culture, influenced by the ongoing importation of Africans to coastal South Carolina. Writes Joseph, "Living in relative isolation, these Africans and later African Americans formed their own creole culture, known as Gullah in South Carolina and Geechee in Georgia" (2016, 94). The Gullah peoples and culture are well documented in studies of creolization and Lowcountry history. They too, are well known for vessel-making: the production of the popular "Gullah baskets" or "sweetgrass baskets." Although documentation of interactions between enslaved peoples inland in South Carolina and those living in the Lowcountry are difficult to locate, the thriving marketplace of Charleston as well as the illicit use of ferries and waterways by black ferrymen to transport goods, materials, and information from community to community suggest that there would have been some contact between the Gullah people and other African and African American people working in less clearly creolized regions, such as Edgefield.

Given this diversified and illicit marketplace economy, it is very likely that Dave did receive some cash from his work, perhaps in exchange with other enslaved artisans and laborers. However, there is an ambiguity in this couplet. Although he takes authorship of the vessel, he does not specify who benefits from the cash. The second line reveals some of the complexities implied here. "Though it is called lucre trash," is cheeky, intelligent, and heartbreaking. The word "lucre" was likely learned through Biblical study, a recurring theme throughout Dave's work.[4] Appearing in the King James Bible in six different verses (Samuel 8:3; Timothy 3:3; Timothy 3:8; Titus 1:7; Titus 1:11; and Peter 5:3), this term refers to money earned through distasteful or dishonest means. It may appear initially as if Dave is referring to the jar as trash. However, the Biblical context makes clear that he is referring to *cash* as trash; sordid and wrongly gained. In the essay "Inscribing Economic Desire," Xiomara Santamarina says of this couplet that "This ironic gap between speaker and sentiment enables Dave to challenge his master's ownership of himself and his jars" (2018, 83). That is, Dave's words denounce the financial situation in which he is trapped; he has made the jar for cash that is immoral as long as it is tied to Transatlantic Slavery.[5] The jar itself, with its deep burnt umber colour, dripping yellow glaze, and gently tilted rim cannot be separated from the lucre with which it is associated; it is as much a receipt as it is a sale.

Dave's boldness in writing upon these vessels is particularly surprising and risky, given South Carolina laws that prohibited slave literacy. De Groft notes that "in 1837 South Carolina made it illegal to teach slaves to read or write and for slaves to actually practice these skills if they had already been taught" before giving this suggestion as to why Dave's writing may have been allowed:

> His inscriptions may have been tolerated, even favored, by Miles and his overseers because they seemed harmless and whimsical. Still, they may have had very different meanings for those who handled his pots daily. Anyone familiar with the history of the division of labor on southern plantations will know that the heavy storage pots would have been handled by slave labourers.
>
> (1998, 244)

Given that the pots "would have been handled by slave labourers," could the nonliterate markings that J.W. Joseph identifies be a part of a network of exchange that is abstract to the contemporary viewer, and certainly would have been also to the historical white viewer, but significant and legible in the ongoing exchange of symbols and signs within enslaved communities?.

Joseph's conclusions are controversial, particularly within archaeological discourse, with Leland G. Ferguson responding:

> Unfortunately, as neat as they are, those kinds [Joseph's] of interpretations are often trivial. Dealing with serious and complicated issues, like the secrets of plantations and the covert symbolism of slaves, requires brainstorming, perhaps for many years, with inconclusive evidence. Archaeologists must work with ambiguity, making neither too much of limited data, nor too little – accepting that value accrues from pondering these issues even if unassailable conclusions are never reached.
>
> (2011, 165)

I find it worthwhile to include his suggestion and to imagine what the potential meanings of these markings could be, even when we are unable to make definitive connections and conclusions. Baron and Cara include the idea of "masking" from white people in the ongoing construction of creolization, writing that "often provoking and defying elite or dominant powers through mockery, irony, humor, and other subversive measures, Creole formulations nevertheless remain intimately grounded and entwined in the everyday exigencies of their own Creole communities. In this respect, Creole enactments are counterhegemonic in their challenge to cultural dominance, making creolity nothing but revolutionary" (2011, 7). There is something deeply counterhegemonic and, indeed, radical, in the possibilities that these inscribed earthenware vessels spark, particularly because they were created under a legal system that outlawed access to communication tools. In sum, these markings may never be decoded, translated, or made legible to the lay person, academic investigator or archaeologist, but that too is part of their power.

In Glissant's *Poetry of Relation,* he writes of the potential of language emerging out of the linguistic constrictions of colonial rule:

> Whatever, coming from a tradition, enters into Relation; whatever, defending a tradition, justifies Relation; whatever, having left behind or refuted every tradition, provides the basis for another full-sense to Relation; whatever, born of Relation, contradicts and embodies it. Anglo-American pidgin (something, therefore, spoken neither by the English nor by the Americans) is a negative écho-monde, whose concrete force weaves the folds of Relation and neutralizes its subsistence.
>
> (93)

He concludes that the results of a violent clash of Relation "are unpredictable, but the beginnings of the capacity to endure are detectable" (95). Broken down into engravings, smudged fingerprints in glaze and carved slashes, enslaved artisans creating earthenware make material the "capacity to endure" and to create, despite the cruelty of the institution that they were forced to endure. Glissant goes on to write that

> at every node of Relation we will find callouses of resistance. Relation is learning more and more to go beyond judgments into the unexpected dark of art's uprisings. Its beauty springs from the stable and the unstable, from the deviance of many particular poetics and the clairvoyance of a relational poetics. The more things it standardizes into a state of lethargy, the more rebellious consciousness it arouses.
>
> (138–139)

Such "callouses of resistance" are perhaps meant metaphorically in *Relations*, but can be taken literally when studying pottery. Michael Chaney, in the introduction to an anthology of essays on David Drake, considers the placement of the engraved lettering of his poetry within a material, stating "One works upon the other materially at the dissolving intersections of the linguistic and the plastic. At this level, language is made up of bumps and ridges, tufts and plateaus" (Chaney 2018, 15). Language, both Chaney and Glissant suggest, is composed of more than words. The poetics of creolization may have existed within the physical ridges of text and engravings for enslaved African and African American people working in Edgefield and the surrounding regions, as they made, transported, and used the earthenware it was written upon.

Ethan Lasser says that "Dave's inscriptions initially read as abstract marks from most vantages. They only gradually cohere, upon close inspection, into letters" (2018, 134). I would like to offer the possibility that even when his poems did not "gradually cohere" and become recognizable to the literate, both they and other nonalphabetic engravings created by enslaved artisans of the region could embody a resistant poetics of Relation. Says Sanya Ruth Mulira, "Poetics appear when the dust settles from cultural collision and the products of the impact begin to take shape. Poetics, in this case, can be likened to culture" (2015, 117).

Section Two

After being thrown, engraved, and left to set, the jugs and vessels would be glazed and fired. Earthenware requires glaze for it to be able to hold liquids, meaning that the vast majority of the works produced in Edgefield were glazed. According to Jamie Arjona, "Dipped in earth-toned glazes with an occasional swirl of slip decorating the surface, most ceramics produced for consumption were utilitarian vessels used for food preparation and storage" (2017, 175). Mastering ceramic glazes requires an understanding of chemistry as well as artistic inclination. Anthropologist Tatiana Niculescu, who wrote a detailed article on South Carolina ceramic glazes, says "Working with glazes requires one to understand the intricacies of production, including how to apply a glaze, how a particular formulation will behave, and how location in the kiln can impact the end product"(2017, 201). Indeed, many writers on the process of glazing speak with a kind of alchemical awe, recognizing the magic of the material. Rice, for example, defines ceramic glazes as "a particular kind of glass, a non-crystalline substance cooled rapidly from a melt of earthy materials" (2015, 98).

Basic alkaline glazes are made of clay, sand, lime, or wood ash, all materials that can be easily found in the Edgefield area. According to Niculescu, "Potters can add small amounts of several other ingredients to the basic alkaline glaze recipe to produce additional variations in color and texture. These additives can include chrome, ground up glass, feldspar, or flint" (2017, 200). In Edgefield, most of the pieces found are shades of green, grey, yellow, and brown, resulting from a combination of the glaze's elemental components and oxygenation while firing (Figure 2.3). Like the dragon kilns, the pieces would later be fired within, the glazes used in Edgefield had roots in Asian pottery: similar alkaline glazes were first produced in China around 1500 BC. Curiously, no scholars have come to agreement about how Abner Landru, who pioneered the use of alkaline recipes in Edgefield, came to know about the Asian technique. Carl Steen writes, "The use of this variant ash and lime based alkaline glaze is a tradition shared by South Carolina and Asians that seems to have bypassed England and Europe" (2011, 22). This is yet another example of the unexpected, undefined, and unpredictable plurality that exists within each of the objects produced at Edgefield, and the exquisite clash of cultures that is found within their material bodies.

Figure 2.3 David Drake, *Jar* (1859), height: 28.75 in.; diameter: -21.75 in., Courtesy of The Charleston Museum, Charleston, South Carolina, OBJECT ID 1919.5.1. Engraved with "Made at Stoney bluff, for making dis ole gin enuff."

Yet among these forced collisions, subtle resistance and assertion of independence can be found. Among the many grey and brown vessels, the dominant glaze colour is dark green. Niculescu gives the following enticing suggestion as to why this may have been:

> The dark green pieces could simply be the result of workers trying to stretch out the last bit of a glaze mixture by adding more clay or wood ash. This would have been economical for owners, but could also be seen as a moment of quiet resistance in which an enslaved person decided to put off making a fresh batch of glaze, which would have required more effort.
>
> (2017, 200)

Here, she suggests that the colours of the vessels may reveal the decisions of the enslaved labourers and an insertion of independence into a process that was imposed upon them. Like the markings Joseph examines, Niculescu recognizes that subtle assertions of independent choice, communication, and resilience may be present in the earthenware, not only in established written languages but in other material details. Once the works were glazed, whether in resistance, in creativity, or simply in frustrated boredom, they would be left in a drying room for several hours before being transferred to the kilns.

The final step in creating the body of an earthenware piece of pottery is its firing. The firing of large vessels involves intense labour, tricky temperature maintenance, and a careful watch of the materials. An extensive 2011 excavation at Pottersville found that the large-scale kilns in Edgefield could be as big as 105 feet long and 12 feet wide (Calfas, 2013). The design found was similar to the "dragon kilns" most commonly seen in southeastern China (Calfas, 2013). In the dragon kilns of Edgefield, the syncretism of the region is made clear: pottery production made use of technology from Asia under the labour of Africans and African Americans for the benefit of white Europeans. Calfas gives a summary of the structure of dragon kilns. I offer it in full:

> Dragon kilns take 72 hours to fire stoneware at 1,200 degrees Celsius, which makes working along a kiln heat-intensive labor. Images of modern-day dragon kiln operations depict potters covered from head to toe with perspiration and ash. To access the stoking ports on a dragon kiln, Dave and other workers would have used a walkway along the hot exterior of the kiln. This walkway allowed them to traverse the incline of the kiln during firing operations. One feature discovered at Pottersville has been interpreted as just such a walkway. We must therefore conclude that the Asian design and style of the kiln informed the pottery production that flourished in the Old Edgefield District. Indeed, the large 40-gallon vessels for which Dave is most famous are comparable in size and color to contemporary Chinese stoneware.
>
> (2013, 66)

While some enslaved people would have been responsible for loading and unloading earthenware into and out of the kiln – which was in itself a difficult task, requiring labourers to "descend into a tight chamber with a relatively steep incline to stack vessels for firing … with remarkably tight quarters and minimal lighting while balancing vessels on other wares and kiln furniture" – others would do the work of maintaining the kilns' 1,140–1,300°C temperature (Arjona 2017, 181–182).[6] The process of firing is neither simple nor safe. Yet the use of dragon kilns was developed specifically out of low-wage practices in "the pottery production centre of Jindexhen … Workers were not enslaved but were paid very low wages … In South Carolina the least expensive labor cost was represented by the availability of enslaved African-American workers" (Fennell 2017, 68). Here, the connections of international industry expansion and the servitude, enslavement, and low-wage labour on which it relied comes to the surface. That dragon kilns appear in two geographically disparate regions of pottery production links not only to the availability of wood, ash, and clay in those areas but also to access to cheap labour.

In a 2013 study, Calfas made use of records of land agreements, kiln capacity, and market demand to "estimate that each potter working at Pottersville in a 12-hour work day turned approximately 25 six-gallon vessels. African-American labourers each contributed different skill sets during ordinary workdays" (Calfas 2013, 269). Some of these skill sets, as has been articulated in this chapter, included the many-step process of creating each of these twenty-five vessels. The various stages of processing and transforming clay may seem to blur together in a production line, where each person working acts as an impersonal participant. Yet, as Glissant recognizes, within any creation and industry existing with cultural flux, "This is not a passive participation. Passivity plays no part in Relation" (1993, 137). This statement is reminiscent of the quotation from Beaudry, Cook, and Mrozowski that objects are not "a passive product of economic behavior, but an instrumental component of symbolic actions" including the projection of desired social positions or roles. Arjona echoes both of these sentiments in this imagined scene:

> At Pottersville, enslaved laborers became attuned to the rhythms of production. Potters listened to the demands of the kiln's ascending chamber visible to workers below. Work animals kicked up dust, pulling a creaky cross-axle in endless circles. Pottery wheels

whirled into motion with a steady kick while potters improvised jug finishes and applied jug handles. Slabs of clay were obediently shaped into utilitarian vessels and half-formed pots rebelliously collapsed ... Enslaved workers forged individual rhythms of production abounding with idiosyncratic calls to action and technical tricks. Each isolated maneuver – perhaps a specific glaze recipe or a specific hand jerk to finish a pot – transformed clays into bodies that extended beyond production

(Arjona, 1998, 191)

Passivity, for Beaudry, Cook, and Mrozowski, for Arjona, and for Glissant, plays no part in the creation of culture, objects, or earthenware. Each person actively engages with their surroundings against a system that attempted to reduce them to simply a production line, to a singular culture or language, and to anonymity. The objects produced in Edgefield help to encapsulate this site of activity not through the sales records of white benefactors and owners but rather through the hands, words, smudges, and creations of enslaved workers themselves.

Section Three

Yet this labour of enslaved workers did not end with the creation of earthenware pieces but also extended into the transport and future uses of the works. Turning to Dave's poetry again proves useful. The mobility of earthenware work necessitates what art historian Alex Potts calls "a kinesthetic viewing," a term which he applied to sculpture. Potts writes that "taking in sculpture is manifestly not just a matter of looking and scanning but also ... of taking the time to walk round it" (2001, 9). On April 12, 1858, Dave engraved,

A very large jar which has four handles / pack it full of fresh meat – then light candles

Here, the first half of the couplet refers to a vessel's exterior structure, while the second refers to the filling of it with food. Yet in both of these parts the text makes direct reference to its reader's actions. A "very large jar" with "four handles" is instructive as much as it is reflective. Four handles implies the possibility of four hands, meaning that this vessel would have optimally been carried by at least two workers, engaging in an entwined dance as they moved it from kiln to marketplace to kitchen. Thus, Dave's work once again invites analysis of another theme of creolized culture and materials: the complex dance of interdependent movement for labour.

Given the culinary and domestic context in which the large jugs were created, they cannot be simply separated from the cured and spice-drenched meats that pressed firmly against their alkaline-glazed interiors. Dave himself seems to draw attention to this, as several of his verses make use of the word "filled." Firstly, on April 8 he wrote,

This noble jar will hold 20 / fill it with silver then you'll have plenty[7]

Then, just two weeks later, on April 21, he engraved,

When you fill this jar with pork or beef / Scot will be there to get a peace (Figure 2.4)

Finally, on his most recently identified work, a butter churn dated 1858, the same word appears again,

This Is a Noble Churn / Fill It Up It Will Never Turn

Figure 2.4 David Drake, *Storage Jar*, (1858), alkaline-glazed earthenware, height: 22 5/8 in.; diameter: 27 in., 82 lbs (37.2 kg); approx. 25 gallon capacity, Metropolitan Museum of Art, New York City. Engraved with "April 21, 1858" and "When you fill this jar with pork or beef / Scot will be there to get a peace."

As Michael Chaney succinctly states, "For a vessel, being filled is self-actualization" (Chaney, 2014, np).This draws attention to the intertwined relationship between the (mostly male) workers who created jugs and jars and the (mostly female) workers who would fill them. Like the medium of pottery itself, food storage involves a physical closeness between the creator and the material. Arjona poetically calls attention to earthenware's subtle physical reminders of, "fleeting intentions, distractions, obsessions and apathies drifting through an ordinary workday" (Arjona 1998, 184). Pottery, like butchering, cooking, and curing meat, requires people to deeply embed their hands in the material, to press against all sides of its body, and to leave a small bit of the self in what you are making: a fingerprint, a drop of sweat, a small smudge. While the permanence of earthenware obviously differs from the impermanence of food, they nonetheless exist in kinship with each other, as a vessel is created to be filled and food cannot be prepared without being held. In order for contemporary scholars to consider Dave's beautifully engraved jars, jugs, and vessels as objects of significant material history, the absence of the consumables with which they were to be "filled" must be included.[8] In the words of Sidney Mintz, "The goods eaten have histories associated with the pasts of those who eat them; the techniques employed to find, process, prepare, serve and consume the foods are all culturally variable, with histories of their own" (1996, 5).

Section Four

The final section of this chapter will briefly consider what I call the "afterlife of earthenware." By this I mean its potential uses once it has been broken, discarded, or otherwise deemed "nonfunctional." The reason for including this afterlife in my analysis is twofold. Firstly, it is important for material and visual studies of enslavement to consider how remnants may have been taken up in significant and creative ways by the enslaved, most of whom would have been stripped of material comforts and limited in their access and ownership of necessary supplies. How might this repurposing be viewed as evidence of enslaved resilience? Secondly, I am personally invested and interested in an art history that values broken objects and that attempts to situate fragments in their own histories of life, death, reuse, and repurpose, rather than only in reference to when they were whole. Writes Mulira, "The crack cannot be filled unless it is acknowledged, just as a wound cannot be healed that is not cared for. The crack has both a presence and an absence. The cracked earth disrupts the path to progress, and the voided space perpetuates the suffering" (2015, 10). In attempting to write against a space that perpetuates suffering, and which does not acknowledge cracks, this final section looks at the placement and use of broken objects, including ceramics, upon the graves of the enslaved.

In *Go Down, Moses*, William Faulkner writes of a Black grave that it was covered with "shards of pottery and broken bottles and old brick and other objects insignificant to sight but actually of a profound meaning and fatal to touch, which no white man could have read" (1942, 135). In South Carolina's pottery district, the practice of placing broken earthenware on graves is particularly well documented (Grinsell 1961, Vlach 1978). In an 1891 issue of the *Journal of American Folklore*, H. Carrington Bolton offers a detailed description of a Black cemetery on the edge of town where "the numerous graves are decorated with a variety of objects, some arranged with careful symmetry, but more often placed without regard to order. These objects include oyster shells, white pebbles, fragments of crockery of every description, glass bottles, and nondescript bric-a-brac of a cheap sort, all more or less broken and useless" (214). Given the date of his writing, it is unclear if this cemetery had been established after abolition or if it contains the graves of both free and enslaved individuals. Establishing this is particularly difficult in Edgefield, because South Carolina was active in continuing an illegal slave trade from Africa well after the 1808 law forbidding it, with 170 newly captive Congolese people documented arriving in the town as late as 1858 (Fennell 2017, 27).

While there are many different scholars who mention the presence of broken objects in letters and reports, different explanations are offered. One suggestion is that this practice is linked to the Bantu tradition of marking grave mounds with small white shells, and that broken pottery may mimic the same ritual. Anthropologist Robert Farris Thompson noted African-Carolinian gravesites with objects that had holes "very carefully chipped out of the bottom, as if to break the objects without spoiling them, to prepare them as items of broken crockery, which traditionally covered the graves of Carolinians of African descent" (1981, 178). A careful chipping of the graveside objects has been found in parts of Egypt, among Sudanese tribes, and in the Blantyre region of Malawi, to name a few locations (Grinsell 1961). In *A Great and Noble Jar,* Cindy K. Baldwin notes that

> This analysis of stoneware vessels produced in Edgefield by African-American potters reveals a process identified by anthropologists as "syncretism," whereby elements of two diverse cultures that are most similar are interwoven, creating a new entity or cultural hybrid.
>
> (2014, 88)

In other words, the Edgefield practice of slave burial evidences the syncretistic process of creolization.

It is impossible to state with certainty if Dave participated in or even knew of the placement of broken earthenware on graves. As is the case in speculating about the intentionality of non-textual markings on his vessels, this is a possibility that opens up questions about the evolution of community spiritual practice and communication, of resilience and compassion. Lasser asks:

> But it is not unreasonable to suppose that this decision represented a choice, a choice to decorate a pot with words rather than some other ornamental motif, and a choice to inscribe words onto a pot rather than some more conventional medium like paper. What is the significance of using a stoneware pot as a platform for one's prose?
>
> (2018, np)

If Dave was aware that there was a chance that the vessels he created would end up on the graves of loved ones, of strangers, of family bought and sold far away from Edgefield, would that not have impacted his desire to decorate and engrave them? Can the potential afterlife of these pieces tell us something, therefore, about the desire to write on them? These questions have no answers. The archives of Dave's life are incomplete and the poetry he wrote does not reveal specific answers. Yet, as Glissant reminds us, "The poetic axiom, like the mathematical axiom, is illuminating because it is fragile and inescapable, obscure and revealing" (1993, 85). As many precious questions as Dave Drake's writing answers, it poses many more.

Conclusion

One of the earliest engraved vessels attributed to Dave has just a single word on it, followed by a date: "Concatination" (sic), June 12, 1834. Concatenation refers to the linking of things or a series of interconnected objects or events. Arthur Goldberg suggests that this was written in reference to the chains or bonds of slavery, yet I find this reading reductive (2017, 252). The interconnected web that Dave lived within included links to other people, communities, and creations. It included the powerful influences of both his white owners and fellow enslaved workers, and an intimate understanding of the interdependent stages of pottery production. There are a myriad of connections that Dave could have referred to beyond the image of chains that have come to represent enslavement. Instead, I offer that "concatination," engraved in the same slanting handwriting that distinguishes all of Dave's text, is a single word that embodies much of what the pottery of Edgefield can teach us.

"Concatination" speaks to the syncretism of Edgefield. The word is material, with looping O's, crossed T's, and the high arch of A's that you can imagine being gently traced by an index finger. The word is theoretical, with philosophical implications and Latin etymology ("*con*" meaning "with" or "together," and *catena* meaning "chain"). It is a series of things united, a series of things that depend on each other to create a whole, links with indeterminate beginnings or ends. It is written on a vessel produced by an African-descended person born into slavery around 1800 on Native American land and owned for his lifetime by Scottish descendants. It is engraved on the same kind of glaze that has been found in ancient objects in the Middle East and Asia, on an object fired in a kiln used for the production of Chinese ceramics. The vessel itself may have stored meat that people from varying regions of Africa relied on throughout long years working on plantations across the American South. "Concatination" is an unexpected summation of the work of David Drake and carries in its thirteen letters an extraordinary history of Edgefield.

Notes

1 After the Civil War in 1865, it appears that Dave Drake took the last name "Drake," likely in reference to one of his first "owners" in Edgefield, Harvey Drake. In the 1870 USA census, he is listed as "David Drake, Turner," but most references to his work use his first name, "Dave," exclusively, because that

was how he signed his pieces (U.S. Bureau of the Census, 1870, Edgefield Country. South Carolina Department of Archives and History). See also Baldwin (2014, 89).
2 As stated by Aaron De Groft, "The lack of written records leaves more speculation than fact about the lives of these slave potters. Dave is no exception; however, glimpses of the man and his art tell an unfinished story of one who used his craft as a means of personal and political expression" (1998, 249).
3 This system is particularly well documented in Charleston, where "Slave Badges" were produced, designed to control and legislate the hiring and renting of enslaved labour. See Harlan Greene's 2008 book, *Slave Badges and the Slave-Hire System in Charleston, South Carolina, 1783–1865* for an extensive analysis of such badges.
4 It is important to note here that one of Dave's enslavers was the Edgefield Reverend John Landrum, a patriarch of the family within which Dave was repeatedly bought and sold. According to Michael Chaney, the Landrum philosophy involved a "Christian paternalism [that] responded to the fear brought about by the Denmark Vesey revolt of 1822 with renewed conviction in the religious instruction of slaves. Through literacy, it was thought, the slave may be Christianized and hence encouraged to accept rather than resent his condition" (2018, 3). This suggests that not only was Dave immersed in a Christian context, but he also may have become literate through Biblical study.
5 A third verse that also interrogates authorial presence and money earned through enslaved labour appears on an 1840 double-handed jug, which has the following engravings: on one side, ": Mr L. Miles 27th June: 1840/Dave," and on the opposite side, "Give me silver or either gold / though they are dangerous; to our soul," using the collective "soul" and pronoun "our" in reference to the dangers of money while simultaneously signing both the names of the enslaver and enslaved on the reverse. Although this essay does not have the breadth to analyse all of Drake's verses as much as they demand, this one struck me as particularly interesting and relevant.
6 Wood was burned in a kiln's "fire box" in order to maintain such high temperatures. Although little scholarly research has been dedicated specifically to the labor of heating such kilns, it is very likely that the arduous process of finding, gathering, and chopping wood relied on enslaved laborers.
7 When an image of the vessel's engravings was not available, Dave Drake's couplets cited in this essay are as they appear in Leonard Todd's *Carolina Clay*.
8 To learn more about the production, storage and consumption of food on American plantations, the 1881 cookbook, *What Mrs. Fisher Knows About Southern Cooking*, provides an excellent and engrossing history through the recipes compiled by the formerly enslaved chef Abby Fisher, giving the contemporary reader an intimate insight into the diets of enslaved Black workers, as well as the food that would be cooked for white enslavers.

References

Arjona, Jamie M. "Jug Factories and Fictions: A Mixed Methods Analysis of African-American Stoneware Traditions in Antebellum South Carolina." *Journal of African Diaspora Archaeology and Heritage* 6, no. 3 (2017): 174–195.

Baldwin, Cinda K. *Great & Noble Jar: Traditional Stoneware of South Carolina*. Columbia: McKissick Museum, The University of South Carolina, 2014.

Bolton, H. Carrington. "Decoration of Graves of Negroes in South Carolina." *The Journal of American Folklore* 4, no. 14 (July 1, 1891): 214.

Burton, Orville Vernon. *In My Father's House Are Many Mansions: Family and Community in Edgefield, South Carolina*. Chapel Hill: The University of North Carolina Press, 1985.

Calfas, George. "Nineteenth Century Stoneware Manufacturing at Pottersville, South Carolina: The Discovery of a Dragon Kiln and the Reinterpretation of a Southern Pottery Tradition." PhD. Dissertation, University of Illinois at Urbana-Champaign, 2013.

Cara, Ana C., and Robert A. Baron. "Creolization as Cultural Creativity." Introduction to *Creolization as Cultural Creativity*, 4–18. Oxford: University Press of Mississippi, 2011.

Chaney, Michael A. "Dave the Potter and the Churn of Time." *Michigan Quarterly Review*, 53, no. 1 (Winter 2014), unpaginated.

Chaney, Michael A., "The Concatenate Poetics of Slavery and the Articulate Material of Dave the Potter." In *Where Is All My Relation? The Poetics of Dave the Potter*, edited by Michael A Chaney, 114–132. New York, NY: Oxford University Press, 2018.

De Groft, Aaron. "Eloquent Vessels/Poetics of Power: The Heroic Stoneware of 'Dave the Potter,'" *Winterthur Portfolio* 33, no. 4 (1998): 249–260.

Faulkner, William. "Go Down, Moses." In *Go Down, Moses, and Other Stories*, 120–142. New York, NY: Modern Library, 1942. https://archive.org/details/in.ernet.dli.2015.509930/page/n5/mode/2up

Fennell, Christopher C. "Innovation, Industry, and African-American Heritage in Edgefield, South Carolina." *Journal of African Diaspora Archaeology and Heritage* 6, no. 2 (2017): 55–77.

Ferguson, Leland G. "'Crosses, Secrets, and Lies: A Response to J.W. Joseph's' … All of Cross'—African Potters, Marks, and Meanings in the Folk Pottery of the Edgefield District, South Carolina." *Historical Archaeology* 45, no. 2 (2011): 163–165.

Glissant Édouard. *Poetics of Relation*. Translated by Betsy Wing. Ann Arbor: The University of Michigan Press, 1997.

Goldberg, Arthur F., and Goldberg, Deborah A., "The Expanding Legacy of the enslaved Potter-Poet David Drake." *Journal of African Diaspora Archeology and Heritage* 6, no. 3 (2017): 243–261.

Greene, Harlan, Hutchins, Harry S., and Hutchins, Brian E. *Slave Badges and the Slave-Hire System in Charleston, South Carolina, 1783–1865.* Jefferson, NC: McFarland, 2008.

Grinsell, L. V. "The Breaking of Objects as a Funerary Rite," Folklore 72, no. 3 (1961): pp. 475-491.

Joseph, J. W. "Crosses, Crescents, Slashes, Stars: African-American Potters and Edgefield District Pottery Marks." *Journal of African Diaspora Archaeology and Heritage* 6, no. 2 (2017): 110–132.

Joseph, J. W. "Meeting at Market: The Intersection of African American Culture, Craft, and Economy and the Landscape of Charleston, South Carolina." *Historical Archaeology* 50, no. 1 (2016): 94–113.

Kenline-Nyman, Brooke. "Manufacturing Social Class: Ceramic Entrepreneurs and Industrial Slavery in the Old Edgefield District." *Journal of African Diaspora Archaeology and Heritage* 6, no. 2 (2017): 155–169.

Maharaj, Sarat. "Perfidious Fidelity: The Untranslatability of the Other." *Global Visions: Towards a New Internationalism in the Visual Arts.* 1994, unpaginated https://southasastateofmind.com/article/perfidious-fidelity/

Mintz, Sidney. 2008. "Creolization and Hispanic Exceptionalism." *Review (Fernand Braudel Center) 31 (3) The Second Slavery: Mass Slavery, World-Economy, and Comparative Microhistories* Part II: 54–55.

Mulira, Sanyu Ruth. "Edouard Glissant and the African Roots of Creolization." *Ufahamu: A Journal of African Studies* 38, no. 2 (2015): 115–128.Niculescu, Tatiana. "Tides of Celadon: Glaze Color Chronology from the Edgefield Pottery District, South Carolina." *Journal of African Diaspora Archaeology and Heritage* 6, no. 3 (2017): 196–224.

Potts, Alex. *The Sculptural Imagination: Figurative, Modernist, Minimalist*. New Haven, CT: Yale University Press, 2001.

Rice, Prudence M. *Pottery Analysis: a Sourcebook*. Chicago, IL: University of Chicago Press, 2015.

Shlensky, Lincoln. "Édouard Glissant: Creolization and the Event." *Callaloo* 36, no. 2 (2013): 353–374.

Steen, Carl. "Alkaline Glazed Stoneware Origins." *South Carolina Antiquities* 43 (2011): 21–31.

Todd, Leonard. *Carolina Clay: The Life and Legend of the Slave Potter Dave*. New York, NY: W. Norton, 2009.

Vlach, John Michael. *The Afro-American Tradition in Decorative Arts: Basketry, Musical Instruments, Wood Craving, Quilting, Pottery, Boat-Building, Blacksmithing, Architecture, Graveyard Decoration.* Cleveland, OH: Cleveland Museum of Art, 1978.

3 "[A] tone of voice peculiar to New-England"

Fugitive Slave Advertisements and the Heterogeneity of Enslaved People of African Descent in Eighteenth-Century Quebec

Charmaine A. Nelson

The *Montreal Gazette* issued its first paper on 25 August 1785.[1] That the first runaway slave advertisement (Guthrie 1785 in Mackey 2010, 328) appeared the following month on 29 September 1785 demonstrated the local white settlers' knowledgeable use of print technology to perpetuate the colonial racial order through which their ownership of black people was justified and secured (Figure 3.1). Although an archive of slave sale, auction, and fugitive advertisements exist alongside other legal, private, and government documents, for the provinces of Ontario, Quebec, New Brunswick, Nova Scotia, Prince Edward Island, and Newfoundland, Canadian participation in Transatlantic Slavery under the French and British Empires is little known both inside and outside of the nation. The prolific ignorance about Canadian Slavery has been strategically cultivated by Euro-Canadians who have, over generations, created the Canadian myth of racial tolerance enshrined in a federal policy of multiculturalism.

This chapter is an attempt to disrupt this dominant Canadian narrative by remembering the centuries-long presence of people of African descent – both free and enslaved – in the regions which became Canada. I also wish to highlight fugitive slave advertisements as an important form of print culture which became an essential part of the colonial archive. The mass production and circulation of such advertisements and their use as a terrain to codify blackness and conflate it with the status of slave became an essential component of a transatlantic discursive strategy for the subjugation of people of African descent.

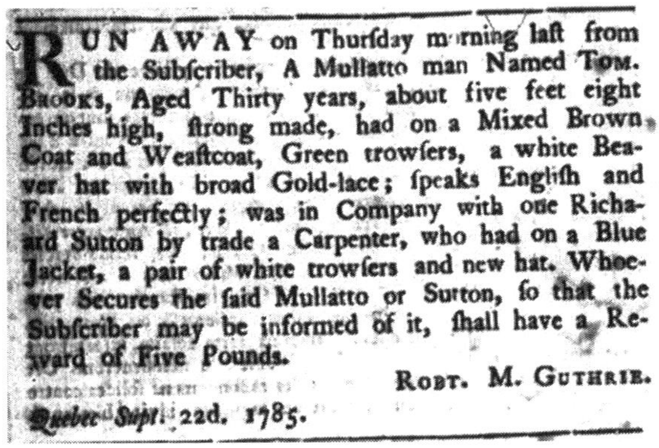
RUN AWAY on Thurfday morning laft from the Subfcriber, A Mullatto man Named Tom. Brooks, Aged Thirty years, about five feet eight Inches high, ftrong made, had on a Mixed Brown Coat and Weaftcoat, Green trowfers, a white Beaver hat with broad Gold-lace; fpeaks Englifh and French perfectly; was in Company with one Richaard Sutton by trade a Carpenter, who had on a Blue Jacket, a pair of white trowfers and new hat. Whoever Secures the faid Mullatto or Sutton, fo that the Subfcriber may be informed of it, fhall have a Reward of Five Pounds.

ROBT. M. GUTHRIE.

Quebec Sept. 22d. 1785.

Figure 3.1 Robt. M. Guthrie, "RUN AWAY on Thursday morning last," *Montreal Gazette*, Thursday, 29 September 1785, vol. I, no. 6, p. 4; Bibliothèque et Archives nationales du Québec (BANQ), Montreal, Canada.

DOI: 10.4324/9781003357117-4

What replaces slavery in the Canadian national imagination is celebratory narratives of the Underground Railroad, the period between 1834 when the British abolished slavery by an act of parliament and 1865 when the Civil War in the United States of America ended. A national cohesiveness of memory has been produced through the almost universal teaching of Underground Railroad histories in both elementary and high school curricula (particularly in February during Black History Month). Canadian education therefore plays a central role in the indoctrination of prepubescent Canadian youth who are taught from a young age that Canada is both racism-free and race-blind. But popular media has also played a central role. Many Canadians have been raised on "Heritage Minutes," one-minute historical short films about various aspects of Canadian history created by *Historica Canada* that air nationally on Canadian television.[2]

One such short entitled "Underground Railroad" (1991) represents a white Quaker woman comforting a formerly enslaved black woman, Eliza, as they wait anxiously in Canada for news of Eliza's enslaved father who is en route out of slavery in the USA. The film ends with Eliza's father emerging from a wooden bench, in which he had been hidden on a wagon trip north, to embrace her and his unnamed son. The father then exclaims "we're free," to which Eliza responds emotionally "Yes Pa weez in Canada!" (*Historica Canada*). The constant recitation and celebration of the Underground Railroad has allowed Canadians to erroneously disassociate Canada from a two-century history of Transatlantic Slavery and to enshrine a period of three decades, casting themselves as the liberators of enslaved African Americans. These myths allow white Canadians to celebrate their difference (mainly from a white American-ness which they actively associate with a pro-slavery American South) as a citizenry made up of "good" people whose white settler ancestors presumably exploited no one in their quest for land, power, and capital. This hierarchization of whiteness is not solely built upon a fabricated history of a completely anti-slavery north (Canada) and a completely pro-slavery south (USA). Instead, when Euro-Canadians do concede that slavery happened in Canada, they routinely attempt to distinguish and valorize their own slaving histories as somehow superior (meaning more benevolent and less violent) based upon the ludicrous assumption that slave minority societies were fundamentally less physically and psychologically brutal for the enslaved than slave majority ones.

In sharp contrast, the unacknowledged histories of Canadian participation in Transatlantic Slavery – by the state and popular media alike – have bred a collective amnesia resulting in an appalling lack of national support for the academic study of Canadian Slavery; the knock-on effect of which is the absence of the serious study of topics of obvious and accepted importance in the field of Slavery Studies. The study of Canadian Slavery lags far behind other regions in the quantity, scope, and foci of the scholarship. The number and disciplinary diversity of the scholars devoted to the study of slavery in the US South, the Caribbean, and the northern parts of South America has led to a host of specialized studies on slave culture, diet, dress, family structures, literacy, maternity, resistance, and the detailed study of population size and mortality. Significantly, while the analysis of fugitive slave advertisements has been an important sub-field in American,[3] Caribbean,[4] and South American Slavery[5] since the 1970s, my publications are among the first to undertake a similar study of Canadian notices.[6] Furthermore, while important sources on Canadian Slavery provide regional overviews and other important information, the majority do not prioritize the lives or experiences of the enslaved.[7]

Another scholarly deficit in the study of Canadian Slavery is the absence of studies of the cultural and ethnic makeup of enslaved communities of African descent. Instead the term "black" is employed in ways which undermine a clear understanding of the complexity of this enslaved community. Despite its usefulness, I would like to offer alternatives for the catchall racial term black, which in its homogenizing universality assumes a creolized subject; a person who was born in a colony (in this case the Americas) or who has undergone a process of creolization, which for the enslaved was always under duress.[8]

In what follows, I analyze Canadian fugitive slave advertisements within a broader diasporic context in order to understand how Quebec enslavers cited birth origins as a means to identify and recapture enslaved fugitives. This study is focused upon slavery in British Quebec and therefore encompasses the period between 1760 (the date of the British conquest of New France) and 1834, the date of British abolition of slavery. However, in reality, the Quebec fugitive notices were published between 1765 and 1798.[9] The fugitive slave notices at the center of this study were collected and transcribed by Frank Mackey, who however, only subjected them to very brief analysis (Mackey 2010, Appendix I, 307–340).[10] I also employ other historical sources to deduce the birth origins and cultures of the enslaved arguing that a key marker of the distinctiveness of the enslaved black population in eighteenth-century Quebec was its profound heterogeneity.

While the flight of the runaway or fugitive, and their often-premeditated acts of redefinition and passing, sought to unbind them from the category of slave, the advertisements sought not only to reconstitute this connection but also to naturalize it. Thus, the slave owning classes sought to criminalize demonstrations of agency by the "self-motivated" (Waldstreicher 1999, 248) people who were enslaved, to code running away as what Marcus Wood has termed "an act of theft, albeit a paradoxical self-theft" (Wood 2000, 79). Against this colonial act of dehumanization, I would like to position the fugitives not as criminals, but as freedom seekers, and the act of running away as a defiant and extremely perilous act of self-(re)definition.[11] However, at the same time, given the deep reticence and indeed hypocrisy of Euro-Canadian populations – displayed in their active and ongoing negation of their colonial and slaving histories – I have consciously chosen to use the terms runaway and fugitive, not because that is what the enslaved people were in any essential way but because that is how they were historically viewed and categorized by the white slave owning classes who sought to immobilize, imprison, and re-enslave them and by the judicial, legal, and political infrastructures, also controlled by the same whites.

The Fugitive Slave Archive

The runway slave advertisement is a primary source with prescribed limits. The limit of the slave advertisement is that it confirms only that someone, socially deemed to be a slave, was thought to have run away from the person who claimed to own the runaway. It is important to note that the archive, however, can never fully capture the extent of resistance through flight in any given region. Since colonial newspapers were often published only weekly, an enslaved person's quick recapture foreclosed the need for the printing of a fugitive notice. We can therefore surmise that many more people escaped than were ever documented in such notices.

Runaway slave advertisements can provide for us a window into the lives and worlds of the enslaved.[12] Each example was about the recapture of an individual or individuals who had fled, and as such required that their enslavers share details that illuminated what made the runaways unique, both in manner and appearance. As such runaway slave advertisements, ubiquitous across the Americas, are repositories of data on enslaved populations. As David Waldstreicher has noted, such advertisements were generally premised on four categories, "clothing, trades or skills, linguistic ability or usage, and ethnic or racial identity," the manipulation of which could alter the perception of one's class and race (Waldstreicher 1999, 249). Accents were also used both to identify how a fugitive might sound when encountered and to indicate to where they might be fleeing. For example, when the merchant John Turner Sr. placed a notice for the return of "a Negro Slave named Ishmaël" in the *Quebec Gazette* on 29 July 1779, he described

Figure 3.2 John Turner, "TEN DOLLARS REWARD," *Quebec Gazette*, 29 July 1779, vol. 726, p. 3; Bibliothèque et Archives nationales du Québec (BANQ), Montreal, Canada.

him as having a "tone of voice peculiar to New-England, where he was born" (Turner 1779 in Mackey 2010, 321–322) (Figure 3.2). But the appearance of the fugitive's body both biological (skin color, hair color and texture, height, build, etc.) and how the fugitive adorned themselves (the color, material, type and style of clothing and footwear, wigs, scarification, etc.) were paramount.

The advertisements, in and of themselves, are testaments to the necessity of deception as a survival tactic of the enslaved. Since advertisements regularly included descriptions of the dress and speech of the fugitive, even when the enslaver did not explicitly document the regional origins of the enslaved person, they are evidence of the ethnicity of the slave population, their Creoleness, or African-ness.

I would like to do something that scholars of Canadian Slavery rarely undertake, that is to place my case study within a broader transatlantic context which includes other sites of both temperate (Nova Scotia) and tropical plantation slavery (Jamaica).[13] My focus is British Quebec between the dates of 1760 and the early 1800s. Frank Mackey has provided a great service to (Canadian) Slavery Studies scholars by compiling and transcribing the Quebec slave advertisements (fugitive, auction, and sale) for enslaved and free black people. However, he does not provide extensive analysis of the advertisements nor does he develop a specific argument about creolization and visual culture. Instead, his book animates the lives of enslaved black people under British rule and their complex relationships with white enslavers in a society where slavery was embedded in the fabric of daily life. Mackey has determined that "ninety-four notices concerning the sale of black slaves and the flight of black prisoners, ship deserters, servants, and slaves" were published in early Quebec newspapers (Mackey 2010, 307). While around forty enslaved men, women, and children were offered for sale in forty-three notices (the last advertised in 1798), forty-five people of African descent took part in fifty escapes (the last also in 1798) and were listed in about fifty-one fugitive notices (Mackey 2010, 307–308).[14] The multiple escapes of certain individuals account for the fact that the number of notices is greater than the number of enslaved people (Mackey 2010, 308).

The Power of Naming: Names, Ages, and Racial Types

Certain categories of naming reoccur, even dominate in fugitive slave advertisements. While the first name of the enslaved person was almost always provided in fugitive slave advertisements, family names were rare since the process of enslavement customarily entailed the stripping of

"[A] tone of voice peculiar to New-England" 57

the African's entire name and the imposition of the enslaver's family name. Significantly, this pattern is the reverse of slave sale advertisements in which the name of the enslaved person was commonly withheld. The namelessness of the enslaved person heightened their commodification for the potential buyers, dehumanizing them and driving home the idea that they were merely an object for sale. But surely too, this deliberate refusal to provide what was arguably (in regions where enslavers were familiar with each other's slave holdings) the most obvious identifying information was a means to impede potential buyers from ascertaining troubling information about an enslaved person.

This was certainly the case when the merchants James Johnston and John Purss placed an enslaved woman named Bett for sale in a *Quebec Gazette* advertisement of 5 July 1787 (Anonymous 1787 in Mackey 2010, 329) (Figure 3.3). According to an earlier fugitive notice placed for her, Bett had absconded from the pair only a few months prior during the winter on 7 March 1787 (Johnston and Purss 1787 in Mackey 2010, 329) (Figure 3.4). Alarmingly, the notice described Bett as being in a state of advanced pregnancy, "big with child, and within a few days of her time" (Johnston and Purss 1787 in Mackey 2010, 329). As such, Johnston and Purss's description of the pregnant Bett not only disclosed the heightened value of the fleeing woman who, according to colonial legal discourse, literally carried what was tantamount to *their* property in *her* womb, but in the eyes of many white settlers, tainted her as irresponsible and rash. Clearly then, withholding Bett's name in their subsequent slave sale notice was a strategy of disassociation.

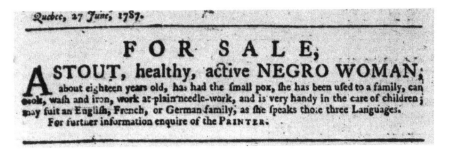

Figure 3.3 Anonymous, "FOR SALE, A STOUT, healthy, active NEGRO WOMAN," *Quebec Gazette*, 5 July 1787, vol. 1142, p. 3; Bibliothèque et Archives nationales du Québec (BANQ), Montreal, Canada.

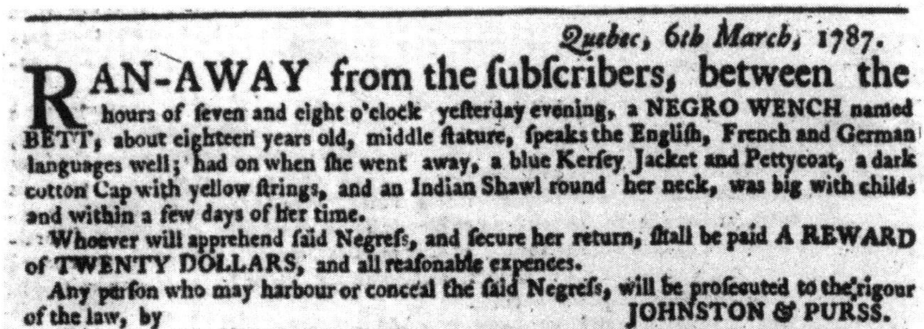

Figure 3.4 Johnston and Purss, "RAN-AWAY from the subscribers," *Quebec Gazette*, 8 March 1787, vol. 1125, p. 2; Bibliothèque et Archives nationales du Québec (BANQ), Montreal, Canada.

Whereas it was rather common to withhold an enslaved person's first name in a slave sale advertisement, the same was not true of fugitive slave notices. In a rare example where the first name was withheld, the 1 September 1766 fugitive notice of the merchant Isaac Werden claimed that "A NEGRO GIRL, of about 24 Years of Age" had absconded on Saturday, 22 August (Werden in Mackey 2010, 314). Although he described her appearance ("pitted with the Small-pox"), language acquisition ("speaks good English"), and dress ("Had on a black Gown and red Callimanco Petticoat"), Werden oddly did not provide her first name.

The Virginia planter, Robert "King" Carter (the richest planter in the state), instructed his overseer to initiate the process of renaming enslaved Africans at the point of purchase (Berlin 1996, 251–252). The process of renaming must have been a moment of great conflict. Although renaming was frequently a process wherein the enslaved person's removal from Africa could be cemented through the imposition of a European name, naming practices in Jamaica and elsewhere in the Americas indicate that enslavers and their overseers often imposed names that deliberately recalled not just the African birth origins, but also the specific ethnicity of the enslaved.

Jamaican Hope Estate's *A List of Negroes on Hope Plantation in St. Andrews* (1788) listed 135 men, 41 boys (176 males), 133 women and 42 girls (175 females), several of whom were given such names including: Eboe Sampson (# 116), Angola Sampson (# 117), Eboe Toney (#120), Eboe Fanny (#266), Eboe Nancy (# 276), Congo Sukey (#283), Angola Sukey (# 284), Eboe Phillis (# 301), and Eboe Dolly (# 302) (Anonymous 1788, unpaginated) (Figure 3.5). This practice was not merely rooted in a bid to easily distinguish between the enslaved but also proved useful in the white desire to differentiate and hierarchize Africans on the basis of potential resistance as supposedly rooted in ethnicity.[15]

Contrarily, the retention of African names, naming practices, and the documentation of specific African origins and ethnicities are almost impossible to detect at the level of white interference or official documents in Nova Scotia and Quebec. This is largely due to the fact that the African-born portion of the slave minority population in both regions surely comprised the smallest percentage of the communities. It followed then that enslavers in these regions were less acquainted with African-born people and less capable of identifying them by ethnicity. Instead, enslavers in these two regions either proclaimed the African birth explicitly or implied it through a comment on language or accent. The reason for the smaller population of African-born people was the nature of merchant shipping enterprise in the regions. As I will discuss in further detail below, in the period of British rule, the merchant ships that arrived in ports like Halifax, Montreal, and Quebec City, with enslaved people of African descent, did not do so *directly* from Africa. This is further verified through an analysis of custom house advertisements which routinely indicated outgoing and incoming vessels from British and Caribbean ports, but none from African ones.[16] Although analysis of these vessels and their human cargoes has yet to be undertaken, the Anglo-Caribbean origin of many of these ships, along with the evidence obtained from slave advertisements and bills of sale, strongly suggests that the dominant enslaved population onboard would have been Creole or Caribbean-born people.

Slave ships arriving from Africa were normal in the Caribbean, parts of South America, and the American South. As such, Jamaican fugitive slave advertisements routinely listed the enslaved by both racial type and/or African ethnicity. However, there were also regions in the American North where enslaved African-born populations became normal. Ira Berlin and Leslie M. Harris have linked the growth of the slave population in eighteenth-century British New York to the increasing arrival of slave ships directly from Africa. It was the growth of this African-born population through which "white New Yorkers learned to distinguish between Kongos and Angolans, Mandes and Mandingos, as they became familiar with the differences among African peoples" (Berlin and Harris 2005, 10–11).

"*[A] tone of voice peculiar to New-England*"   59

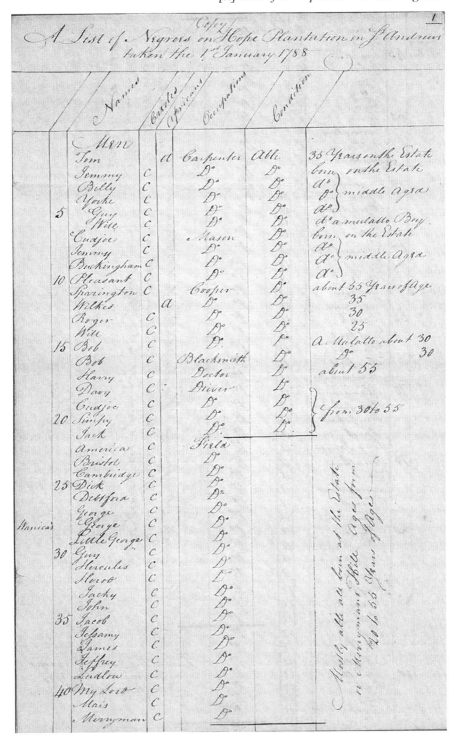

Figure 3.5 A List of Negroes on Hope Plantation in St. Andrews (1788), paper, 32.39 × 20.3 cm, ST West Indies Box 3(1), The Huntington Library, San Marino, California.

White Canadian knowledge of African-ness surely paled in comparison. This deficit is revealed in how African-born enslaved people were identified within fugitive slave notices. Of the fifty-one fugitive slave notices for forty-five runaways which Mackey has identified for Quebec, only five people were described in ways which stated or inferred that they were African-born. Interestingly, all five were males and none of the descriptions provided a specific ethnicity. The first documented enslaved person whose origins appear to have been African was Drummond. However, John McCord's fugitive notice of 27 June 1765 did not explicitly state this fact (McCord in Mackey 2010, 314). Rather, McCord's addendum that Drummond "*Speaks very bad English, and next to no French*" was the striking declaration which marked Drummond as outside of the linguistic norms of a Creole in Quebec (McCord in Mackey 2010, 314). William Gilliland's 19 September 1771 fugitive notice for "a Negro Man" named Ireland (who had allegedly escaped with a white indentured servant named Francis Freeland) stated that Ireland "speaks English tolerably plain, but no other Language, except that of his native Country, *Guinea*" (Gilliland in Mackey 2010, 318). While enslavers commonly referred to slave ships as *Guineamen*, having the African nation stand in for the continent, since Gilliland was a slave owner from New York State, he may actually have intended to use Guinea as a national or ethnic identifier for Ireland.[17]

The five fugitive slave notices placed by William Brown were more direct than McCord's or Gilliland's. Perhaps the explicit statement of the origins of the fugitive can be related to Brown's position as the owner of the *Quebec Gazette*. Arguably, more than any other enslaver in Quebec City, and indeed the province, William Brown would have been familiar with the possibilities, reach, and power of the fugitive slave advertisement, all of which hinged upon the printing of specific and often intrusive details about the enslaved person. Significantly then, all of Brown's five fugitive notices for Joe's escapes on 22 November 1777, 25 January 1778, 22 December 1778, 16 September 1779, and 18 February 1786 proclaimed that Joe had been "born in Africa" (Brown in Mackey 2010, 319, 320, 321, 322, 328–329).[18]

Although there is not enough evidence to state it definitively, the fourth and fifth Quebec fugitive slave notices, published fourteen years apart, that disclose the African birth origins of a runaway may have been for the same person described as a "Negro man Named JACK," 5 feet 8 inches tall. While the first notice placed on 21 May 1778 by the fur traders James Finlay Sr. and John Gregory (Finlay and Gregory in Mackey 2010, 320) reverted to the linguistic paradigm describing Jack as speaking "no other tongue but English, and that upon the Guinea accent," the French notice placed by William Grant on 15 March 1792 described Jack as "né en Afrique" [born in Africa] (Grant in Mackey 2010, 335).

Interestingly then, only one of the fugitive slave notices placed to recapture these five enslaved males may have provided any indication of their ethnicity and only two stated explicitly that the runaways had been born in Africa. But of course, the absence of statements of African-ness in other Quebec fugitive slave advertisements does not mean that other enslaved fugitives were not also born in Africa. Other sources become useful in discerning the size and scope of this minority population. For instance, although the brothers and business partners Mathew and John Macniders identified the enslaved "NEGRO MAN" fugitive named Caleb by age, height, and clothing, his origins can be ascertained through his deed of sale (Macniders in Mackey 2010, 330). Mackey has determined that Caleb, who was purchased on 26 June 1786 from the carpenter William Mackenzie for £35, was named in the deed as a "native of Guinea, about thirty years old" (Mackey 2010, 539, note #50).

Different groups of enslaved people surely coped with enslavement in different ways. For the African-born, depending upon their age at embarkation, the nature and intensity of their memories of home surely informed their relationship to other enslaved people, their experiences of their new societies and their enslavers, and their ability to retain their African cultures. One means of cultural retention was the preservation of African names. Berlin has noted that enslaved Africans remembered and used their real names as a form of resistance citing runaway slave advertisements from Georgia where an enslaver conceded that the fugitives he had renamed Abel and Bennett, actually went by the names Golaga and Abbrom, respectively (Berlin 1996, 252, note #4). Similarly, Philip D. Morgan also discussed enslaved people with both African and Anglo-Jamaican names at Vineyard Pen, St. Elizabeth, Jamaica where Thomas Thistlewood was the overseer (1750–1751) (Morgan 1995, 52).[19] Whether fighting to hold onto their chosen African or European names, this practice seems to have also existed in British North America.

In a runaway advertisement placed by Azariah Pretchard in Quebec for "A NEGRO MAN," who he named as Isaac, Pretchard was also forced to concede that he "calls himself *Charles* some times" (sic) (Pretchard in Mackey 2010, 337). In another Quebec case, an advertisement placed by James Frazer noted that an escaped "Negro Man" went by the name Robin or Bob and a "Negro Woman" by Lydia or Lil (Frazer in Mackey 2010, 338–339). Similarly, in a notice placed by Michael Wallace in Nova Scotia for the return of "a Negro Man Servant ... named BELFAST," he admitted that the "likely, stout-made fellow" of about twenty-seven years of age "goes by the name of BILL" (Wallace 1794, 1).[20] In yet another case in Nova Scotia, when Abel Michener of Falmouth advertised for the return of an Irish indentured male named John M'Neil and an enslaved female named Philis, he admitted that the latter called herself Betty (Michener 1789, 2).

In their bid to assimilate and "civilize" the enslaved, white enslavers regularly imposed traditional European names upon them. For instance, males were frequently given the Irish name Mungo (Mongo). One fugitive slave advertisement placed by Benjamin Dewolf of Windsor, Nova Scotia in the *Halifax Gazette* on 24 October 1780 listed "a Negro Boy named Mungo, about 14 Years of Age" who had run away on Tuesday, 17 October (Dewolf 1780, 3). As Beth Tobin Fowkes asserts, "Mungo was a common name for African slaves" and was popularized in plays like Frances Burney's *A Busy Day* (1801) in which the white heiress Eliza has a black servant named Mongo and Isaac Bickerstaff's *The Padlock: A Comic Opera, in Two Acts* (1768) which also included a black servant named Mungo.[21]

Descriptions of the enslaved body commonly included an age, age range, or at least an indication of adult or child status and also a description of the body type or weight (like stout), height, and importantly, complexion or racial type. However, due to the infrequency with which the enslaved were issued standard identity documents like birth certificates, the supposed age of the enslaved was often mere guesswork. In the context of Jamaican plantation slavery, annual ledgers similar to those used to track livestock extended to the regulation of the enslaved populations and would often list slave births, but by the year only. Far less specific were the age ranges given for enslaved children and adults. The plantation ledger *A List of Negroes on Hope Plantation in St. Andrews* (1788) did not provide specific ages for each enslaved person but rather provided only estimates or grouped people in various age ranges. An example of the former practice was three male coopers listed as an African Wilkes about thirty-five, a Creole Roger about thirty, and another Creole Will about twenty-five. In the same ledger, marginal notes grouped the enslaved across the diverse ages of one month to six years, six to fourteen years (a group that the ledger indicated was employed as a weeding gang), twenty to fifty-five, or simply as old and infirm. More specific, but still elusive, enslaved males named East, West, North, South, Short, Long, and Swift were noted as "part of the 20 new Negroes purchased October 1787 ages from 20 to 25" (Anonymous 1788, unpaginated).

In Jamaica, the term Negro often became interchangeable with the word slave. For instance, Christer Petley has demonstrated that the uber-wealthy white Jamaican planter Simon Taylor, who owned four estates and managed several others for absentee planters (making him responsible for the management of some 4,000 enslaved people), frequently referred to the enslaved on his plantations as "Negroes" (Petley 2009, 51).[22] However, the term did not necessarily indicate an African birth origin.

African-born people were far less likely to be mixed race and were commonly described as having dark complexions and scarification. Enslaved Creoles could indeed also be racially unmixed and have dark complexions. Thus, while the naming of mixed African and European racial heritage in fugitive advertisements normally indicated that the enslaved person was a Creole, care must be taken to recall the heterogeneity of African corporeality which transcended the idea of a uniform dark complexion and tightly curled hair. In a case related by Shane White and Graham White, James Brittian recalled the beauty of his African-born enslaved grandmother who had hair, "fine as silk and hung down below her waist" (White and White 1995, 68).[23] The British Atlantic spawned a peculiarly detailed list of racial terms for people of African ancestry. Terms like sambo, mulatto, and quadroon indicated a supposedly definitive racial mixture of African and European ancestry and as such revealed, almost always, a Creole.[24]

Ethnicity and Complexion: Naming Practices

Just as enslavers in tropical locations like Jamaica paid careful attention to the African ethnicity of the enslaved and expressed concern for the resistance of certain groups, similar preferences, albeit broader, seem to have taken root in northern regions. For instance, in regard to the selection of laborers for his plantation Mount Vernon, George Washington preferred to buy Creole West Indian (or Caribbean) people, who were, according to R.F. Dalzell and L.B. Dalzell, "thought to be preferable to Africans since they were already familiar with plantation ways" (Dalzell and Dalzell 1998, 130).[25] Meanwhile in Quebec, when the co-founders and co-owners of the *Quebec Gazette*, William Brown and Thomas Gilmore (who died in 1773) were searching for reliable labor for their printing office, they wrote to their former employer William Dunlap in Philadelphia and specified that they wanted a "Negro Boy" who was "fit to put to press, and who has had the Small Pox, *is Country born*, and can be recommended for his Honesty" (italics mine) (Brown and Gilmore 1768, 1).[26]

The description offered by Brown and Gilmore was precise and detailed. While the mention of smallpox reveals that enslavers were preoccupied with the health and mortality of their enslaved laborers, it also underscores the commodification of labor which was at the heart of slavery. Their preoccupation for the male's fitness and age highlights the demands of the intellectual *and* physical nature of the work to which they intended to set their new "Negro Boy." While the request that Dunlap's choice be honest was of obvious relevance to any enslaver, the request that the black boy also be "country born" demonstrates the white preference for Creoles, blacks who, through their birth in the Americas, were thought to be "seasoned" and less resistant. While it is as yet undetermined if this preference for Creoles existed in other northern regions like Nova Scotia, I would argue that evidence will eventually bear out that this too was the case, in part because enslavers in the regions that became Canada were far less familiar with African-born people than various groups of Creoles (African Canadian, African American, and African Caribbean people).

Whereas the practice of identifying the enslaved by ethnicity persisted in Jamaica even after the British abolition of the slave trade in 1807 (since African-born people were still residing on the island), the use of the term Negro as a generic term for people of African ancestry seems to have pervaded racial discourse in Nova Scotia and Quebec. Significantly, the frequent use of the term Negro implies that white enslavers did feel it necessary to name race in such advertisements, perhaps in part, to differentiate between enslaved indigenous people [panis(e)] or Africans in Quebec.[27] While Jamaican racial naming was comprised of a six-pronged hierarchy including: Negro, Sambo, Mulatto, Quadroon, Mustee, and Musthiphino, Quebec naming practices for enslaved blacks as indicated in slave advertisements included only Negro, Negro-Mulatto, or Mulatto. Although the archive of slave sale notices in Nova Scotia is less definitive, known auction, fugitive, and sale advertisements use the terms black, Negro, and mulatto.[28]

Within the slave minority context of Canada, the term Negro – as a common stand-in for black, African, and slave – disrupts our ability to understand to what extent African ethnicity or Creole status was discernable within the enslaved and free black populations. Since the history of slavery in the region under the French (as New France) dates back to the 1600s, without a doubt, African Canadians (or those whose creolization had dominantly occurred in the region) were definitely present. The history of African American fugitives fleeing north (not to freedom at this time, but simply away from their specific enslavement and toward a community that would hopefully not identify them as enslaved) as well as the forced relocation northward of enslaved blacks by their white American enslavers (mainly Loyalists) meant that African Americans were surely also present in significant numbers in (British) Quebec, starting in 1760.

Besides Creoles who were of African Canadian and African American origins, the eighteenth- and nineteenth-century black populations in Nova Scotia and Quebec were augmented by the steady arrival of other Creoles; the enslaved people of African descent who arrived as the "secondary cargo" or commodities on ships that originated from Caribbean ports, ships also loaded with primary cargoes of slave-produced plantation goods like sugar, rum, and molasses. Printed in the *Halifax Gazette*, on Saturday, 30 May 1752, the notice entitled "Advertisements, JUST imported and to be sold by Joshua Mauger" listed six enslaved people for sale. While the word "just" worked to further objectify the people listed in the advertisement by emphasizing the newness of the arrival of Mauger's human commodities and his desire for a quick turnaround, the word "imported" announced the enslaved people as foreigners. The first person to be described in this notice was "A very likely Negro Wench, of about thirty five Years of Age, a Creole born" (Mauger 1752, 2). Creole, as it was used in this context, was a way to describe a Caribbean origin. However, this advertisement may also have disclosed the presence of African-born people among the group, a point detectable in the lack of English language fluency in arrivals from the British Caribbean. The notice continued, "Also 2 Negro Boys of about 12 or 13 Years old, likely, healthy and well shap'd, and understand some English" (sic) (Mauger 1752, 2).

Unlike more southern port settlements in British North America (later USA), the primary port in Nova Scotia, Halifax, and the two primary ones in Quebec, Quebec City, and Montreal do not appear to have received merchant ships directly from Africa. Instead, late eighteenth- and early nineteenth-century newspaper notices for shipping affairs routinely listed vessels arriving from or bound for Britain and the Anglo-Caribbean. Such information was commonly printed in notices reporting harbor news, custom house activity, or those placed by individual ship captains advertising space for passengers and/or freight. In one such case, an advertisement printed on Tuesday, 26 March 1799 in *Royal Gazette and Nova-Scotia Advertiser* exposes the profound economic transatlantic connections between Halifax and the Anglo-Caribbean. The notice informed the public that the brigs Lord Nelson and Nymph, captained by Rundle and Pryor, respectively, had arrived from St. Vincent, along with Captain Hughes brig Friends from St. Thomas in twenty-eight days and an unnamed brig from Jamaica (Anonymous 1799, 3).[29]

Fugitive Slave Advertisements as Evidence of Ethnicity and Birth Origin: Quebec

While the ubiquity of the term Negro elides the specificity of African or Creole origins in Quebec, some of the fugitive advertisements disclosed more specific information about the ethnicity of the enslaved. Within the fifty-one Quebec fugitive notices this information can be grouped into four categories: (1) those that disclose African birth, (2) those that disclose birth or origin in the region that became the USA, (3) those that indicate a Caribbean origin, and finally (4) those that betray some anomalous characteristic unusual to eighteenth- and nineteenth-century residents of Quebec. This last category is the most uncertain since it is based on my educated reading of what is stated and withheld in the notices.

The first category, African birth, has already been discussed above (9.8% of fugitive notices and 11.11% enslaved fugitives). In the second category, six people can be potentially identified as African American Creoles (11.76% of fugitive notices and 13.33% of enslaved fugitives) – potentially only, since the notices do not always indicate the USA as their place of birth, but instead their place of residence prior to their forced migration to Quebec. The mulatto Andrew who fled from James Crofton of Montreal was listed as born in Maryland (Crofton 1767 in Mackey 2010, 315), a "Negro" named Cesar was purchased by Jean Orillat on 25 August 1773 from Garret Van Vliet of New York (Orillat 1775 in Mackey 2010, 318), a "Negro Slave" named Ishmaël was described by his owner John Turner as possessing a "tone of voice peculiar to New-England, where he was born" (Turner 1779 in Mackey 2010, 321–322), the "Negro Lad" Nemo was described as being born in Albany (Ritchie 1779 in Mackey 2010, 323), and finally a man named Tight (Saul 1784 in Mackey 2010, 326–327) and woman named Ruth (Saul 1789 in Mackey 2010, 332) (described as a married couple) who were listed in separate fugitive notices published over five years apart, had been purchased in Albany, New York (Mackey 2010, 536–537, note # 40).

However, of the six, only Andrew, Ishmael, and Nemo seem to have been *born* in as opposed to *from* what became the USA. It is important to note that due to the dates of these notices, only the ones for Ishmael, Nemo, Tight, and Ruth were placed after the USA had declared its independence from Britain. Further, it is unclear if any of the fugitives was young enough to have been born after the declaration itself and therefore born precisely in the USA (as opposed to British North America). However, regardless, the political upheaval of the late eighteenth century which led to war and the clearer articulation of distinctive regional US cultures – like Ishmaël's peculiar New England accent – were certainly also already present during the period when these people were born.

In the third category, Caribbean origin, although only one Quebec notice proclaimed this explicitly, three more enslaved fugitives appear to have shared this origin (7.84% of fugitive notices and 8.89% enslaved fugitives). A "Negro man" named Lowcanes who escaped from the merchant and ship captain William Gill on 18 November 1775 was likely of Caribbean origin (Gill 1775 in Mackey 2010, 319, 534, note # 27). The enslaved man may have been named after a place. Mackey has deduced that the name Lowcanes may have been an Anglicization of the French name Léogane, the name of a town in the French Caribbean colony of St. Domingue, a center for sugar and coffee production (Gill 1775 in Mackey 2010, 319, 534, note #27). Furthermore, the fact that Lowcanes purportedly spoke "good French" but "no English" would align with an experience of enslavement in a French colony.

A fugitive notice placed by Mr Simon Fraser asked the public to aid him in the recapture of JNo. Thompson who he described as "a black Boy ... height about 5 feet 3 or 4 inches, born in Spanish-Town, Jamaica" (Anonymous 1779 in Mackey 2010, 322) (Figure 3.6). Placed in

"[A] tone of voice peculiar to New-England" 65

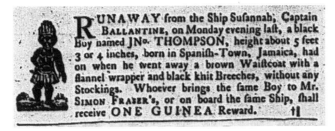

Figure 3.6 Anonymous, "RUNAWAY from the ship Susannah, Captain Ballantyne," *Quebec Gazette*, 30 September 1779, vol. 735, p. 3; Bibliothèque et Archives nationales du Québec (BANQ), Montreal, Canada.

the early autumn, the September weather was likely still warm enough to embolden the young Thompson who was accustomed to a tropical climate. That Fraser, who asked for Thompson to be brought to his residence or "on board the same Ship" used the title Mr, would indicate that he was most likely a passenger, as opposed to a crew member. But it is unclear if Fraser had just arrived, or was preparing to sail and thus also, if Thompson had arrived on the same ship from elsewhere with Fraser (perhaps his native Jamaica) or had been purchased or hired in Montreal to accompany Fraser on an impending voyage. It seems more likely that Fraser was leaving the settlement since if he had intended a prolonged visit or to reside in Montreal, he would likely not have given the option for the public to return the boy to the ship. The fact that the black youth had a family name and was not explicitly named as a slave may indicate that he was free. However, enslaved black sailors like Pompey (who was listed in a Quebec fugitive notice on 15 August 1771) were present in Quebec and Fraser's advertisement insists upon some contract that Thompson had supposedly violated with his flight (Johnston and Purss in Mackey 2010, 317–318).[30]

A "Negro man" named Snow was, like Thompson, also likely from the Caribbean. Although listed in a fugitive notice along with another black man named Tight from Albany (Saul 1784 in Mackey 2010, 326–327), the ship captain René Hippolyte Laforce who was involved in West Indian trade owned the tall and slender, bilingual, and ironically named Snow (Mackey 2010, 537, note #41). Laforce's travels to the Caribbean increase the possibility that Snow might have been purchased in that region. Meanwhile, although listed as a Negro servant by his female enslaver the Widow Perrault (Perrault 1787 in Mackey 2010, 329), Mackey claims that Alexis was a mixed-race slave, the "mulatto" son of the Guadeloupe-born Catherine[31] who had been purchased in February 1755 by the prosperous merchant Jacques Perrault for 1,275 livres (Mackey 2010, 536, note #39).[32] Since Catherine was a French Caribbean Creole, her son Alexis necessarily shared her Caribbean heritage, even if his father was most likely a white man. Since Perrault purchased Catherine alone in 1755 and Alexis was supposedly eighteen in 1775, it seems that he was born into slavery in Quebec when Perrault owned his mother. Given the prolific sexual exploitation of enslaved black females within slavery, it behooves us to ask if the white Perrault was Alexis's father and, if so, if the Widow Perrault's slave sale notice for Catherine in the *Quebec Gazette* on 4 March 1784 was a punitive attempt to separate mother and son (Perrault 1784 in Mackey 2010, 326).

The fourth category is the most nebulous since it is comprised of notices that did not feature specific descriptions of the regional origins of the enslaved. Nevertheless, five enslaved fugitives can be assigned to this category: Will, Drummond, Bell, Pascal, and Isaac (9.8% of fugitive notices and 11.11% enslaved fugitives). In a fugitive notice of 15 July 1768, an enslaved man described as "a Mulatto named WILL" draws attention due to his description by the enslaver, the Quebec merchant Eleazar Levy, as speaking "French, English and *Spanish*" (Levy 1768 in Mackey 2010, 315)[33] (italics mine). While the first two European languages were common among the free and enslaved inhabitants of Quebec, Spanish was not. Since enslavers customarily advised the readers of the language proficiency of the enslaved – as when John McCord explained that the enslaved "Negro Man" Drummond "*Speaks very bad English, and next to no French*" – the absence of similar clarification of Will's language skills would seem to indicate that he spoke and comprehended all three languages well (McCord 1765 in Mackey 2010, 314). As such, as a mixed-race man and almost certainly a Creole, Will may have been born and/or raised in a region where Spanish had been spoken, regions which included the southern regions of what was to become the USA, Mexico, Central America, South America, and Caribbean islands like Cuba, Puerto Rico, and the region of Santo Domingo (today, the Dominican Republic) on the island of Hispaniola.

Drummond's language skills also prompt questions about his origins. Since many enslaved people who had been born or spent significant time in Quebec quickly became proficient in both English and French – like Tom Brooks who was described in a Montreal fugitive notice of 1785 as speaking "English and French perfectly" (Guthrie 1785 in Mackey 2010, 328) – Drummond's "very bad" language skills may indicate that he was African-born or purchased in a region where neither language was common.[34] Furthermore, we can speculate that Drummond had not lived long enough in Quebec to perfect these languages. Similar to Drummond, Nemo, supposedly born in Albany was described, suspiciously, as speaking English and French only tolerably (Ritchie 1779 in Mackey 2010, 323). While the lack of French fluency makes sense for a man from Albany, the lack of English fluency does not. A comparison with Nemo's female accomplice, Cash, leads me to believe that she was African Canadian. Specifically, it is their enslaver Hugh Ritchie's failure to provide a birth origin for the twenty-six-year-old Cash, along with an acknowledgment that her French and English were very fluent, that leads me to believe that Cash may have been born in Quebec.

An enslaved mixed-race female Bell seems to have shared a similar experience of a recent migration like Drummond. Bell was listed in two fugitive advertisements in the *Quebec Gazette* on 20 August 1778 and 5 November 1778. According to Mackey, her enslaver the butcher George Hipps had purchased her at auction from Thomas Venture, a ship captain (Hipps 1778 in Mackey 2010, 321, 535, note #32). The history of her sale by Venture and the nature of his employment indicate that Bell could have been forcibly migrated on Venture's ship from outside of Quebec. This history and her mixed-race identity mean that like Will, she was most likely Creole.

The mixed-race man Pascal Puro was also likely from outside of Quebec. Although Constant Freeman placed the advertisement for his escape, it explained that Puro, described as a "Mulatto," was the property of John Sargent, a Loyalist from Salem, Massachusetts who settled in Barrington, Nova Scotia after the War of Independence (Freeman 1788 in Mackey 2010, 331, 539, note #52). Puro had apparently escaped from the schooner Lucy, also owned by Sargent (Mackey 2010, 539, note #52). Sargent's own origins in the USA, his residence in Nova Scotia as a prosperous merchant, his possession of a ship, and Puro's escape directly from it, all increase the likelihood that Puro was not from Quebec (Mackey 2010, 539, note #52).

Like the mixed-race man Will who peaks interest due to his proficiency with Spanish, Isaac's language skills similarly point toward his potential foreignness to Quebec. Isaac, listed as a "NEGRO MAN" in a notice, had escaped on 29 April 1794 from Azariah Pretchard, Sr. at New Richmond "in the district of Gaspié" (Pretchard 1794 in Mackey 2010, 337). Pretchard described Isaac (who called himself Charles) as capable of speaking "good English and some

Table 3.1 Fugitives listed by ethnicity or regional origins with date of first or only escape

African	African American	Caribbean	Foreign to Quebec
Ireland (1771)	Andrew (1767)	Lowcanes (1775)	Drummond (1765)
Joe (1777)	Cesar (1775)	Thompson (1779)	Will (1768)
Jack (1778)	Ishmael (1779)	Snow (1784)	Bell (1778)
Caleb (1788)	Nemo (1779)	Alexis (1787)	Pascal (1788)
Jack (1792)	Tight (1784)		Isaac (1794)
	Ruth (1789)		

broken French and *Micmac*" (sic) (italics mine) (Pretchard 1794 in Mackey 2010, 337). Since Mi'kmaq people were indigenous to the Maritimes and the Gaspé Peninsula of Quebec, Isaac's knowledge of this language indicates his experience with these communities or individuals. Isaac's potential connection to these regions aligns with Pretchard's history.[35] A Connecticut Loyalist, after the War of Independence (according to Mackey) Pretchard "was persuaded ... to lead a group of refugees to the Gaspé" (Mackey 2010, 541, note #64). Therefore, while Charles may have been an African Canadian who Pretchard encountered and purchased in the region, he could also have been an African American who was forcibly relocated by Pretchard to New Richmond from the USA.

If my deductions are correct across these four categories, of the forty-five people of African descent listed in fifty-one Quebec fugitive advertisements, as many as twenty may have been foreign, or, put another way, not African Canadian. If we remove Ireland who had fled from New York and one of the two men named Jack (in the event that the two Jacks were the same person), we are still left with a sizable number of people of African descent, eighteen, who were from elsewhere (40% of enslaved fugitives) (Table 3.1).

Conclusion

Due to the lack of slave ships transporting enslaved Africans from the African continent directly to ports like Halifax, Montreal, and Quebec City, African-born people almost assuredly comprised the smallest portion of the enslaved black population in both Nova Scotia and Quebec. The lack of direct shipping routes between Africa and Canada and the infrequency and lack of sophistication with which Quebec enslavers named African-born people in fugitive slave notices – especially given the pervasive belief in the heightened resistance of this group – would indicate a comparatively small population. While enslaved people of African birth make up approximately 17%, 21%, or 25% of this regionally and ethnically-defined population (depending on whether Ireland and both Jacks are counted), without further information, it is still premature to conclude that African-born people were more likely to resist through flight than their black Creole counterparts, as was the popular notion among white enslavers in Jamaica. As I have discussed elsewhere, Jamaican planters and overseers quickly recognized that plantations with greater numbers of African-born people were more likely to have rebellions.[36] The enslaved populations' knowledge of the Maroon communities in Jamaica, combined with the continual influx of large groups of Africans on slave ships, must have had a serious influence on this pattern.

However, whether African or Creole, many enslaved blacks identified primarily with their African identity and culture. In Quebec, the enslaved male Jean-Baptiste-François who apparently, upon gaining his freedom, renamed himself Jean Beaucour *dit* l'Africain or Jean-Baptiste L'Africain is a case in point (Mackey 2010, 72, 168; Nelson 2016, 146). Thus far, in the Quebec fugitive slave notices, twenty of forty-five fugitives (44%) can be identified by regional origin, either through the details stated in the notices or in other archival sources. The enslaved populations of tropical colonies like Jamaica came to be composed primarily of two groups: an ethnically-diverse group of Africans and an ever-increasing African-Jamaican or regional Caribbean Creole community due to an inter-island slave trade. In contrast, the black enslaved population of British Quebec was augmented through migration in two primary ways: (1) the inland migration of Creole African Americans and others from the regions that would become the USA and (2) the transatlantic traffic of merchant ships from the Anglo-Caribbean which docked at ports like Montreal and Quebec City. Further study of the dress and cultural habits of enslaved people of Quebec will shed light on how they retained or adapted their African and African Creole cultures and hopefully how they interacted and perceived each other and resisted their enslavement.

Some of the most important questions are as yet unanswerable: (1) could the enslaved in Canada distinguish the ethnicity and birth origin of their fellow bonds-people? (2) If so, how could they discern such things, and what did it mean to their intra-group politics, interaction, and communication? (3) How aware were the enslaved of the transformations in their cultural and social practices as they were changed over a lifetime and across generations from Africans into Creoles? (4) If Creoles by definition were more apt to be "seasoned" or "broken," what did this mean for cross-ethnic alliances in terms of resistance and rebellion?

While much scholarly attention has been given to the question "what was blackness," I would like to ask instead *when was blackness*? In Jamaica where hundreds of enslaved people lived together on plantations thousands of acres in size, did a black majority, many of whom were African-born, translate into greater opportunities for the performance and preservation of one's African ethnicity? Did what Ira Berlin has called the "radical separation of master and slave and the creation of the worlds of the Big House and the Quarters" create a physical buffer which provided the enslaved with the unsupervised room to preserve their African cultures? (Berlin 1996, 284) Or did the immediate expropriation of their African past inhibit the practice and maintenance of cultural knowledge (Berlin 1996, 284). Contrarily, did the proximity of the enslaved to their enslavers in the urban spaces of Halifax, Montreal, and Quebec City and the "heavy burdens of continual surveillance" inhibit cultural preservation? (Berlin 1996, 283).

The diasporization of Africans implies their creolization or their transformation in places like Canada and Jamaica from African to African Canadian and African Jamaican, respectively. But I am interested not only in the question of *what* creolization looked like but *when* it occurred. Under the burden of white-imposed slave codes, laws, and prohibitions, when did Africans lose their ethnic specificity and become something else? The archive of fugitive slave advertisements can be helpful in answering such questions. Joe, enslaved in Quebec City, fled at least five times from William Brown, the co-founder and owner of the *Quebec Gazette*.[37] While listed as a "Negro Lad" with tolerable English and French in the first fugitive slave notice of 27 November 1777 (Brown 1777 in Mackey 2010, 319), in the last notice dated 4 May 1786 he was described as the fluently bilingual pressman of the newspaper (Brown 1786 in Mackey 2010, 328–329) (Figure 0.5) Significantly then, Brown's notices not only documented Joe's determined resistance but the very process and progress of his creolization.

This chapter represents an attempt to understand complexity within blackness, by beginning to uncover the specific regional and ethnic origins of the enslaved population of African descent in Quebec. It is with this knowledge that we will be able to better comprehend the cultural, linguistic, social, and spiritual complexity of this community and if and how they worked to preserve their African and African American (continental) ways of life while living and laboring under the strategic material impoverishment, cultural prohibitions, social surveillance, and physical brutality of the white slave owning classes of Quebec.

Notes

1 All of the Quebec fugitive slave advertisements have been transcribed in Frank Mackey. 2010. "Appendix I: Newspaper Notices." *Done with Slavery: The Black Fact in Montreal, 1760–1840*. Montreal: McGill-Queen's Press, 307–344.
2 Historica Canada. 1991. "Underground Railroad." *Historica Canada*. Accessed 2 June 2021. https://www.historicacanada.ca/content/heritage-minutes/underground-railroad
3 See for example: J. Christopher Lehner. 1978. *Reaction to Abuse: Maryland Slave Runaways, 1750–1775*. Baltimore, MD: Morgan State University; Lathan A. Windley. 1983. *Runaway Slave Advertisements: A Documentary History from the 1730's to the 1790*. Westport, CT: Greenwood Press. The volumes include: #1 – Georgia, #2 – Maryland, and #3 – South Carolina.; Billy G. Smith and Richard Wojtowicz, eds. 1989. *Blacks Who Stole Themselves: Advertisements for Runaways in the Pennsylvania Gazette, 1728–1790*. Philadelphia: University of Pennsylvania Press; Philip D. Morgan. 1985. "Colonial South Carolina Runaways: Their Significance for Slave Culture." *Slavery and Abolition* 6(3): 57–79; Freddie L. Parker. 1993. *Running for Freedom: Slave Runaways in North Carolina, 1775–1840*. New York: Garland; Graham Russell Hodges and Alan Edward Brown, eds. 1994. *"Pretends to be Free": Runaway Slave Advertisements from Colonial and Revolutionary New York and New Jersey*. New York: Garland Publishing, Inc.; David Waldstreicher. 1999. "Reading the Runaways: Self-Fashioning, Print Culture, and Confidence in Slavery in the Eighteenth-Century Mid-Atlantic." *The William and Mary Quarterly* 56(2) April: 243–272.
4 See for example: Patricia A. Bishop. 1970. *Runaway Slaves in Jamaica, 1740–1807: A Study Based on Newspaper Advertisements Published During that Period for Runaways*. Kingston, Jamaica: The University of the West Indies; Michael Craton. 1978. *Searching for the Invisible Man: Slaves and Plantation Life in Jamaica*. Cambridge, MA: Harvard University Press; Orlando Patterson. 1982. *Slavery and Social Death: A Comparative Study*. Cambridge, MA and London: Harvard University Press.
5 See for example: Gilberto Freyre, Sylvio de Vasconcellos, and Virgilio B. Noya Pinto. 1979. *Os Escravo nos Anúncios de Jornais Brasileiros do Século XIX*. 2nd edition. São Paulo: Companhia Editoria Nacional; Ana Josefina Ferrari. 2006. *A voz do dono: uma análise das descrições feitas nos anúncios de jornal dos escravos fugidos*. Campinas, SP, Brasil: Pontes; Silmei de Sant'Ana Petiz. 2006. *Buscando a liberdade: as fugas de escravos da província de São Pedro para o além-fronteira, 1815–1851*. Passo Fundo: Universidade de Passo Fundo, UPF Editora.
6 Charmaine A. Nelson. 2017. "'Ran away from her Master … a Negroe Girl named Thursday': Examining Evidence of Punishment, Isolation, and Trauma in Nova Scotia and Quebec Fugitive Slave Advertisements." Chap. 5 in *Legal Violence and the Limits of the Law*, edited by Joshua Nichols and Amy Swiffen, 68–91. NYC: Routledge; Charmaine A. Nelson. 2018. "Servant, Savage or 'Sarah': Examining the Visual Representation of Black Female Subjects in Canadian Art and Visual Culture." Chap. 1 in *Women in the "Promised Land"?: Essays in African Canadian History*, edited by Wanda Thomas Bernard, Boulou Ebanda de B'béri, and Nina Reid-Maroney. 43–74. Toronto: University of Toronto Press.
7 William Renwick Riddell. 1920. "Slavery in the Maritime Provinces." *The Journal of Negro History* 5(3) July: 359–375; William Renwick Riddell. 1923. "Notes on the Slave in Nouvelle-France." *The Journal of Negro History* 8(3) July: 316–330; William Renwick Riddell. 1923. "The Slave in Upper Canada." *Journal of the American Institute of Criminal Law and Criminology* 4(2) August: 249–278; William Renwick Riddell. 1925. "Le Code Noire." *The Journal of Negro History* x(3) July: 321–329; Marcel Trudel. 1960. *L'esclavage au Canada français: Histoire et conditions de l'esclavage*. Quebec: Presses Universitaires Laval; Marcel Trudel. 1990. *Dictionnaire des Esclaves et de leurs Propriétaires au Canada Français*. La Salle: Éditions Hurtubise HMH Ltée; Robin W. Winks. 1997. *The Blacks in Canada: A History*. 2nd ed. Montreal: McGill-Queen's Press; Frank Mackey. 2010. *Done with Slavery: The Black Fact in Montreal 1760–1840*. Montreal: McGill-Queen's University Press.
8 For a discussion of creolization, see Sidney Mintz. 2008. "Creolization and Hispanic Exceptionalism." Review (Fernand Braudel Center) *The Second Slavery: Mass Slavery, World-Economy, and Comparative Microhistories*. 31(3) Part II: 251–265; Linda M. Rupert. 2012. *Creolization and Contraband: Curaçao in the Early Modern Atlantic World*. Athens: University of Georgia Press.
9 For Nova Scotia, the earliest slave sale notice that I have found thus far was published on 30 May 1752, while the earliest fugitive slave advertisement dates from 19 May 1768. The earlier dates of slave notices in Nova Scotia aligns with the earlier project of British colonization, starting in 1713 as

70 Charmaine A. Nelson

a part of the Treaty of Utrecht. However, consistent effort at settlement did not take place until 1749 under Edward Cornwallis, the captain general and governor-in-chief of Nova Scotia. See: Joshua Mauger. 1752. "Advertisements: Just Imported." *Halifax Gazette*. Saturday, 30 May, p. 2; PANS MFM #8151, Reel 8151, 23 March 1752–6 March 1766, printed by John Bushnell, Grafton-Street, Nova Scotia Archives, Halifax, Nova Scotia, Canada; Henry Denny Denson. 1768. "RUN Away, from the Subscriber." *Nova Scotia Gazette*. 19 May. British Library Newspapers.

10 Mackey collected Quebec newspaper notices about black people in the period of (British) Quebec. However, since the analysis of the advertisements was not his focus, his brief remarks about names, ages, origins, status, complexion, and region only spans eight pages (307–314).

11 I am grateful to Sylvia Hamilton for sharing with me her idea of enslaved fugitives as freedom-runners. Conversation between Sylvia Hamilton and author, 7 November 2015, Halifax, Nova Scotia.

12 An examination of the transcribed fugitive slave advertisements published in Mackey's book (2010) reveals various details about the bodies (height, build, movement), dress practices (hair styles, head-wrapping), labor, illness (smallpox), suffering (marks and scars), skills (violin playing), literacy, familial bonds, and birth origins of the enslaved in Quebec. See Mackey. "Appendix I: Newspaper Notices." 307–344.

13 The rarity of comparative Slavery Studies scholarship which includes Canadian sites is a product of three issues: (1) there is simply not enough Canadian Slavery Studies being generated, (2) most scholarship focuses on tropical or semi-tropical regions with slave majorities, and (3) most comparative studies focus on similar sites (population, climate, labor, etc.).

14 The last slave sale notice was placed anonymously and ran in the 22 January 1798 *Montreal Gazette* for a woman described as "An excellent Negro Wench aged about 30 years."
Anonymous. 1798. "FOR SALE. An excellent Negro Wench." *Montreal Gazette*. 22 January; transcribed in Mackey. 2010. "Appendix I: Newspaper Notices," 338. The last fugitive notice was: James Frazer. 1798. "NINE DOLLARS REWARD. RAN away from the Subscriber." *Montreal Gazette*. 20 August; transcribed in Mackey. 2010. "Appendix I: Newspaper Notices," 338–339, 542 n #68.

15 In Jamaica, enslaved people's ethnicity was taken as a predictor of their resistance and the most feared ethnic group was the Coramantee (Akan from West Africa's Gold Coast).
Diana Paton. 1997. Tacky's Rebellion (1760–1761). *The Historical Encyclopedia of World Slavery*, ed. Junius P. Rodriguez, vol. II L-Z. Santa Barbara, CA: ABC-CLIO, Inc. 623.
Michael Mullin. 1992. *Africa in America: Slave Acculturation and Resistance in the American South and British Caribbean, 1736–1831*. Urbana: University of Illinois Press. 24, 26. According to Richard Sheridan, the Maroon leaders were mainly comprised of Akan-speaking Coromantee enslaved people from the Gold Coast.
Richard Sheridan. 2010. "The Jamaican Slave Insurrection Scare of 1776 and the American Revolution." Chap. 2 in *Origins of the Black Atlantic*, edited by Laurent Dubois and Julius S. Scott. New York: Routledge, 27.

16 One printed custom house notice listed the vessels that had arrived in Halifax from Barbados, Jamaica, London, St. Vincent, and St. Thomas. See: Anonymous. 1799. "Halifax March 26." *The Royal Gazette and Nova-Scotia Advertiser*. Tuesday, March 26. xi (585): 3; PANS MFM #8168, Reel 8168, 3 October 1797–14 October 1800. Nova Scotia Archives, Halifax, Nova Scotia.

17 Marcus Rediker. 2007. *The Slave Ship: A Human History*. New York: Penguin Books. 50.

18 Joe's 18 February 1786 escape was actually from the Quebec City jail alongside a white criminal named John Peters and he was initially hunted by the sheriff, James Shepherd, and jail-keeper, John Hill in a fugitive notice dated 23 February 1786. This indicates that Joe had escaped from Brown some time before this jailbreak. Brown followed up running fugitive notices for Joe starting on 4 May 1786. James Shephard and John Hill. 1786. "BROKE out of His Majesty's Goal." *Quebec Gazette*. 23 February. transcribed in Mackey. 2010. "Appendix I: Newspaper Notices." 328; William Brown. 1786. "BROKE out of His Majesty's Gaol." *Quebec Gazette*. 4 May. transcribed in Mackey. 2010. "Appendix I: Newspaper Notices." 328–329.

19 See also: James H. Sweet. 2006. *Recreating Africa: Culture, Kinship and Religion in the African-Portuguese World, 1441–1770*. Chapel Hill: University of North Carolina Press.

20 The advertisement describes Bill's frustrated attempt to board a ship bound for Newfoundland.

21 Tobin's assertion is based upon the scholarship of Tara Ghoshal Wallace.
Beth Fowkes Tobin. 1999. "Bringing the Empire Home: The Black Servant in Domestic Portraiture." Chap. 1 in *Picturing Imperial Power: Colonial Subjects in Eighteenth-Century British Painting*. Durham, NC: Duke University Press. 30.

"[A] tone of voice peculiar to New-England" 71

22   Petley reveals that Taylor, who was born on 23 December 1738, had and annual income of £47,000 and an estate estimated at £1,000,000 when he died in 1813. Petley further notes that in the British Isles between 1809 and 1839, only 905 people died having achieved a personal wealth of £100,000 (46).

23   The beauty of her hair, and no doubt its similarity in texture to that of Europeans, inspired the jealous rage of the white female enslaver who had the woman whipped, cut her hair off, and ordered that his grandmother henceforth wear it shaved to the scalp. The white mistress redirected her anger toward her husband at the enslaved female victim of his sexual violence. The issue of misdirected anger and rage is also evident in the actions of enslaved females who bullied or sometime used physical violence against the enslaved males with whom they were forcibly, sexually paired.
See Thomas A. Foster. 2011. "The Sexual Abuse of Black Men under American Slavery." *Journal of the History of Sexuality* 20(3) September: 457–458.

24   The enslaved Creoles who defy this description are what Ira Berlin refers to as Atlantic Creoles. Atlantic Creoles were mixed-race peoples, usually born of African mothers and European fathers on the west African coast and were, "Familiar with the commerce of the Atlantic, fluent in its new languages, and intimate with its trade and cultures, they were cosmopolitan in the fullest sense."
Berlin, Ira. 1996. "From Creole to African: Atlantic Creoles and the Origins of African-American Society in Mainland North America." *The William and Mary Quarterly*. Third Series. 53(2) April: 254.

25   For more on the slaving practices of George Washington, see Ryan Kluftinger. 2016. "In the Shadow of the Big House: Mount Vernon's Architecture of Slavery." *Chrysalis: A Critical Student Journal of Transformative Art History* 1(3) Winter. Accessed August 15, 2024. https://blackmaplemagazine.com/research/chrysalis/

26   This letter is partially transcribed in the lecture: Neilson, Colonel Hubert. 1906. "Slavery in Old Canada: Before and After the Conquest at the Literary and Historical Society of Quebec." 2 March, 32. It would appear that Brown and Gilmore did not get what they asked for since a series of six fugitive notices were printed in their newspaper (five by Brown and one by the sheriff, James Shepherd Esquire) for the "NEGRO MAN SLAVE named JOE, *born in Africa*" who in terms of the act of running away, appears to be the most resistant enslaved person known to date in the history of Canadian Slavery (italics mine).
For transcriptions of these advertisements see: Mackey. 2010. "Appendix I: Newspaper Notices." 319, 320, 321, 322, 328–329.

27   In Quebec where enslaved people of African and indigenous ancestry were enslaved together, the term panis was used for enslaved indigenous males and panise for females, regardless of ethnicity.

28   I have deduced this from my own research and the notices compiled in: Harvey Amani Whitfield. 2018. *Black Slavery in the Maritimes: A History in Documents*. Peterborough, Ontario: Broadview Press.

29   The name of the brig from Jamaica was not printed and the captain's name is partially illegible but may be Sprot.
Anonymous. 1799. "Halifax March 26." *The Royal Gazette and Nova-Scotia Advertiser*. Tuesday, 26 March. xi(585): 3; PANS MFM #8168, Reel 8168, 3 October 1797–14 October 1800, Nova Scotia Archives, Halifax, Nova Scotia, Canada.

30   The advertisement lists Pompey as "lately bought of Mr. Perras" who Mackey describes as a grain and flour merchant (532 n #23).

31   Mackey suggests that Catherine (alias Catiche, Catherine Martin) was the woman offered for sale by the Widow Perrault in a curt fugitive notice in the *Quebec Gazette* dated 4 March 1784. As Mackey had also noted, the odd advertisement listed no price, physical description, or list of her skills. Madame Perrault. 1784. "A VENDRE UNE NEGRESSE." *Quebec Gazette*. March 4; transcribed in Mackey. 2010. "Appendix I: Newspaper Notices," 326.
Mackey claims that Catherine was a free woman (a "naigresse Libre") by 1799 when she was admitted as a patient to the hospital Hôtel-Dieu from 6 to 28 January (536 n #39).

32   Mackey claims that the Widow Perrault, Louise Charlotte Boucher de Boucherville, purchased Catherine and Alexis (at the supposed ages of fifty and eighteen, respectively) for £66.13s.4d at the auction of her husband's estate after his death in 1778 (538 n# 48).

33   Sarah Levy was presumably a female family member of Eleazar (Mackey, p. 531, n # 17).

34   Mackey argued that Drummond's language skills likely indicated, that "he was a recent arrival from overseas" (p. 530 n #11).

35   It appears that the first attempts to transcribe and translate the Mi'kmaq language into English were in the late nineteenth century. Therefore, Charles could not have learned the language from a book.
Reverend Silas Tertius Rand. 1875. *A First Reading book in the Micmac Language: Comprising the*

Micmac Numerals, and the names of the different kinds of Beasts, Birds, Fishes, Trees, &c. of the Maritime Provinces of Canada. Also, some of the Indian names of places, and many familiar words and phrases, translated literally into English. Halifax, N.S.: Halifax Printing Company and Reverend Silas Tertius Rand. 1888. *Dictionary of the Language of the Micmac Indians, who reside in Nova Scotia, New Brunswick, Prince Edward Island, Cape Breton and Newfoundland.* Halifax, N.S.: Halifax Printing Company.
36 See: Charmaine A. Nelson. 2016. *Slavery, Geography, and Empire in Nineteenth-Century Marine Landscapes of Montreal and Jamaica.* London: Routledge/Taylor and Francis, 78; Steeve O. Buckridge. 2004. "Dress as Resistance." Chap. 2 in *The Language of Dress: Resistance and Accommodation in Jamaica, 1760–1890*. Kingston, Jamaica: University of the West Indies Press, 71.
37 Although Joe was initially enslaved by William Brown and Thomas Gilmore, Gilmore's premature death in 1773 meant that he never printed fugitive slave advertisements for Joe's escapes (1777–1786). Five notices were placed by William Brown and one by the Quebec City sheriff and gaol-keeper, James Shepherd and John Hill.
Mackey. 2010. "Appendix I: Newspaper Notices." 319, 320, 321, 322, 328–329.

References

Anonymous. 1788. *A List of Negroes on Hope Plantation in St. Andrews* paper, 32.39 × 20.3 cm, ST West Indies Box 3(1), Huntington Library, San Marino, California, USA.
Anonymous. 1799. Halifax. March 26. *The Royal Gazette and Nova-Scotia Advertiser.* Tuesday, March 26. xi (585): 3; PANS MFM #8168, Reel 8168, 3 October 1797–14 October 1800. Nova Scotia Archives, Halifax, Nova Scotia, Canada.Underground Railroad. *Historica Canada* https://www.historicacanada.ca/content/heritage-minutes/underground-railroad (accessed 30 April 2019).
Berlin, Ira. Berlin. 1996. "From Creole to African: Atlantic Creoles and the Origins of African-American Society in Mainland North America." *The William and Mary Quarterly.* Third Series 53(2) April: 251–288.
Berlin, Ira and Leslie M. Harris, eds. 2005. "Introduction: Uncovering, Discovering, and Recovering: Digging in New York's Slave Past Beyond the African Burial Ground." In *Slavery in New York*. New York: The New Press, Published in Conjunction with the New-York Historical Society.
Brown, William and Thomas Gilmore, Quebec City. 1768. Letter to William Dunlap, Esq. Philadelphia, April 29. Library and Archives Canada, Ottawa, Ontario, Canada.
Dalzell, R. F. and L.B. Dalzell. 1998. *George Washington's Mount Vernon: At Home in Revolutionary America.* New York: Oxford University Press.
Denson, Henry Denny. 1768. "RUN Away, from the Subscriber." *Nova Scotia Gazette.* May 19. British Library Newspapers, London, UK.
Dewolf, B. 1780. "RAN AWAY, From BEJAMIN DEWOLF of Windsor." *Halifax Gazette*, xi(751) 24 October: 3; PANS MFM #8158, Reel 8158, 6 September 1774–26 December 1780, Nova Scotia Archives, Halifax, Nova Scotia, Canada.
Mackey, Frank. 2010. *Done with Slavery: The Black Fact in Montreal 1760–1840.* Montreal: McGill-Queen's University Press, 307–344.
Mackey, Frank. 2010. "Appendix I: Newspaper Notices." In *Done with Slavery: The Black Fact in Montreal 1760–1840*. Montreal: McGill-Queen's University Press.
Mauger, Joshua. 1752. "Advertisements, JUST imported and to be sold by Joshua Mauger." *Halifax Gazette*. Saturday, 30 May, p. 2; PANS MFM #8151, Reel 8151, 23 March 1752–6 March 1766, printed by John Bushnell, Grafton-Street, Nova Scotia Archives, Halifax, Nova Scotia, Canada.
Michener, Abel. 1789. "RUN Away from the Subscriber on Monday." *The Royal Gazette and Nova Scotia Advertiser* 1(14) 30 June: 2; McGill University Library, Montreal, Quebec, Canada.
Mintz, Sidney. 2008. "Creolization and Hispanic Exceptionalism." *Review (Fernand Braudel Center) The Second Slavery: Mass Slavery, World-Economy, and Comparative Microhistories* 31(3) Part II: 251–265.
Morgan, Philip D. 1995. "Slaves and Livestock in Eighteenth-Century Jamaica: Vineyard Pen, 1750–1751." *The William and Mary Quarterly*. Third Series 52(1) January: 47–76.

Nelson, Charmaine A. 2016. *Slavery, Geography, and Empire in Nineteenth-Century Marine Landscapes of Montreal and Jamaica*. London: Routledge/Taylor and Francis.

Petley, Christer. 2009. "'Home' and 'this country': Britishness and Creole Identity in the Letters of a Transatlantic Slaveholder." *Atlantic Studies* 6(1) April: 43–61.

Tobin, Beth Fowkes. 1999. "Bringing the Empire Home: The Black Servant in Domestic Portraiture." Chap. 1 in *Picturing Imperial power: Colonial Subjects in Eighteenth-Century British Painting*. Durham, NC: Duke University Press, 27–55.

Waldstreicher, David. 1999. "Reading the Runaways: Self-Fashioning, Print Culture, and Confidence in Slavery in the Eighteenth-Century Mid-Atlantic." *The William and Mary Quarterly* 56(2) April: 243–272.

Wallace, Michael. 1794. "Twenty Dollars Reward." *The Weekly Chronicle*. Saturdays, 8 February. vii (402), p. 1; 15 February. vii(403), p. 1; February 22. vii(404), p. 1; 15 March. vii(407); MFM 8165, Nova Scotia Archives, Halifax, Nova Scotia, Canada.

Whitfield, Harvey Amani. 2018. *Black Slavery in the Maritimes: A History in Documents* Peterborough, Ontario: Broadview Press.

White, Shane and Graham White. 1995. "Slave Hair and African American Culture in the Eighteenth and Nineteenth Centuries." *The Journal of Southern History* 61(1) February: 45–76.

Wood, Marcus. 2000. "Rhetoric and the Runaway: The Iconography of Slave Escape in England and America." Chap. 3 in *Blind Memory: Visual Representations of Slavery in England and America, 1780–1865*. Manchester: Manchester University Press, 78–142.

4 Creolization on Screen

Guy Deslauriers' *The Middle Passage* as Afro-Diasporic Discourse [*Le passage du milieu*]

Sophie Saint-Just

Le passage du milieu (1999) is a French Caribbean docu-fiction directed by Guy Deslauriers (1999, 2001), edited by Aïlo Auguste, and known in the English-speaking world as *The Middle Passage* (2001). It is based on a screenplay written by Claude Chonville and Patrick Chamoiseau. Completed on a €700,000 budget[1] and released in France on 14 February 2001, the French, Senegalese, and Martinican coproduction *Le passage du milieu* (1999) was bought by HBO Television and adapted in English[2] as *The Middle Passage* (2001) before it was shown on that premium cable television channel, albeit to a restricted audience, on 9 February 2002. The American HBO Television version became available on VHS tape and on DVD via HBO Video in 2003. The challenging ways in which *Le passage du milieu* subverts cinematic conventions[3] matched the cable channel's cutting-edge and trend-setting reputation. The film's abstract cinematic language proved a perfect fit for HBO's 2002 Black History Month programming. There, *The Middle Passage* joined a small number of francophone historical films chronicling the African experience: one week earlier, HBO had also premiered a biopic on *Lumumba* (2000) by Haitian diaspora filmmaker Raoul Peck.

The "story" told in *The Middle Passage* is literally the journey of a slave ship and its human cargo leaving the African coast of Senegambia to the Americas. It is a narrative presented from the point of view of an unidentified African captive, a ghostly male narrator who refers to himself as: "just another black body in a sea of dark despair" (Deslauriers 2003) and yet functions as an all-knowing historiographer. This historiographer, heard but never seen, confronts a collective traumatic past by visually rewriting, for a twenty-first-century audience, the Middle Passage as a seminal moment in the history of the African Diaspora. In the film, the conventional figure of the historian is replaced with that of a ghost, an omniscient African captive, who sees the past, the present, and the future and whose non-linear account, whose very presence and absence collapse time, and disrupt hierarchies of knowledge. This narrative is bookended by scenes that show a French Caribbean teenager in contemporary Martinique as the recipient of the African captive's aural and visual cinematic narrative. The long buried history of his ancestors is presented as *his* story.

Framing *The Middle Passage* as Visual Discourse

Informed by Deslauriers' and Chamoiseau's commitment to the *devoir de mémoire* (the insider's task of recovering and reconstructing hitherto erased or distorted cultural memory), *The Middle Passage* is a visual reconstruction of the Transatlantic Slave Trade (*la Traite*) that oscillates between affirmation and contestation. By repurposing the title of his 1962 travelogue, *The Middle Passage: The Caribbean Revisited*, the film speaks back to V.S. Naipaul's idea of Martinique as an assimilationist French colony, rejects conventional French (and Western) historiographies of the

Caribbean, and replaces them with Caribbean and Afro-diasporic frameworks: visual tropes by Kamau Brathwaite (1982), Derek Walcott (1979), and Paul Gilroy (1993) filtered via the writings of Edouard Glissant (1981; 1990). It also affirms and depicts at its very beginning the process of creolization as the affirmation of a transformative diasporic identity that begins to emerge during the forced crossing of Africans to the Americas. The film provides more than a Glissantian "prophetic vision of the past" (Glissant *Le discours antillais*, 132), it offers a visual recognition of historiographies that define the African Diaspora in its quest for memorialization and in its formulations of a collective historical imaginary. *The Middle Passage* visually embeds creolization within these theories to anchor the French-Caribbean to Afro-diasporic frameworks.

Among all of Guy Deslauriers' and Patrick Chamoiseau's film collaborations, *Le passage du milieu* (France, 1999) or *The Middle Passage* (US version, 2001)[4] is the film that mostly belies the filmmaker's and novelist's tendency to focus exclusively on the History, stories, and culture of the island of Martinique.[5] Rather than solely embrace a distinctive Martinican perspective, Deslauriers and Chamoiseau (1999, 2001) channel the theories of Edouard Glissant and other male Caribbean poets and theorists whose work redefined Caribbean historiography to situate their film within a wider Pan-Caribbean perspective and in a larger tradition of African Diasporic discourses. Their cinematic translation of theories is achieved through shot composition, juxtaposition of European and African musical legacies, casting, title, and voice-over narration.

According to Sarah Kozloff (1989), the use of voice-over offers many advantages. Historically, it has helped overcome financial limitations and representational constraints since "narration provide[s] the perfect means of conveying all the discursive and expository information relevant to non-fiction subject matter: of linking materials from various times and locales, and of amalgamating archival, stock, re-enactments, graphics, and location footage" (28). Deslauriers (1999; 2001) and Aïlo Auguste (1999; 2001), his editor, play with voice-over to add discursive layers and complexity. They use voice-over for its "intermixture of narration with exposition, argumentation, instruction and poetry" (Kozloff 1989, 2) to not only structure the film but also to shape its poetics, the (re)vision of the Middle Passage that it presents to the world. When Deslauriers (2006) was asked: "Did you immediately opt for voice-over narration to recount that story?" he responded, "Yes, voice-over narration immediately made sense," going on to cite the millions of Africans who were captured, enslaved, and deported to the Americas. He continued, "Thus, with the exception of these Afro descendants, the others remained anonymous. Voice-over narration made sense because it made it possible to tell this story in one voice," a voice that speaks in the name of millions of missing and irrecuperable souls (Deslauriers 2001). A fluid organizing device, voice-over gives access to "characters' thoughts and feelings," and affords "freedom in time and space," what Kozloff calls "multifariousness" (80). Last but not least as Kozloff describes: narrators "tend to voice the ideological/and or moral agenda behind the film" (80).

Deslauriers, Chamoiseau, Memorialization: The Docu-fiction as *lieu de mémoire*

In a 1998 interview conducted with *Africultures* while he was still in the pre-production stage of *Le passage du milieu*, Guy Deslauriers (2006) explained to Olivier Barlet (2006) how directing the film as a docu-fiction helped him formulate the film's oppositional language and overcome financial and representational limitations in the reimagining of the Middle Passage as a "holocaust":

> Combining documentary and fiction narrative deepens the sense of reality in a great number of scenes and allows for greater dramatization. While many written documents exist, there are few images. Engravings do not translate this reality in its entirety because

they reproduce the perspective of the [colonizing] Other on the hold. It was of prime importance for us to translate that narrative onto the screen differently. *The Middle Passage* is a narrative that arises from the hold. It is the omniscient narrative of a slave that includes re-enactments of scenes viewed from the hold.

(80)

Partly financed with French state funds, *The Middle Passage* began as an Afro-diasporic project. As Savrina Parevedee Chinien (2008) mentions, it was "produced and distributed by Jean-Marie Téno, a cinéaste from Cameroon, the voice-over narration in French is done by Maka Kotto, an actor from Cameroon (in the US version it is done by Djimon Hounsou, an actor from Benin)." The film in its US version continued to expand its reach within the African Diaspora when it caught the attention of two prominent members of the New York and Los Angeles African American cultural community. Sam Martin from HBO Films saw the docu-fiction at the Sundance Film Festival and selected it for programming in February for Black History Month. The film was adapted in English from the French with the help of renowned novelist Walter Mosley. The production of the film was also part of a larger push (McCusker 2007, 3–4) toward a more inclusive "approche mémorielle" that included acknowledging France's colonial past by recognizing the Algerian War, "the war without a name," and also slavery—among other *mémoires*—as part of French historiography. In the 1990s, the seminal exhibition *Les anneaux de la mémoire: Nantes-Europe "Afrique" Amériques* held from December 1992 to February 1994 at the Château des Ducs de Bretagne in the French city of Nantes was a turning point in the process of memorializing the slave trade in France. *Les anneaux de la mémoire* acknowledged Nantes' past as a *port négrier* (slave-trading port) and the role that the slave trade played in developing the economy and infrastructures of the French nation, helping it achieve economic prosperity in the seventeenth and eighteenth centuries.

Subsequently in 1998, on the 150th anniversary of the 1848 abolition of slavery in the French West Indies, a series of remembrances and commemorative events were held in France and in the French Caribbean. They reactivated issues, such as the recognition of France's imperial and colonial past and reframed politics of identity in the French Caribbean. In Paris, for instance, "Racines noires 98: rencontres des cinémas du monde noir," a film festival dedicated to cinemas of the African Diaspora was organized at la Vidéothèque de Paris and in several art house theaters in Paris and its *banlieue*. The same year in Martinique, the *Cap 110* memorial, Laurent Valère's monumental white sand, gravel, and concrete sculptures of African captives, was erected at the Anse Caffard in the township of Le Diamant to pay tribute to the transported Africans who in 1830 drowned in a shipwreck at the same location.

Deslauriers explained in a personal interview that he found the idea for the film in archives in Nantes in the journal of the captain of a slave ship. The log entry stated that several African women threw themselves overboard and engaged in a mutiny,[6] an even harder film to get financed, produced, and completed, by Deslauriers' own account. The idea for the film also originated in Chonville's, Chamoiseau's, and Deslauriers' desire to recover the voice of the African captive and to make visible one (of many) lost narrative(s) of origin for the African diaspora. During an interview at the Sundance Festival with Robin Gatto and Yannis Polinacci, Deslauriers (2001) explained:

The perspective shown in the film isn't that of an outsider nor is it the view from the deck, the point of view of a sailor or of the captain. On the contrary, the aim was to depict those people as shadows, as silhouettes. The aim was not to identify with them but to identify with the captives.

Chonville, Chamoiseau, and Deslauriers were motivated by the desire not to let their history be told by others. In the film, the captive's perspective is mediated by the juxtaposition of shots that depict European and African legacies and prefigure the beginning of creolization. These shots—shots of baobab trees, masks, the door of no-return, and in a sequence in direct conversation with Alain Resnais and Chris Marker's *Les statues meurent aussi* (1953), African masks and shots of whips, shackles, the fiddle, the mast, bell, anchor, deck of the slave ship, and the slave ship—function as African and European iconographies of the Middle Passage. Visual images of European and African cultural legacies, symbols of the dispersal of African peoples and modes of transportation and technologies of conquest and subjugation represent the various elements that set creolization in motion during the Middle Passage, a process that continues within the space that negates the indigenous presence, the "New World."

As their respective filmography and bibliography and collaboration on film show, Guy Deslauriers and Patrick Chamoiseau are both invested in memorialization. Before directing *Le passage du milieu,* Guy Deslauriers honed his craft making fiction and documentary films about Martinican religious practices, nineteenth-century history, and the social conditions of French Caribbean women. Although he was born in France, Deslauriers, like Chamoiseau, grew up in Martinique and it is there that during his teenage years, he developed a passion for photography and cinema. His first exposure to the burgeoning local filmmaking practice began with audio-visual workshops held at the Service Municipal d'Action Culturelle (SERMAC), a cultural center created by Mayor Aimé Césaire in the 1970s in Fort de France to support interdisciplinary artistic production of Martinique. The goal of the SERMAC was to transform Martinican men, women, and children—who were consumers of French culture—into producers of culture. As Deslauriers participated in workshops at the SERMAC, his commitment to learning the craft of cinema increased. Internships in advertising agencies and for local film production companies making documentaries opened another crucial door for him. Deslauriers worked on Euzhan Palcy's seminal film *Rue Cases-Nègres* as an assistant director and that film played a decisive role in his trajectory as a filmmaker. The challenges encountered during principal photography served as a pivotal training ground and Deslauriers (2001), then a French literature major destined to a career as a high school teacher, decided to leave Martinique for France to become a filmmaker.

In the 1980s and 1990s, Deslauriers began to direct short, *moyen-métrage*, documentary and feature-length fiction films, some conceptualized and written with Patrick Chamoiseau and Claude Chonville, a history teacher from Martinique. In 1996, Deslauriers, Chamoiseau, and Chonville worked together on a documentary about the Martinican poet, essayist, playwright, and novelist Edouard Glissant. Deslauriers and Chamoiseau have embraced Glissant's theoretical legacy and, in many ways, they see themselves as his heirs. Deslauriers, for instance, is quoted in the HBO Films DVD of *The Middle Passage* saying that he directed this docu-fiction to reconstruct and recover historical narratives that are not part of the collective consciousness in the French Caribbean: "I wanted to tell this story because it's my story and one that I did not know" (DVD). Here his vision as a filmmaker directly echoes that of Glissant, who has stated:

There is an entire part in the history of my country that remains unknown, that remains submerged because of the Western education that we received both as benefit and as suffering. Retrieving this past is where some of my greatest efforts lie as a writer[7]

(Baudot 1993)

Likewise, Chamoiseau makes no secret of Edouard Glissant's lasting influence on his work and he has explained:

> I believe that there is practically no theme in my novels or in *what I develop* (emphasis mine) that is not in a certain way announced, approached, explained by Edouard Glissant, both in his analytical work, this (sic) poetic work, his novelistic work, and in all the roads he has explored. It is thus perhaps the formidable capacity for investigation in the Antilles that allows me today to move forward in the shelter of the formidable literary project of Édouard Glissant (Chamoiseau in Perpignan 143).
>
> (Kemedjio 2002, 216)[8]

In her extensive examination of Patrick Chamoiseau's literary production and collaborations with Martinican photographers and filmmakers, Maeve McCusker (2007) notes that Marianne Hirsch's concept of post-memory informs Chamoiseau's œuvre in so far that post-memory "is not mediated through recollection but through an imaginative investment and creation (McCusker 6)." As a didactic visual reconstruction of the Middle Passage mediated via the genre of the docufiction, *The Middle Passage* offers a way to prevent "the loss of collective memory" (*Le discours antillais* 473) and to perform the recovery of this diasporic memory via the cinematic gesture of the "devoir de mémoire" (Deslauriers 2003). What Nora (1989) calls "the will to remember" (19), in his essay "Between Memory and History: les lieux de mémoire" is also a will—that explains the film's didacticism—to inscribe and transmit through the moving image given that "Ours is an intensely retinal and powerfully televisual memory" (Nora 17). This "will to remember," as a *sine qua non* of the *lieu de mémoire,* is one of the *raisons d'être* of the film.

Deslauriers, Chonville, and Chamoiseau's collaboration on *The Middle Passage* can thus be framed as a work of post-memory intended for the twentieth and twenty-first offspring of the transported Africans, who as members of the African Diaspora convene to watch the film and do the work of remembering and recognizing themselves as members of this larger group for "Memory is blind to all but the group it binds" (Nora 19). The docu-fiction *The Middle Passage* is therefore reimagined as a *lieu[x] de mémoire*: it exists because there are no "*milieu de mémoire*, real environments of memory" (Nora 7) marked by insiderism. As Pierre Nora (1989), who coined the term, specifies: "*[l]ieux de mémoire* originate with the sense that there is no spontaneous memory, that we must deliberately create archives" and that "[t]he defense by certain minorities, of a privileged memory that has retreated to jealously protected enclaves in this sense intensely illuminates the truth of *lieux de mémoire*—that without commemorative vigilance, history would soon sweep them away" (12).

Beginnings and Continuum: Archiving Visual Memory

The film begins with a series of three brief white intertitles against a sobering black background. The first intertitle retraces the economic origins of the triangular slave trade while the second intertitle dwells on the human cost of the slave trade and locates the forced "migration" and commodification of African captives as a site of origin for the African Diaspora. The third intertitle introduces the Middle Passage as a theoretical concept and as the route/ root to formulations of identity within the African Diaspora that memorializes the victims of the slave trade. In the opening sequence, the film title, *The Middle Passage*,[9] appears in white letters against the rolling of dark waves seen from a large ship. This sequence introduces the film's non-conventional abstract language and the slave ship and the sea, a sea that is "never blue, always black" (Parevadee Chinien 2008), as tropes: symbols, metaphors, synecdoches as "[h]istory cannot [.] make the past mean without creating abstractions" (Rosenstone 1995, 8).

Initially, only faint diegetic sound (from a source visible onscreen)—the sound of the mast and the cracking sound of a large wooden structure swayed by the wind—and the movements and position of the camera that follows the rolling—a high-angle shot from the "point of view" of the ship—suggest the presence of a slave ship. Sound, camera position, and movement create a disorienting sensory experience. The dedication, "In memory of my father, Georges ..." that closes the opening sequence introduces the theme of transmission, perhaps unintentionally implying that the production of cultural memory, in *The Middle Passage*, is considered through the prism of a continuum of male cultural producers and situated in that genealogy.[10]

The heaviness of the opening sequence is counteracted by a considerable leap in time and in tone. While, in the opening sequence, intertitles place the time frame of the slave trade between the seventeenth and nineteenth century, the following sequence is set in present-day Caribbean. It shows a black teenage boy arriving on a white sand beach bordered by palm trees and walking, his back to us, toward a deep blue sea (Figure 4.1). His deliberate pace, his presence on the beach, and the way he warily scrutinizes the ocean question dominant representations of the Caribbean as an ideal tourist destination. The scene is interrupted by a disembodied and dignified "African" voice who begins the film's narration.[11] The sea the narrator describes in voice-over is archive, record, repository, and the tomb of the teenager's African ancestors. Expectant but slightly reluctant, the teenager sees nothing yet that the African captive is describing but his staring at the sea begins to recast the latter as a "vault" (Walcott, 1979), as a primordial source of knowledge, encompassed in Walcott's (1979) seminal poem "The Sea is History" and as a visual rhetorical device through which the colonized returns the gaze and speaks back to the colonizer. The duty of the disembodied narrative voice is to depict the Middle Passage as a long agony to accompany the teenager—that is

Figure 4.1 Guy Deslauriers, *Le passage du milieu* (France, 1999), *The Middle Passage* (US version 2001) film still, scene: "It is beyond him to understand what took place." Kreolimages, Paris, France, 1 hour 15 minutes (France), 1 hour 18 minutes (USA).

accompany us, the (un)informed audience—to a reconstruction of the voyage in the hold. The trope of the sea as burial ground, memorial site, historical vault originates in recent literary and theoretical works from the Anglophone Caribbean. At times, the film functions as a (re)construction of the "sea [as] history" as quoted by Glissant (1990) in *Poétique de la relation* and *Le discours antillais* (1981) of both Brathwaite's (1982) "The Unity is Submarine" in *Sun Poem* and Walcott's poem "The Sea Is History" in *The Star-Apple Kingdom* (1979). Derek Walcott's (1979) marine trope of recovery of Caribbean history in his seminal poem "Sea Is History" in *The Star-Apple Kingdom* is repurposed throughout the film:

> Where are your monuments, your battles, martyrs?
> Where is your tribal memory? Sirs,
> In that gray vault. The sea. The sea
> Has locked them up. The sea is History.

This recovery is apparent in the unusual title of the film. As the Anglicism of the French title indicates, the construction of this historical narrative does not take place in a vacuum. The docu-fiction directly inscribes itself in a Caribbean theoretical continuum and offers itself as a *lieu[x] de mémoire*. In the previously mentioned 1998 *Africultures* interview, Deslauriers explained the film's title:

> It comes from the English Middle Passage, a term that designates the second leg of the triangular voyage between Europe, Africa, the West Indies, and Europe. Slaves were displaced from one continent to the other and experienced a definite break with the land of their ancestors, what some Caribbean authors have described as the death of the African and the rebirth of a new being.
>
> (Deslauriers and Barlet 2006, 80)[12]

The French title *Le passage du milieu* directly alludes to the sea and the slave ship presented as a "material, symbolic, and physical" *lieux de mémoire* (Nora 1989, 19). The circular structure of the film suggests that this memorial site is obfuscated and yet ongoing when another ship, the contemporary cruise ship, symbolizing the capitalist tourist economy as a continuing form of imperialism (Watts 2014, 1), offers an implicit present-day evocation of the Middle Passage, is seen by the teenager, at the end of the film, leaving the bay of Fort-de-France.

The Slave Ship as Trope

The slave ship is a recurring image and visual motif in *The Middle Passage*. Panoramic shots of the slave ship alternate with the captives' inhuman living conditions in the hold and the crew's hurried interactions with them. The omnipresent African narrator voices the captives' subjectivity by relaying their questions about their fate as silent, brief and rare flashbacks of their previous lives remind them of their humanity. Shot from above, high-angle panoramic shots reconfigure the ship as visual concept (Figure 4.2).

In the *Black Atlantic, Modernity and Double Consciousness* (1993), Paul Gilroy designates the slave ship as one of several "new chronotopes" (4) and "structures of feeling, producing, communicating, and remembering what [he] ha[s] heuristically called the black Atlantic world" (3). Aware that "In delivering the image from a bird's eye point of view, the shot[s'] graphics more easily lend themselves to symbolic use" (Van Sijll 192), Deslauriers evokes and repurposes Gilroy's "image of the ship—a living, micro-cultural, micro-political system in motion" (4).

Figure 4.2 Guy Deslauriers, *Le passage du milieu* (France, 1999), *The Middle Passage* (US version 2001) film still, scene: "Many such ships were seen in the African slave ports." Kreolimages, Paris, France, 1 hour 15 minutes (France), 1 hour 18 minutes (USA).

As Dominique Curtius argues in "Construire une mémoire postcoloniale de l'esclavage dans *Passage du milieu*," Deslauriers rejects the idea of patrimony "as monuments and statues that still perpetuate colonial official history"; instead he replaces state-sponsored monuments with the concept of the slave ship as cultural "patrimony" (Curtius 531–532). The director deploys the slave ship as a metonymy familiar to Caribbeanists, a visual trope that speaks to Afro-descendants but perhaps remains puzzling, opaque, or less recognizable as form of discourse to a mainstream audience accustomed to traditional film narratives and unfamiliar with the Middle Passage. Recurrent yet always ever changing wide-angle shots of the ship gliding across the ocean mark the passing of time and the voyage's progress but they also imbue the iconic image of the ship with a different meaning.

Panoramic shots redefine the Transatlantic Slave Trade as a process. For Paul Gilroy (1993), the ship's voyage to the "New World" epitomizes "a counterculture of modernity" of which "the image of ships in motion across the spaces between Europe, America, Africa, and the Caribbean [i]s a central organising symbol." It is precisely Gilroy's use of "*across the spaces between*" that Deslauriers repurposes throughout the film. Deslauriers (1999, 2001) uses the ship as a motif that rewrites Western historical narratives, by implying that modernity is a reciprocal process. The "formation" of Europe happens in its imperial and capitalist relationship to the African continent and the Americas of which the ship is a fundamental allegory in Africana and Caribbean studies. The interior space of the slave ship carries with it a "racialized sense of historical formation or degrading social process" (Hesse 2002, 149). Recurrent panoramic shots convey through the discursive space created by the film a visual recreation of the Middle Passage that depict "the expansive, repetitive nature of enslavement" (Hesse 2002, 149). *The Middle Passage* therefore claims the slave trade, the commodification of African people on an industrial scale, and the ensuing establishment of the plantation economy as the central conditions to Europe's modernity as a route to represent what I call proto-creolization.

The film's distinctive editing, Aïlo Auguste's insertion of aerial shots of the ship between brief more legible repetitive sequences, posits the ship as the "first island" (per Glissant's concept) and as a site where creolization begins. Originating in the history and ethnography of the colonial Americas, the term creolization refers to an ongoing cultural process where different cultures forcefully come into contact, combine, fuse and re-emerge as a new culture. Although transformed by the other elements with which they came into contact, elements of that new culture may simultaneously be discrete and yet still recognizable as part of their former original legacy. While *The Middle Passage* does not depict the process in its entirety but only the initial stages of the forced contact between Indigenous, European, and African peoples that inaugurate the process of creolization, it uses the ship as a point of departure to allude to ways in which this process begins. The film's innovative editing style creates a visual discourse out of "the *bateaux négriers* that crossed the Atlantic as the original agent of linguistic and cultural creolization in—or, rather on the way to—the Caribbean" (Watts, 2014, 85).

The beginning of the creolization process is first briefly shown as Glissantian "dispossession" (Glissant 1981, 112). Right before the chained captives enter the slave ship, the hands of a sailor strip an African captive of a cowrie necklace and bracelet the young man wore on his neck and his arms, parts of the body that will be chained. This violent gesture is a clear allusion to Glissant's (1981) notion of the transported African as a "naked migrant,"[13] unable to bring "his tools, the image of his gods, his everyday instruments" (112). The use of slow motion in this scene also evokes trauma (Van Sijll 2010, 76) to portray the conditions that set in motion creolization. In addition, Deslauriers and his director of photography, Jacques Boumendil, privilege diagonals and symmetry, to characterize the subaltern position of the captives (Figure 4.3). The lined bare torsos of young African men framed as a descending diagonal capture the moment when the men will be led, chained, and crammed in the hold. Furthermore, the downward movement of descending diagonals signal to the viewers the inevitability of their fate (Van Sijll, 2010, 8) but also characterizes their destination, the hold as a descent to hell.

Figure 4.3 Guy Deslauriers, *Le passage du milieu* (France, 1999), *The Middle Passage* (US version 2001) film still, scene: "The downward movement of descending diagonal." Kreolimages, Paris, France, 1 hour 15 minutes (France), 1 hour 18 minutes (USA).

The Hold: Gehenna, Matrix, Genesis

If panoramic shots of the slave ship symbolize the formation of a "Black Atlantic counterculture of modernity," the bottom of the ship, the hold, is where several components of creolization begin to merge in hellish conditions. Citing "La barque ouverte" in *Poétique de la relation,* Joanne Chassot (2015) notes that the hold is for Glissant (1990) "the tomb and the womb" (101–103), a womb that she contends gives birth to the African Diaspora (102). At the very beginning of *Poétique de la relation,* Edouard Glissant (1990) uses the plural form of Gehenna to evoke a place of great suffering and to describe the unbearable experience of the Africans packed as cargo in the hold of a slave ship (17). In Judaism and in the New Testament, Gehenna or hell is the valley of a Hinnom, a place near Jerusalem where children were sacrificed to Baal, a fertility God. I am suggesting here that Deslauriers carves the hold as a womb-like space of proto-creolization. The hold described in *Poétique de la relation*'s "La barque ouverte" ("The Open Boat") is: "[your] matrix, a mold that nonetheless expels you "(18); it is the unbearable environment in which creolization begins to develop. Lateral camera movements suggest process and transformation. For the African captives who will survive the Middle Passage, the hold is Gehenna, matrix, and Genesis. As a space of prolonged agony, the hold inflicts disease, physical death or remakes the transported Africans who survive the Middle Passage into new beings.

The hold is also one of the vantage points from which the captives observe the Europeans and the environment in which a new identity emerges, born out of conditions in which they are kept. It is the space that begins to break and remold the transported Africans, the space that starts to modify and shape their worldview. It functions as another site of origin where forced contact sets in motion modes of formation. The visual language expresses the very conditions that prepare the terrain for proto-creolization. Deslauriers and Boumendil's stylized spatialization of the ship already evokes, within the space of the hold, the carceral environment of the plantation. Cinematographer and director use frame composition and diagonals to render this spatialization and portray the transported African captives and European sailors' reciprocal fear and prolonged contact. Vertical lines and grids render imprisonment and confinement. Diagonals ascending from left to right, because they "go against the reading eye and work against gravity" (Van Sijll 8), denote difficulty and visually illustrate the plight of the captives described in the voice-over narration: their interrogations and observations, maneuvers and strategies for survival, attempts at mutiny, privations (lack of movement, of light, of food), the violence that they experience, (rape, whipping).

Visualizing Proto-Creolization in the Hold

By itself, the hold cannot account for the entire process involved in the formation of Creole languages, a process that takes place between the remaining indigenous population, the white settlers and enslaved Africans, and other groups over a period of time within the indigenous space of the "island," in the Americas, on the plantation. *The Middle Passage* suggests more than it shows the conditions that lead to the emergence of Creole languages in the hold. Deslauriers, Chonville, and Chamoiseau (1999, 2001) convey that formation of a Creole language begins in the hold by portraying the interactions between the transported captives and the crew of the ship—the captives viewing the latter as "angry birds"—as silent. Paradoxically, this silence along with a lack of dialogue and medium close-ups of silent African men infer that the creation of a new mother tongue began in the historical space of the slave ship as a necessity.

The film specifically hints at the necessity of creating a new language when the narrator introduces the captives' different origins: "Hausas, Fantis, Ashantis, Huedas, Yorubas, Wolofs from Senegambia" but also "Mandinkas, Peuhls, Bambaras." This list foregrounds the process of linguistic creolization. Men, women, and children who are "from every corner of the continent," unable to communicate with each other, are experiencing a simultaneous loss of language. Bathed in a spectral blue light, the bottom of the slave ship is represented as a crowded maze of chains where the sailors, fearful of the captives, hastily accomplish their tasks. Its symmetrical horizontal and vertical lines suggest that it is a structured environment that coerces its occupants into developing a new way of being. The hold appears as a transformative zone of contact, as a traumatic conduit for those who survive violence, diseases, hunger and who are forced to pick up external elements to re-create the self and adapt.

In the appendix to the HBO Film DVD, Deslauriers (2003) alludes to the centrality of the hold in creating a new, proto-Creole identity:

> The film is about slavery, the process that takes the slave from Africa to the Americas. What happened before the slave reached the plantation? What were the conditions in which the slave was brought to the Americas? That's why it was important to use the boat.

The director's use of the terms "slavery" and "slave" to refer to the transported Africans is telling: it already gestures toward the captives' transformation and and the changes that will constitute changes that will constitute their new identities, changes that start on the ship and continue in new lands. Aural and visual images show how this process begins at sea and continues when the cargo and crew reach lands inhabited by indigenous populations.

The juxtaposition and confrontation of European and African[14] musical legacies and the transported captives' use of dance also make proto-creolization visible. The score of *The Middle Passage* includes three main musical themes repeated throughout the film to set and maintain the mood of the film, express the transported Africans inner and outer worlds, and elicit an emotional response from viewers. The first musical theme expressed by string instruments and the piano conveys melancholia throughout the film. The sailors' music constitutes the second theme visually represented by string instruments, such as the fiddle that the sailors play onboard to keep their "human cargo" in shape during the one daily hour of movement as "exercise." The third musical theme is drum-based and it is the music that the transported Africans carried in their heads with them and conjured to retain their humanity and express their views of the world. It is the sounds and rhythm that they summoned to resist and endure and that they transformed in their attempt to recreate it and stay connected to their African ancestors.

Deslauriers and Chamoiseau (1999, 2001) use the narrator's voice-over to express how the captives abhor the music that the sailors play, to foreground the captives own musical traditions and to hint at the fact the transported captives—later as enslaved persons and their descendants—will produce new creolized forms of music that combine European and African musical legacies and more:

> They forced us to dance to their despicable tunes. We, who have so much music in us. We, whose descendants will gather together to create music with such great power. The music of the future. One day our music will change the world.
>
> (Deslauriers 2003)

The juxtaposition and confrontation of European and African musical legacies show that, on the ship, musical traditions started to forcefully combine and that proto-creolization was already at play. The Middle Passage is the chasm that symbolizes the route to becoming a new people. Like the genre of the docu-fiction, it is an in-between space that breaks and transforms. At the end of the screening, audience members, like the chained Africans, are beginning to be transformed by their viewing experience.

Conclusion: From Didacticism to Creolization

Part of the challenge of watching *The Middle Passage* is to accept that the film is deliberately crafted as a non-pleasurable didactic experience. Experiential cinematic language replaces traditional depictions of the transatlantic experience endured by the enslaved. Guy Deslauriers (1999, 2001) and his editor, Aïlo Auguste, make viewers endure a grueling and monotonous cinematic experience that attempts to mirror the plight of those chained to each other in the hold. For some viewers, Wendy Knepper (2012) notes *The Middle Passage*'s "lack of dramatic tension," its "plodding pace and strangely pacific tone are at odds with the representation of the horrors of and violence of the enslavement" and she adds, "The physical suffering of the African is undermined rather than intensified by the use of the voice-over narrative" (188). Lars Eckstein (2008), who like Knepper (2012) writes about the film's "alienating techniques" (81), adds that "images and frames are often repeated and convey a sense of the dullness of an Atlantic crossing" (79). The African captives experience a long transformative agony from which some are "reborn" into "a new being" and the film in its design to teach and its refusal to entertain, inflicts upon its viewers recurrent abstract images, an unhurried and protracted pace that mirrors the transported Africans' oppressive conditions.

Another challenge for the spectator is that the voice-over narrator's identity cannot be ascertained. Trained by cinematic conventions to identify with one protagonist, viewers throughout the film, keep looking for the narrator among the collective group of chained captives—who untypically look directly at the camera—only to discover that they are unable to physically identify him. This clever bait and switch scheme increases the discomfort of the viewer who is perpetually being lost and misled. Heard but not seen, the African captive exists as a spectral presence that provides narrative continuity to a fragmented storyline. He morphs into an omniscient narrator who seamlessly links the film's numerous temporal ellipses: transporting viewers back to his village in Senegambia or recurrently punctuating his rumination with panoramic shots of the slave ship gliding across the sea. Viewers lulled or nauseated by the movement of the slave ship are thus guided by the narrator's words yet disoriented by the physically unidentifiable yet authoritative historical narrative voice of the male narrator. The absence of the plot and having no immediate understanding of the protagonist or their identity until the end of the film, interferes with the pleasure of watching. In its refusal to provide a central heroic character as a point of reference to the audience, *The Middle Passage* forces the audience to seek out the meaning of the film's visual dimension and to view the film as a non-traditional narrative but also as a discursive rendition of the Middle Passage.

Speaking for and to the African Diaspora, Deslauriers, Chamoiseau, Chonville, and Auguste characterize the Middle Passage as a pivotal moment in the making of the diaspora, expressed by the voice-over narrator as: "We were all foreigners to each other but it will not be long before we became one people." In "Framing the 'Black' in Black Diasporic Cinema," Michael T. Martin (1995) proposes a definition of "Black Diaspora" that partly echoes the focus of *The Middle Passage*:

> [t]he black diaspora exists over time and space and is a historical formation of the capitalist world system. It is dynamic, plastic and transnational, intersecting First and Third World, across Africa, the Americas, and Asia to the metropolises of western Europe and North America. Migration and displacement, social oppression and resistance are among its key features.
>
> (4)

86 Sophie Saint-Just

By Martin's definition, the concept of African Diaspora provides a discursive space that has the potential of calling into question-dominant Western historical narratives, to denounce what Glissant (1981) calls in *Le discours antillais* an "official" and "univocal" "capital H History" (275–276).

In this chapter I have explored the ways in which Guy Deslauriers' film *The Middle Passage* can be framed as a narrative of origins that translates pivotal Afro-diasporic theories onto the screen. The discursive dimensions of the film are staged visually in recurrent panoramic shots of the slave ships, of the sea, and of the captives' untenable living conditions in the hold and framed by film elements that cast the slave ship as a symbolic "first island" where proto-creolization begins. The slave ship and the hold hint at the process in which: "A population [that] changes itself *into another people* … and thus [that] enters into the always renewed variance of relationality [la Relation] (of the Relay, of the Relative)" (Bongie 1998, 59). Embedding the idea of creolization within that framework, Guy Deslauriers deliberately reimagines the Middle Passage as a *lieu de mémoire* for an audience beyond the French Caribbean. To gesture toward the African Diaspora, he centralizes orality as an authoritative form of knowledge as: "lengthy oral tradition create[s] a poetic, metaphoric relationship to the past" (Rosenstone 1995, 9). Deslauriers and Chamoiseau visually align themselves with Edouard Glissant's ideas of creolization in an attempt to disengage themselves from French cultural hegemony, reach a larger audience and exist on the cultural world stage within a continuum of Afro-diasporic identities that interrogates Western colonial historiography.

While the film does not negate the central place the African continent occupies in Afro-diasporic narratives of origins, its idea of pre-colonial Africa is limited because it is mediated through the male gaze and a French Caribbean lens. The docu-fiction uses the voice-over narration of an African captive as "a narrative that is so to speak a diary" (Curtius 2006, 534) to interrogate previous visual (lithographs, Hollywood films) and written (a captain's journal) representations of the Middle Passage and written accounts. The film's visual aesthetics and narrative strategy bring to mind one of Glissant's (1990) definitions of creolization quoted by Chris Bongie: "a completely new dimension that permits each and every one of us to be both here and elsewhere, rooted and exposed, lost in the mountains and at liberty under the sea, harmoniously at rest and restlessly wandering" (46). The "multifarious" (Kozloff 1989) position of the ghostly African narrator who is "both here [in the diegesis] of the film and elsewhere [non-visible, a "wandering" ghost]," his erudite commentaries mirror the initial process of fragmented positionings of the subject who is becoming creolized in the matrix and womb-like space of the hold.

Notes

1 Guy Deslauriers estimated the budget for the film and shared it with me during a personal interview in 2005.
2 *Le passage du milieu*'s unusual trajectory to becoming HBO's *The Middle Passage* can be explained both by its successful integration into the circuit of film festivals attended by professionals in the television and movie industries and its unconventional narrative style. First selected at the Toronto Film Festival in September 2000, then at the Sundance film festival in January 2001, the French-Caribbean film was noticed by African American producer Sam Martin at HBO Films. Coincidentally, the African American novelist Walter Mosley, who had already worked with HBO Television on the screen adaptation of his novel *Always Outnumbered, Always Outgunned* (1998), attended a private screening of *Le passage du milieu*. Mosley was immediately won over by "the tension between the language (poetic) and the images (stoic)" but thought that the translation done by a francophone translator "did not work" and that the voice-over narration "did not have the same drama as the French" (Mosley, Personal Interview). He then collaborated with that French translator on the English version of the French text written by Claude Chonville and adapted into a screenplay by Patrick Chamoiseau. The

French translator's and Mosley's commitment to maintaining *Le passage du milieu*'s literary integrity prohibited the film from being lost in obscurity and being easily dismissed. That Patrick Chamoiseau was already well known at American universities in Francophone and Africana academic circles as the recipient of France's highest literary prize, the Prix Goncourt, for his 1992 novel *Texaco* and as a co-author of the ground-breaking essay *Eloge de la créolité/In Praise of Creoleness* (1993) only gave the HBO version of the film more *cachet* and a limited audience. Martin and Mosley surmised that the diasporic dimension of the film would strike a chord in Caribbean and African American communities and beyond.

3 According to Bordwell and Thompson these conventions include a seamless narrative style achieved through characterization, verisimilitude, continuous editing, sound, and mise-en-scène with little if any narration.
4 I am first using the original French title *Le passage du milieu* but will otherwise mostly use the English title in translation *The Middle Passage* when I am referring to the US DVD version produced by HBO.
5 In their expansive analysis of the Martinican's intelligentsia attempts at "appropriat[ing] and subvert[ing] central ideas associated with modernity," anthropologists Richard and Sally Price identify the limits of the Créolistes' arguments. In "Shadowboxing in The Mangrove," Price and Price denounce the ideological "insularity" present in Bernabé's, Chamoiseau's, and Confiant's manifesto *Eloge de la Créolité*. According to them, " 'the Créolistes' lack a pan-Caribbean perspective, in any but a superficial programmatic sense, combined with a (French-inspired) notion of that one nation normally equals one culture, leads them to be genuinely intrigued when they discover that, in the French Antilles, things are different. The idea of multiple identities then becomes not the normal human or Caribbean) state of affairs but a phenomenon in need of explanation, and celebration (11)."
6 The same log may have inspired Fabienne Kanor (2006) for her novel *Humus*.
7 This is my English translation of Glissant's statement in French: "Il y a toute une partie de l'histoire de mon pays qui demeure inconnue, qui reste noyée par l'éducation que nous avons reçue de l'Occident comme un bienfait et comme une souffrance. Récupérer ce passé, c'est l'un des grands principes de mon effort d'écrivain," taken from the "Thématique" webpage of his website, http://www.edouardglissant.fr/fiche1.html
8 This is my English translation of Chamoiseau's French original statement: "Je crois qu'il n'y a pratiquement aucun thème de mes romans ou de ce que je développe qui ne soit d'une certaine manière annoncé, abordé, expliqué par Edouard Glissant, à la fois dans son travail d'analyse, son travail poétique, son travail romanesque et dans toutes les pistes qu'il a explorées. C'est donc peut-être la formidable capacité d'investigation aux Antilles qui me permet aujourd'hui d'avancer à l'abri du formidable projet littéraire d'Édouard Glissant," quoted in Cilas Kémédjio's article.
9 Here I am using the English title in translation because I am quoting the voice-over from the DVD produced by HBO.
10 Yet the film is mostly silent on women's perspectives of the Middle Passage, even if it briefly recounts their experience. Deslauriers, Chamoiseau and Chonville revise Western historiography about the slave trade with an invisible male African narrator (as mentioned earlier Maka Kotto in the French/Djimoun Hounsou in the HBO Film English version) addressing an implied male viewer (the black teenage boy who approaches the ocean as a site of diasporic memory to learn *his*tory in its complexity) who is a stand in for the larger audience invested in narratives from the African Diaspora. Fabienne Kanor's *Humus* (2006) and Léonora Miano's *La saison de l'ombre* (2013) are novels that offer polyphonic women-centered perspectives of the slave trade and their lives and experience.
11 The voice-over narrator states:
The child who looks out over this ocean cannot imagine the terror it holds. It is beyond *him* to understand what took place under these waters. No hurricane or mythological sea demon can compare to the dreadful fate visited upon the black skin and humanity. This bloody sea. [Close up on the face of the child staring at the sea many shades of blue]. When it comes time to teach our children [the child frowns slightly] about this malevolent age, we must remember the holocaust in its entirety. This will prove to be a difficult task [extreme close-up of the child's worried face, cut to the blue sea] many of us seek to forget or even deny the monumental genocide and the enslavement of millions. [The boy has now become a black silhouette framed by the blue sea and the white sand] For others, it may seem like some long forgotten past but for me it was only yesterday [sound of tools against shackles, cut to slow motion sepia-colored sequence showing legs of African captives in shackles].
12 Deslauriers original French quotation reads: "Il vient du terme anglais Middle Passage qui désignait le deuxième temps du voyage triangulaire Europe-Afrique-Antilles-Europe. Les esclaves passent d'un

continent à l'autre, en rupture définitive avec la terre des ancêtres, ce que certains auteurs antillais ont décrit comme la mort de l'Africain et la renaissance d'un être nouveau."
13 I translated the original "migrant nu" as the naked migrant.
14 For an in-depth discussion of diegetic and non-diegetic music in the Middle Passage, see Savrina Chinien's "La déconstruction de l'Histoire dans *Le Passage du Milieu* de Guy Deslauriers" (2011, 16–17).

References

Baudot, Alain. 1993. *Bibliographie annotée d'Edouard Glissant*. Toronto: Editions du GREF.
Bongie, Chris. 1998. *Islands and Exiles: The Creole Identities of Post/Colonial Literature*. Stanford, CA: Stanford University Press.
Brathwaite, Kamau. 1982. *Sun Poem*. Oxford; New York: Oxford University Press.
Chassot, Joanne. 2015. "'Voyage through Death/to Life upon these Shores': The Living Dead of the *Middle Passage*." *Atlantic Studies* 12.1: 90–108.
Chinien, Savrina Parevadee. 2008. "*Le passage du milieu*, de Guy Deslauriers." *Africine.org*. 5 Dec. 2008. Accessed 13 July 2016.
Chinien, Savrina Parevadee. 2011. "La déconstruction de l'Histoire dans *Le Passage du Milieu* de Guy Deslauriers." *Interculturel* 15: 227–252.
Curtius, Anny Dominique. 2006. "Construire une mémoire postcoloniale de l'esclavage dans *Passage du milieu*." In *Images de soi dans les sociétés postcoloniales*, edited by Patricia Donatien-Yssa. Paris: Editions Le Manuscrit. 529–543.
Deslauriers, Guy. 1999. *Le passage du milieu*. Les Films du Raphia.
Deslauriers, Guy. 2001. "Un Martiniquais à Sundance: Entretien avec Guy Deslauriers, réalisateur de Passage du Milieu." Edited by Robin Gatto and Yannis Polinacci. *Filmfestivals.com*. N.d. Web. 24 July 2006.
Deslauriers, Guy. 2003. *The Middle Passage*. New York: HBO Video.
Deslauriers, Guy. n.d. "Personal Interview." Edited by Sophie Saint-Just.
Deslauriers, Guy, and Olivier Barlet. 2006. "Le point de vue des captifs." *Africultures* 8 (1998): 80–81. *Africultures.com*. 26 Feb. 2002. Web. 11 July 2006.
Eckstein, Lars. 2008. "The Pitfalls of Picturing Atlantic Slavery: Steven Spielberg's *Amistad* vs Guy Deslauriers' *The Middle Passage*." *Cultural Studies Review* 14.1: 72–84.
Gilroy, Paul. 1993. *The Black Atlantic: Modernity and Double Consciousness*. Cambridge: Harvard University Press.
Glissant, Edouard. 1981. *Le discours antillais*. Paris: Gallimard.
Glissant, Edouard. 1990. *Poétique de la relation*. Paris: Gallimard.
Hesse, Barnor. 2002. "Forgotten Like a Bad Dream: Atlantic Slavery and the Ethics of Postcolonial Memory." In *Relocating Postcolonialism*. Edited by David Theo Goldberg and Ato Quayson. Oxford: Blackwell. 143–173.
Kanor, Fabienne. 2006. *Humus*. Paris: Gallimard.
Kemedjio, Cilas. 2002. "Founding-Ancestors and Intertextuality in Francophone Caribbean Literature and Criticism." *Research in African Literatures* 33.2: 210–229.
Knepper, Wendy. 2012. *Patrick Chamoiseau: A Critical Introduction*. Jackson: University Press of Mississippi.
Kozloff, Sarah. 1989. *Invisible Storytellers: Voice-Over Narration in American Fiction Film*. Berkeley: University of California Press.
Martin, Michael T, ed. 1995. *Cinemas of the Black Diaspora: Diversity, Dependence, and Oppositionality*. Detroit, MI: Wayne State University Press.
McCusker, Maeve. 2007. *Patrick Chamoiseau: Recovering Memory*. Oxford; New York: Oxford University Press.
Miano, Léonora. *La saison de l'ombre*. Paris, Grasset, 2013.
Mosley, Walter. "Personal Interview." Edited by Saint-Just Sophie. 16 Oct. 2004.

Naipaul, V. S. 1962. *The Middle Passage: The Caribbean Revisited*. New York: Vintage Books. Reprint, 2002.

Nora, Pierre. 1989. "Between Memory and History: Les lieux de mémoire." *Representations* 26: 7–24.

Peck, Raoul. 2001. *Lumumba*. New York, NY: Zeitgeist Films.

Price, Richard and Sally Price. 1997. "Shadowboxing the Mangrove." *Cultural Anthropology* 12.1: 3–36.

Resnais, Alain and Chris Marker. 1953. *Les statues meurent aussi*. Paris: Présence Africaine Editions.

Rosenstone, Robert A. 1995. *Revisioning History: Film and the Construction of a New Past*. Princeton, NJ: Princeton University Press.

Van Sijll, Jennifer. 2010. *Cinematic Storytelling: The 100 Most Powerful Film Conventions Every Filmmaker Must Know*. Studio City, CA: Michael Wiese Productions.

Walcott, Derek. 1979. *The Star-Apple Kingdom*. New York, NY: Farrar, Strauss, and Giroux.

Watts, Richard. 2014. "Floating Signifiers: Cruise Ships and the Memory of Other Voyages." *Journal of Romance Studies* 14.2: 78–90.

5 Baskets of Rice

Creolization and Material Culture from West Africa to South Carolina's Lowcountry

Matti Turner

From the 1670s until emancipation, the labor of enslaved Africans on the South Carolina coast produced more rice than anywhere else in the Western Hemisphere and the region "gloried in one of the greatest concentrations of wealth in the world "(Carney 2001, 78). Recent scholarship demonstrates that this exceptional productivity, of both rice and wealth, was the result of not only the labor of enslaved people but also their knowledge systems and technological expertise which were extracted, appropriated, and commodified by the plantation system. Complex technological and epistemological systems, which Judith Carney terms "rice culture" (2001, 8), were forcibly transplanted from the "Rice Coast" – the rice-growing region from contemporary Senegal to Liberia – to the South Carolina coast, known as the Lowcountry, where they transformed the landscape and were themselves transformed. Even though rice growing itself has now nearly disappeared, other aspects of "rice culture" persist. Contemporary coiled basket "sewing," a creolized material form closely related to those of West Africa, thrives today. This is a story of dispossession and exploitation, but also one of sophisticated knowledge systems, complex ecologies, and processes of creolization that enabled people to live culturally rich and meaningful lives despite hostile conditions.

This chapter attempts to make four related contributions: (1) to consider some of the material culture of Lowcountry rice history – milling technologies, rice varieties, and especially sewn baskets – as creolized objects and the outcomes of creolization processes; (2) to emphasize the functional component of cultural continuity, transformation, and loss; (3) to argue that these processes happen not only in accelerated moments but extended through time well beyond the first generations of enslaved people in the Lowcountry; (4) and to argue that the protracted nature of creolization is largely the product, on the one hand, of the ongoing disruptive force of shifting economic imperatives and, on the other hand, the simultaneous fostering of cultural continuity and creativity in alternate spheres of life.

The terms "Creole" and "creolization" are, as Stuart Hall writes, "powerfully charged but also … exceedingly slippery signifier[s]" (Hall 2010, 28), the consideration of which has been highly productive in driving better understandings of cultural change and experience in plantation colonies. "Creole" was originally applied to "white Europeans born in the colonies, or those Europeans who had lived so long in the colonial setting, that they acquired many 'native' characteristics and were thought by their European peers to have forgotten how to be 'proper' Englishmen [,] Frenchmen [and Spaniards]" (28). Then it was used to distinguish between enslaved Africans and Creoles who were "born in and thus 'native to,' the island or territory" (28). Essentially, "[t]he first meaning of creole … referred to … someone with foreign origins … that had now become localized and blended [and] distinctive" (Cohen and Toninato 2010, 4). This happened through processes of creolization which "produces a 'third space' – a native or vernacular space, marked by the fusion of cultural elements drawn from

DOI: 10.4324/9781003357117-6

all originating cultures" (Hall, 29). This process is always defined by complex entanglements and extreme power differentials.

The forging of new culture and the plantation economy in the Lowcountry is a fascinating case study in creolization. Sidney Mintz, in his article "Creolization and Hispanic Exceptionalism" (2008), provides a very specific and useful definition of creolization as: "the creative cultural synthesis undertaken, primarily by the slaves interacting with the master class, in tropical New World plantation colonies, through which new social institutions, furnished with reordered cultural content, were forged" (Mintz 2008, 255). By emphasizing the "forg[ing]" of "new social institutions," Mintz defines creolization as constituted by deep changes to the very structure of culture rather than just its content. He elaborates:

> [d]escribing creolization primarily as mixing or hybridization dilutes the reconstructive, creative and institutionalizing aspects of what happened in these first creolizations. I use the word "institution" here in two senses, to mean a group that meets regularly enough and with enough motivation to develop its own internal order; and the rules (e.g., for courtship, say, or burial), that are invoked to guarantee regularity and order. For people in a culture to live and enact that culture, they need institutions. It follows that a great deal of cultural perpetuation involves not simply the cultural materials, but also the social platforms, the lattice works of interaction, that sustain materials over time, giving more exact shape to them through social practice.
>
> (259)

For Mintz, institutional transformation is at the heart of creolization. He sees linguistic creolization as closely tied to cultural creolization. Using language as a model or analogy for cultural creolization, Mintz sees the forging of new institutions rather than just cultural content as corresponding to the transformation of grammatical structures rather than just vocabulary. This linguistic model relates to his belief that the "creative synthesis" of creolization takes place during a short interval. Just as one generation of children can flesh out pidgin into a grammatically complex creole language, creolization supposedly creates its new forms of culture very quickly – usually through the first generation or two (256). In the Lowcountry, enslaved people forged a rich creolized culture complete with a creole language, known as "Gullah" or "Geechee" (Matory 2008, 233).

It is important to consider not just *what* creolization is but *how* it happens. For Mintz, it happens where a "subordinate, culturally and linguistically heterogeneous" slave majority interact with a "dominant, culturally and linguistically homogenous" master class in a plantation colony (2008, 255). These conditions contain two essential features: firstly, catastrophic levels of disruption and, secondly, a sufficient forum in which new cultural practices can be forged, fostered, and take hold. Numerous disruptive forces are apparent as, "enslavement, transportation, and the plantation regimen profoundly disturbed the original institutions of the enslaved who came from many societies" (259). On the other hand, the cultural life of a slave majority provided spaces in which new cultural formations, both institutional and material, could be established and practiced. Since this forum allowed the original cultures of the enslaved to be reformed into new practices instead of being assimilated into or displaced by the culture of the dominant class, this space provided some measure of cultural continuity which would have been otherwise unavailable. In my analysis, disruption and continuity, while opposites, are the necessary constitutive poles that together drive creolization. It should be noted that what measure of continuity exists for Mintz comes through the other side of a radical and rapid transformation of cultures into new creolized forms. Much of Mintz's thinking fits the Lowcountry example;

however, alternate spheres of practice and ongoing disruptive forces, both discussed below, together facilitated always incomplete and ongoing creolization processes in the Lowcountry well past the first moments of "creative cultural synthesis."

The most important recent work on the history of rice and slavery, especially with regards to Lowcountry history is Judith Carney's *Black Rice: The African Origins of Rice Cultivation in the Americas* (2001). Here, she brings together and adds to work done on Lowcountry and environmental history. She draws from Daniel Littlefield who centralizes the role of enslaved Africans and their skilled labor in the formation of Lowcountry culture and agriculture and Peter Wood who places this history in the context of the larger Atlantic Basin (Littlefield 1981; Wood 1974). She also looks to environmental historians (especially Alfred W. Crosby 1972; 1986) who have emphasized the historical influence of flora, fauna, and micro-organisms, though mostly considering only the "portmanteau biota" (Crosby 1986, 270) that accompanied Europeans to and from the "New World." Carney explicitly adds to this scholarship an emphasis on the "portmanteau biota" and indigenous knowledge systems which accompanied West Africans during their forced migration and enslavement in the Americas. Carney thus brings together the human and non-human elements in the history of forcibly transported people, knowledge, and biologies, which together produced a new creolized economy and society in the Lowcountry.

Until relatively recently, scholars held that one domesticated species of rice, *Oryza sativa*, exists and was introduced to West Africa by the Portuguese in the fifteenth century (Littlefield 1981, 84). However, in 1899, French botanists "discovered" another species, *Oryza glaberrima*, grown in West Africa (Carney 2001, 15). Its origin was debated until the 1970s when evidence from numerous fields belatedly forced the consensus that it was domesticated in the Inland Niger Delta around the first century BC (34–36). Domesticated *glaberrima* is a foundational piece in the wealth of culture that was transplanted from the Rice Coast to the Lowcountry.

Rice growing requires complex systems of knowledge and technology. Carney explains that "rice is a knowledge system" (8). She refers to the "underlying knowledge system that informed both the cultivation and milling of rice" (81), both indigenous to West Africa's Rice Coast and made anew in the Lowcountry, as "rice culture" (2). "Rice culture" is constituted by "cultural funds of knowledge" (112), technological systems, and ecological conditions. Carney describes how the interactions of these three components produce a diversity of techniques aimed at subsistence:

> Only by understanding West African rice culture as an assemblage of integrated component parts can one grasp the full complexity of the indigenous knowledge that enabled the crop's adaptation to so many different locales. In planting numerous lowland and upland environments along a landscape gradient, farmers had at their disposal a rich assortment of techniques that could be adjusted to specific soil and water conditions.
>
> (28)

Such a diversity of techniques, adapted to different environments, from upland hills to inland swamps, and tidal mangrove estuaries (57), is typical of subsistence agriculture. The diversification of environments and techniques mitigates the risk of mass crop failure. If one food source fails due to drought or pests, for instance, others, either more genetically resistant or in an unaffected microclimate, still provide. This approach not only diffuses risk but also spreads labor demands through time, and requires no external energy input, therefore making subsistence stable and resilient and providing varied food sources. Subsistence, the desired end, is thus achieved. "The threat of famine," Carney writes of the Rice Coast, "acted as an incentive for developing one of the world's most ingenious cultivation systems" (44). We begin to see the integration of knowledge, technology, environment, and culture in the techniques employed: iron-bladed hoes vary in design depending on use and soil type (54, 55); processing techniques include large mortars and pestles for milling – the process, also known as hulling, by which the chaff is removed from the grain (27) – and parboiling for storage (53); people coil dozens of types of baskets for processing, transportation, and storage as well as other social uses (113, 118); irrigation systems are suited to various drainage conditions and crop needs (60–68); and intercropping and cattle grazing feed the soil and diversify food sources (37, 47).

Gender is an integral part of institutional frameworks that structure knowledge, technologies, and daily practice in West African "rice culture" (Carney 2001, 52). While there is diversity among the gendered divisions of labor among respective groups on the Rice Coast, overall, women possess a near monopoly on rice-related knowledge and, except where heavy land moving is done by men, cultivation work – seed selection, sowing, hoeing – and processing and preparation are all performed by women (58, 108).

Rice itself is foundational to "rice culture." It is the central social and biological technology from which other technologies and cultural practices extend. Through the pressure of deliberate seed selection over time, women bred rice into hundreds of varieties, each adapted to micro-environments, technological regimes, pest resistance, nutritional needs, and culinary desires. As an object of West African material culture, rice itself is highly mobile across institutional contexts and changes function and meaning as it traverses these institutions. In the field, it is seed for cultivation. In the home, it nourishes people as grain. In religious rituals, it nourishes ancestors as offerings (Carney 2001, 31), and in divination practice it mediates between generations of living and dead rice growers (Schildkrout and Rosengarten 2008, 46). Like rice, other aspects of material culture perform shifting functions and carry varied meanings across institutional settings. Mortars and pestles were used for milling grain, but became part of the social institutions that dealt with death and burial as "the deceased's mortar and pestle ... are placed ... on her grave" (Carney 2001, 31). Sewn baskets have many shifting and often fluid functions including rice gathering, winnowing, transportation (Carney, 3, 113, 118), storage (Schildkrout and Rosengarten 2008, 46), grain cleaning and food drying, ritual offerings, divination, and in burial and marriage rituals (Carney, 46, 43, 45, 44). Like rice, a basket is both a utilitarian tool and also a social technology that mediates between its maker, its user, and their ancestors. It locates people cosmologically and within a food system that is integrated into a meaning system. This institutional mobility of material culture, as explored below, facilitates cultural resilience during times of great disruption.

The Carolina colony was founded in 1670 by Barbadian planters and their slaves (Wood 1974, 21). As Carney describes in her book, *In the Shadow of Slavery: Africa's Botanical Legacy in the Atlantic World* (2009), enslaved Africans were soon successfully growing rice, as well as many other crops, in their own provision grounds which they subsisted on during their enslavement (Carney 2009, 150). After failing with numerous crops, the slave-owning class "began to explore the commercial potential of some of [the] slave foods. The search for a viable cash crop, in effect, ended in the food plots of the enslaved" (150). When wealthy whites "understood [rice's] commercial potential, they relied on the knowledge and skills of Africans from rice-growing societies to expand its cultivation" (151). Enslaved workers then built, for their owners, immense rice plantations using techniques adapted from West African practices.

Dependable records on the contributions of enslaved African Americans are very limited in large part due to racial bias making these contributions invisible to those who left lasting records and the historians who have examined them. Carney therefore relies on the relationship between "cultural funds of knowledge" (2001, 112), technologies, material culture, the migrations of specific populations, and rice history to verify that the technical expertise that built the Lowcountry rice economy was of African origin. She writes that "[t]his involves shifting research attention ... to 'rice culture,' the underlying knowledge system that informed both the cultivation and the milling of rice. Thinking about rice as a knowledge system reveals dynamics of agrarian diffusion, innovation, and the origins of specific agricultural practices that promote historical recovery" (81). In the clear continuity of material culture between the Rice Coast and the Lowcountry, Carney finds firm evidence that the techniques and underlying knowledge are of West African origin. Following the evidence in this way, we can also trace material culture through creolization processes.

Of disruption and continuity, the Lowcountry was uniquely suited to facilitating the later. A unique set of conditions made continuity of practice and the incubation of new forms possible (Figure 5.1). Prizing their skills and knowledge, planters paid premium prices for enslaved people from the Rice Coast and Bunce Island, a slave trading fort off Sierra Leone which specialized in selling enslaved, rice-growing peoples to Charleston (Littlefield 1981, 109). While Rice Coast slaves were diverse themselves and many enslaved people were from elsewhere, the effect was a less heterogeneous slave population than in other colonies. Ecological similarities also made practices of "rice culture" highly transplantable: Lowcountry geography lent itself to African rice-growing techniques and Lowcountry grasses similar to those of the Rice Coast made coiled basket sewing possible (Rosengarten 2008a). Techniques adapted to similar conditions, saw continued use. Hoe designs remained almost identical through the history of Lowcountry rice cultivation (Carney 2001, 108–110). As on the Rice Coast, people used large standing mortars and pestles for milling (Carney 2001, 84; 2008, 99). The continuity of conditions and practice extends to many areas of life. Rice, especially *glaberrima* and its associated meanings, was reproduced by slaves in the Lowcountry. John Lawson, an English explorer, noted, in the early days of the colony, the cultivation of black and purple rice – the unmistakable color of African *glaberrima* before milling – and remarked on the great number of varieties grown (Carney 2009, 147–151). Lowcountry culinary tradition still has significant lineage to

Figure 5.1 Scarbough & Cooke, Theodore Gaillard, "For Sale." and James Anderson, R. & W. Lindsay, "Windward Coast Negroes." *Charleston Evening Gazette*. July 30, 1785. 1 (18): 1. Widener Library, Harvard University, Cambridge, MA.

West Africa in part because enslaved people grew African crops for themselves which allowed them to maintain their culinary preferences.[1] The gendering of labor and rice-knowledge mirrored institutional structures of the Rice coast for a time (107–141). Lowcountry slaves leveraged their knowledge and skill, which were coveted by plantation owners, to negotiate the "task system," a creolized labor regime derived from African slavery (100). The task system improved their conditions as it "set normative limits to the number of hours demanded," after which workers controlled their time (99).

On the opposite side of the equation, the extreme disruption from forced migration, mixing, and enslavement drove the creolization of cultural forms. On the question of the degree of cultural loss that led to this creolization, and the mechanics of this loss, I here part ways with Mintz. He emphasizes that those voyaging through the Middle Passage "could only bring with them certain parts ... of their ancestral cultures – what they could carry in their minds" (259). He explains that loss of cultural content undermined institutional structure: "[e]nslavement, transportation, and plantation life compelled the enslaved to lose great quantities of cultural material that were linked to *how* things are done, and because of it, some of the underpinnings for *why* one does things at all ... also melting away" (258). Lowcountry history, however, provides a counterpoint to his account of cultural loss. The tremendous reproduction of rice-related material culture in the new institutional contexts of the Lowcountry, originated from what people carried only "in their minds." This fact demands a different story of disruption, continuity, and loss. Culture does not "melt away" because its material forms are not transported. The difference between the loss or continuity of practice is often a matter of function, the practice of functions in the new context and whether there is sufficient institutional space for continuity. Cultural material can be highly mobile across contexts, as noted previously, but if it no longer successfully performs a function, it will be neglected and lost. For example, mortars and pestles would not function without suitable land, seed, and motivation to grow rice, and would thus be lost. On the other hand, continuity is often the result of practices traversing from one institutional framework to another in order to remain functional in a new setting. The institutional space for drum making and playing was threatened by their prohibition. However, enslaved people managed to keep this space active in secret. Some of the same craftspeople who built mortars and pestles also built drums and Peter Wood even speculates that they sometimes covered the bottom of pestles with animal skins to use them clandestinely as drums (Wood 2008, 90).

Given this functional perspective on creolization processes, it is important to consider how radical functional shifts drove change between the Rice Coast and the Lowcountry. In the former, the ends of social institutions were subsistence, meaning-generation, and social cohesion, while in the latter, the ends were almost singularly capital reproduction. The economic ends of the plantation economy acted as a constant disruptive force driving cultural, technological, and institutional change that extended through the history of Lowcountry slavery. The significance of this can hardly be overstated when considering whether cultural content and social institutions function and survive on the Lowcountry plantations. Baskets, for instance, which had carried food to kitchens and mediated between farmers and their ancestors and the natural and supernatural on the Rice Coast, later carried rice to granaries in the Lowcountry and mediated between enslaved laborers and their enslavers, foreign markets, and British investment capital. Within these new institutional settings, sewn baskets survived as meaningful and functional material culture, but did so by serving wildly different ends.

Furthering the ends of the plantation economy, farmers no longer grew rice to nourish their past, present, and future generations. Instead, laborers toiled to provision global commodity markets for the benefit of their enslavers and their financiers. This new economic regime produced creolized seed technologies with new functions, as the old ones failed to serve the imperative of capital reproduction. Rice, now a commodity, was selected for different traits. The diversity of *glaberrima* mentioned by Lawson, despite superior drought, weed, and salt resistance, was replaced by a few varieties of *sativa*, which is a better commodity species if given high water and nutrient inputs and is far more amenable to mechanical milling (Carney 2008, 99–100).

Social institutions are likewise transportable and mutable, yet need to maintain some function to survive. The uncompromising economic ends of the plantation system inevitably undermined social institutions suited to subsistence regimes. What gender meant on the Rice Coast subsistence farm could not function in the same ways on the plantation where all enslaved people became objectified, interchangeable labor. Gender roles and relations were therefore transformed. The task system, a negotiated and creolized institution, came under ongoing transformative pressure. Once the slave-owning class successfully appropriated and commodified the knowledge and techniques of the enslaved, the ends of capital reproduction further exerted themselves and the plantation system de-skilled and de-gendered labor and further appropriated and remade such knowledge and techniques for itself. Once the enslaved lost the leverage of exclusive knowledge, conditions severely deteriorated throughout the eighteenth century (Carney 2001, 99–100) as people worked very long days in the heat and over highly reflective water and many died of malaria (118). The history of milling technologies is also instructive here. In West Africa, rice is milled briefly each day. As Carney explains, "its pounding for consumption marks the passage of time, as women's rhythmic striking of a pestle against a mortar full of rice grains heralds the beginning of a new day in countless villages of the region" (8). Hand milling on the plantation marked a different kind of time. Workers performed this ceaseless task on an industrial scale for months following harvest. The mortar and pestle was decontextualized from its cultural meaning and recontextualized within the plantation institution. Operating a large mortar and pestle demands both tremendous strength and a light, skilled touch to mill significant quantities without breaking the rice grains (Carney 2008, 99). As the profit motive led to increasing production, all hands, those of skilled women and unskilled men, equivalently instrumentalized, were employed in milling. The result was large quantities of broken grain and lost profits. This may have been the result of a disregard for the fact that this skill was uniquely possessed by women or the flattening effect of commodified labor that seeks to maximize the labor extracted while minimizing investments, such as skill training. Either way, this interaction of gendered labor and the plantation economy drove further technical change. The high incidence of broken grain (lost profit) prompted the mechanization of milling on plantations at the turn of the nineteenth century (Rosengarten 2008a, 107). Mechanization, however, did not improve conditions for the enslaved. Instead, it removed a production bottleneck and thus greatly increased other labor demands.

Enslaved people's alternate spheres of life, which fostered cultural creativity and continuity apart and somewhat autonomous from the dictates of the master class, countered, to some extent, the disruptive force of the plantation regime. In Mintz's account, creolization is a rapidly completed process of transformation. However, alternative spheres of life, such as provision grounds and the slave-domestic attest to the ongoing and incomplete nature of this process.[2] For centuries, enslaved people in the Lowcountry sustained themselves with creolized technological systems in their provision grounds. Here, people grew what Carney calls a "new, robust plant assemblage" (Carney 2009, 99) of old and "New World" crops suited to subsistence. Cultural practices not functional in the plantation field continued to sustain enslaved people physically, socially, and spiritually. The consistency of ends (subsistence, the production of meaning, etc.) between these alternate spheres and Rice Coast farming cultures contributed tremendously to the continuity and elastic resilience of many aspects of Lowcountry culture including creolized food systems. Enslaved people worked to the ends of both subsistence and commodity production in different fields simultaneously. These two spheres would have interacted in ways invisible to many observers as material culture, such as baskets, mortars and pestles, and rice itself would have been mobile and transformable, moving between the respective spheres and shifting functions, meanings, and institutional contexts in each field of practice. While the creolized forms of the plantation economy were established and appear at first glance to be the end results of completed changes, these alternate spheres demonstrate the perpetual incompleteness of these transformations. The ongoing interaction of multiple incompletely creolized spheres provided both ongoing disturbance and the space for cultural creativity and continuity necessary for protracted processes of creolization through time.

The task system is not only significant for its ameliorating effect on the labor conditions but also because through it, enslaved people gained "partial autonomy from claims on their labor" (100). That autonomy secured spaces for cultural continuity and creativity in the alternate spheres of the enslaved. Carney explains that "it provided slaves the opportunity to allocate more time to cultivate their garden plots, hunt, fish, and gather products that could either go toward improving their nutritional status or be sold in local markets for small profits" (99). By securing such alternate spheres of practice so necessary for creolization, the task system, itself a creolized labor regime, facilitated further creolization.

While there is not yet any scholarly proof, it is highly likely that the enslaved were growing varieties of *glaberrima* in their provision grounds well after it passed from favor on the plantation, and possibly well after emancipation as it would have suited culinary preferences, held significant spiritual and worldly meaning, and been better suited to marginal lands and hand milling than *sativa* varieties. Social institutions that depended on these varieties of rice, such as religious practices, would have been better supported in turn. When conditions change, practices that have been functional only in subaltern spheres, such as provision grounds, can expand outwards and regain a broader use. Following emancipation, plantation farming quickly ended and many free blacks, under a new economic regime, acquired land in the Lowcountry and commenced family-farming (Rosengarten 2008a, 115). They used techniques, such as hand milling with mortar and pestle that had become obsolete on plantations, but not on provision grounds (115).

Dramatic examples of cultural practice and technologies embedded in alternate spheres and expanding out into full cultural and technical systems exist in Maroon colony subsistence agriculture. Tinde Van Andel's work in the Saramaccan region of Surinam, a long time Maroon stronghold, provides some insight here. He explains that "*Oryza glaberrima* is still grown, milled by hand, eaten, offered to the ancestors, sold on the market, and even exported to the Netherlands by Maroons. Traditional religion plays an important role in the survival of this ancient rice species" (8). Rice growing Maroon colonies in the Americas have exceptional technological continuity with West Africa compared to those communities that endured the full life of the plantation economy. Every verified location in the Americas of continual *glaberrima* cultivation is a former Maroon colony[3] and the uses of *glaberrima*, such as those noted by Van Andel, are often similar to those of West Africa (8). Rice is still used as a religious communication medium between the living and the dead and Saramaccans grow some varieties exclusively for this purpose (4). Carney writes that "Maroon rice culture has changed little over more than two hundred years of observations" and that it is still a "woman's crop" (Carney 2009, 93). This gendered transmission of rice technology is expressed by the old Saramaccan story of Paanza who escaped enslavement on a plantation after she "scoops up some grains of ripened rice and stuffs this seed rice into her hair" and brought it to the Maroon colony (92). Since the colony was established when the plantation system was well developed, subsistence technologies that came to define Maroon practice, and the gendered structure of these practices, so similar to those of West Africa, had to have been maintained by the enslaved in alternate spheres parallel to the plantation economy which resisted the appropriations and disruptions of the plantation system (92).[4]

Of the practices of Lowcountry material culture focused on thus far–rice varieties, mortars and pestles, and sewn baskets – it is the last of these creolized practices that has endured to the present. The production of "Gullah baskets" or "sweetgrass baskets" thrives in South Carolina today. Dale Rosengarten notes that "African Americans have been making coiled baskets without interruption for more than three hundred years, impelled for the first two centuries by the needs of global commerce, but always in response to their own desires and purposes too" (Rosengarten 2008a, 105). Like rice, the basket is a social and biological technology and an aesthetic object that mediates people's relationships with land, ancestors, other technologies, and with each other. Additionally, baskets are highly valued for their aesthetic properties. They make for an exemplary case of creolization with their history of holding multiple shifting places within constantly changing institutions. A prime example is the fanner basket which was used for winnowing, where milled rice is dropped from a height, then (Figure 5.2) caught as the chaff blows away in the wind. It no longer performs this function in the Lowcountry, but persists as a craft object.

Historical research on basket making practices is made especially difficult by their formal variation in the Lowcountry and their biodegradable nature. There was variation by region and likely from plantation to plantation depending on the mixed ethnic origins of slaves and the availability of specific materials. The knots that bind together the beginning of the first coil are often used to distinguish between otherwise similar methods from different islands or areas (Rosengarten 2008a, 110). According to Rosengarten, "no Lowcountry baskets from the seventeenth century have survived, nor have scholars found written references to baskets in Carolina before 1700" (105). However, because the craft is transmitted through oral teaching, the

Figure 5.2 Winnowing *Rice, Mt. Pleasant, South Carolina* (1974); Arthur Manigault, Sr. winnows rice in a fanner basket made by his wife, Mary Jane Manigault. p. 100, photo: Greg Day. Courtesy The Africa Center/Museum for African Art, from exhibition catalogue, GRASS ROOTS: *African Origins of American Art.*

contemporary existence of the practice confirms its historical continuity.[5] By way of challenges and possibilities for scholarship, Rosengarten states:

> a historian interested in basketry is handicapped by the perishable nature of the vegetable fibers from which it is made, and by the view of the basket as a humble object, useful but replaceable. For the eighteenth century, documentary evidence of basket production is sparse but informative, all of it in texts written by Europeans. Baskets occasionally are mentioned in wills, inventories, account books, and overseers' reports where they are described simply as tools and commodities.
> (105)

Most who documented the Lowcountry before emancipation lacked an eye for the significance or even the existence of basket technologies, many of which would also have been deliberately hidden. As with rice, the history of basket making often leaves only fleeting traces except in its reproduction in the present or the recent past. Between these fragments of evidence and continuities with African technologies, the history must be pieced together.

Tracing the historical origins of the coiled Lowcountry basket is exceedingly difficult. Anthropologist Joseph Opala insists on the Sierra Leonean origins of the craft (Schildkrout and Rosengarten 2008, 24). This theory has found some acceptance but there is significant reason to point elsewhere. Dale Rosengarten and Enid Schildkrout do just that:

> It is remarkable today we still find African baskets which closely resonate with Lowcountry forms. Older baskets ... suggest close ties between enslaved Africans in America and populations in Senegal, The Gambia, Sierra Leone, Angola, and the Congo.
> (Schildkrout and Rosengarten 2008, 20)

Sandra Klopper even argues for the possibility of a complex connection to southern Africa (2008). Lowcountry baskets are virtually all coiled. Long pieces of sweetgrass, bulrush, or long leafed pine needles are bunched together.[6] A "binder" strip of palmetto, a shrub-sized palm plant, or split oak is coiled around the bunch to create a cylindrical row and sewn into the last coil to add another row (Schildkrout and Rosengarten 2008, 42, 59; Rosengarten 2008a, 104, 110). Coiled baskets are found throughout West Africa. However, sewers weave and do not coil fanner baskets in Sierra Leone, further bringing into question the notion of a single origin (Schildkrout and Rosengarten 2008, 42). In a creolized context, however, multiple origins, such as this should not be confounding, but expected.

In considering the role of baskets, one must consider them as embedded in West African "rice culture's" complex systems of relational meaning. Rosengarten and Schildkrout explain:

> While baskets were associated with rice on both continents, in Africa rice was embedded in rich cultural systems that had evolved over centuries, in contrast to the rapidly organizing slave plantation societies that emerged in semitropical America. African rituals of rice [of which baskets were a key part] included masquerades and sculpture, harvest celebrations, and gifts to commemorate important life passages.
> (Schildkrout and Rosengarten 2008, 22)

In this West African context of complex relational meaning, baskets were used for winnowing, transportation, storage, marriage, funeral rituals, social mediation, and more. Subtle changes in form can redefine a basket's function. For instance, the interweaving of a "silk grass" in with the rushes makes it a friendship basket which is gifted and brings "luck and bounty" (Rosengarten 2008b, 131).

Fanner baskets and baskets for the storage and transportation of rice were tremendously important pieces of the Lowcountry plantations' technological system. Planters made their slaves produce them on a very large scale (Carney 2001, 18). Unlike with milling, the plantation economy could not de-skill or mechanize this labor and thus had to rely on those with the skills and those who were taught by older generations. Consequently, the making of these baskets remained gendered – work baskets were produced by men. Enslaved males, often those considered unfit for field work, such as the elderly and injured, were made to produce these baskets. This was also done in larger volume in the winter when other labor demands slackened. The form became suited to mass production, employing oak binding and bulrush bunches for strength and relatively crude coiling for production speed (Schildkrout and Rosengarten 2008, 22). This semi-industrialized production only increased as plantations expanded from inland swamps to rivers in the mid-eighteenth century and again with the mechanization of milling (Rosengarten 2008a, 108). Winnowing was never mechanized even when other tasks were. Thus, the demand for winnowing baskets expanded greatly with production and plantation size increases. Baskets were also a commodity sold between plantations and basket sewing skills added to the commodity value of enslaved people (104, 107).

The Civil War brought further change as basket production was encouraged and organized by the occupying Union Army. "The Port Royal Experiment" organized the labor of freed slaves to "[promote] economic independence, literacy, and civil rights," and to avoid, as the commanding general pointed out, "the evils of idleness" (Rosengarten 2008a, 115). In this transitional moment, large scale production was still supervised by whites, while the impetus shifted from profit to a paternal vision of self-betterment (115). The fleeing of plantation owners also changed production radically. Rosengarten writes that after the war:

> No longer under compulsion to mass produce fanners, basket sewers continued to make agricultural work baskets and household forms as their own needs dictated. In the shift from coerced labour to family farming, growers relied on the old hand tools to process their crops. Gone were the days when schooners docked at plantation levees to load barrels of rice destined for waiting mills, yet rice-growing on a small scale continued. The last rice mill shut down in South Carolina long before the last mortar, pestle, flail, and fanner basket were laid to rest.
>
> (115)

Many of the technologies just mentioned were, like we see in Maroon colonies, sustained through use in the alternate sphere of slave subsistence systems and employed on a larger scale again to suit family-farming – typically a mixed system of both commodity production (usually cotton) and subsistence farming (115). After the war, there was a shift in the dominant form from work baskets to domestic baskets:

> the bulrush 'work' basket, once essential to rice production and traditionally made by men, almost disappeared. Sweetgrass 'show' baskets, on the other hand, based on household forms and made primarily by women, began to be produced for a new market, leading to the artistic efflorescence taking place today.
>
> (Rosengarten 2008b, 128)

These "sweetgrass baskets," also known as "Gullah baskets," would have been invisible to most observers on plantations and, especially if one holds a too-rapid view of cultural change, could have easily been believed to have been lost. However, they did not appear spontaneously. Instead, they were nurtured and practiced continuously in the domestic sphere of the enslaved – a living technological repository akin to and closely related to the provision ground and somewhat autonomous from the dictates of the plantation. We can see in the continuity of practice from the re-emergence of this material culture and its African origins that this continuity was facilitated specifically by the labor of woman, the traditional holders of the necessary knowledge and skill.[7] Domestic baskets were produced and used by enslaved women and their descendants for long enough to bring them back to public life to be transformed again in a series of ongoing creolizations.

As the social institutions surrounding its production transformed, the Gullah basket took new shapes. Sweetgrass, sometimes mixed with long leaf pine needle for contrast, replaces bulrush and is bound by palmetto instead of oak. These materials are chosen for both their aesthetic properties and their pliability, and the time spent on each basket increased with the passing of mass production (Rosengarten 2008a, 120; 2008b, 134, 140). Sewers began to use the preserved techniques and changing materials to produce a "large repertory of functional pieces – bread trays and table mats, flower and fruit baskets, shopping bags, knitting baskets, thermos bottles or wine coolers, ring trays, and wastepaper baskets" (2008a, 120). Around 1970, bulrush was reintroduced due to sweetgrass habitat loss and limits to access. Since it is more structurally robust, it resulted in "a noticeable trend toward big sculptural forms that feature elaborate surface decoration and meticulous stitching" (2008a, 120).

In 1929, with the paving of Highway 17 out-of-state tourist traffic came to the Lowcountry. Basket makers found a new source of income by selling baskets at roadside stands, typically marketing their work as authentically "Gullah" (Rosengarten 2008b, 136). Many sewers sustained their families on the income from this small-scale cultural commodification. Simultaneously, centralized markets also sold their products and kept a share (136–140). The rise of the Arts and Crafts movement also made the basket function as an art object (Figure 5.3). Some of the best sweetgrass baskets are coveted and shown in galleries worldwide (42). The form has transformed to suit new purposes. Once the ends of a basket are a gallery or wall hanging and not a functional container, sewers use traditional techniques to add new flair and creativity to their work. In his article, "Missions and Markets: Sea Island basketry and the Sweetgrass Revolution," (2008) Rosengarten writes:

> Practical and imaginative forms made today and displayed by sewers at their stands and other venues appeal to the hand and the eye as the products of a vibrant artistic culture. Yet the humble coiled basket remains what it always was: a vessel, sewn of bundles of grasses held together by a flexible stitching element and answering a myriad of human purposes.
> (144)

The adaptive dynamism inherent to creolized technologies is evidenced in the ability to "answer" to these many purposes.

Mary Jackson is a celebrated sweetgrass basket sewer, respected both by her peers and the art world. In a *New York Times* interview she explains that the practice of sewing "was important for maintaining my ancestor's identity." She adds that "it reminded us of where we came from and that we came from some place. The techniques were jealously guarded, and it was a cardinal sin to teach it to those outside the family structure, especially to whites" (*New York Times*, June 6, 1993). Clearly, the Lowcountry basket has been both sustained in alternate spheres

Figure 5.3 Mary Jackson, *Low Basket with Handle* (nd), Gift of Marcia and Alan Docter, Accession # 2001.61, Smithsonian American Art Museum, Washington D.C., USA.

and undergone numerous creolizing transformations through time. Baskets in the Lowcountry have been instruments of plant production, religious objects, coveted domestic tools, means of government "uplift" programs, cultural commodities, and valued art. Despite this, the basket still serves some of its original functions. It is regularly used as a domestic tool and it sustains livelihoods through a reformed mode of craft production. In Mary Jackson's statement, we see older African functions take a new form: the act of coiling a basket is not precisely a practice of divination, yet it is a semi-ritualized practice which mediates between past and present (the living and their ancestors), locating people in meaningful ways and across both time and space. It connects its maker with the generations from whom the skill has been passed down, including the enslaved workers who shaped Lowcountry life and their West African forebears, and orients them to an ancestral home. The transmission of these functions through time attests to the resilient capacities of creolized technologies to achieve continuity despite extreme disruption and their almost linguistic function to communicate meaning autonomous from those ascribed by the dominant culture. In this exemplary case of cultural creolization, we see the transformation of the institutional frameworks of religious practice and divination; yet through this transformation, across time, and in new institutional contexts, many of the original functions are still performed! This fits very closely with Mintz's characterization of creolization except with the addition of the protracted nature of the process.

Peter Wood describes more autonomous functions of the basket as well as the related practice of "basket naming":

> Artful coiled baskets ... were used to haul and process white-owned produce grown by the enslaved. But these same baskets could also be used to hold the maker's own beloved newborn, or to shelter an infant at the edge of a field while the mother hoed weeds in the baking sun. The giving of "basket names" is a tradition that outlasted slavery .... From birth, most black Carolinians have two given names. One is an official name used in dealing with outsiders; the other is a "basket name," known only among family and friends, given when a child is small enough to sleep in a basket. And when the great war finally came, the same hands that made scores of flexible fanner baskets for winnowing the master's rice might even sew a basket boat for escaping.
>
> (Wood 2008, 92)

The autonomy of these meanings and functions from the dominant ideology, economy, and system of power is key to the resilience of the culture. This protracted creolization process which produces a great deal of autonomy of meaning and function depended greatly on the incompleteness of creolized change and alternate spheres of life apart from those dominated by slave owners. Basket naming was a practice directed precisely at achieving such autonomy.

Autonomous interventions, such as "basket naming" shift the structure, or grammar, of the relationship between enslaved and enslaver. Linda Rupert connects creolization with economics by referring to "multiple economic interactions that took place in the early modern Atlantic world as conversations, conjuring up the image of social and cultural exchanges interwoven with economic ones" (Rupert 2012, 7). If creolization is a conversational process, in plantation economies, the conversation was exceedingly forceful, even violently one sided. The role of the economics of the plantation economy in this "conversation," as we have observed, has had much more of an unraveling effect than an "interweaving" effect. However, people have endured this and re-woven new lives and technologies precisely by intervening on the terms of the conversation and developing autonomous spaces of their own. Objects of material culture have moved fluidity, traversing and serving new institutions and economic regimes while also serving alternate ends for the enslaved and retaining many of their original functions. Alternate spheres of practice, such as the slave-domestic and the provision ground also change the institutional grammar – they change the language of this conversation in ingenious ways, such as the giving of "basket names" and the weaving of sweetgrass baskets.

Notes

1 For accounts of Lowcountry culinary history pertaining to rice, see Harris (2008) and Hess (1992).
2 While it exceeds the scope of this chapter, it is important to note here the important work of Margaret Washington Creel who "argue[s] for the presence of dynamic, creative, cultural trends of African presence among the Gullahs" (6) in her study on religious continuity between West Africa and the syncretic Christianity of the Gullah. She notes the importance of "functional" aspects of religion to aid in this continuity (3).
3 These communities exist in Nicaragua, Panama, El Salvador, Surinam, and Guyana (Carney 2008, 27).
4 Amerindian contributions to the technologies and survival of Maroon colonies should also not be underestimated (Carney 2009, 84–98).
5 The practice was not acquired from Native Americans in the region who wove and did not sew their baskets (Wood 2008, 81).
6 Bulrush has long been associated with the story of Moses as a baby in a bulrush basket. For many Gullah, Moses is an emancipator and the plant, still used has religious and political significance as a result (Rosengarten 2008a, 110).

7 More detailed study on how gendered knowledge and skill defined the slave-domestic and provision grounds and thus fed into broader creolization processes would be an important and fascinating contribution. The examples we have seen – baskets, milling, and Maroon subsistence systems – are hopefully suggestive of the process and its importance.

References

Carney, Judith A. 2001. *Black Rice: The African Origins of Rice Cultivation in the Americas.* Cambridge: Harvard University Press.

Carney, Judith A. 2008. "Rice in the New World." In *Grass Roots: African Origins of an American Art*, edited by Theodore Rosengarten, 94–103. New York: Museum for African Art.

Carney, Judith A. 2009. *In the Shadow of Slavery: Africa's Botanical Legacy in the Atlantic World.* Berkeley: University of California Press.

Cohen, Robin and Paola Toninato, 2010. "The Creolization Debate: Analysing Mixed Identities and Cultures." In *The Creolization Reader: Studies in Mixed Identities and Cultures*, edited by Robin Cohen and Paola Toninato, 1–21. London: Routledge.

Crosby, Alfred W. 1972. *The Columbian Exchange: Biological and Cultural Consequences of 1492.* Westport: Greenwood Press.

Crosby, Alfred W. 1986 *Ecological Imperialism: The Biological Expansion of Europe, 900–1900.* Cambridgeshire: Cambridge University Press.

Hall, Stuart, 2010. "Créolité and the Process of Creolization." In *The Creolization Reader: Studies in Mixed Identities and Cultures*, edited by Robin Cohen and Paola Toninato, 26–38. London: Routledge.

Harris, Jessica B. 2008. "Carolina's Gold: Three Hundred Years of Rice and Recipes in Lowcountry Kitchens." In *Grass Roots: African Origins of an American Art*, edited by Theodore Rosengarten, 122–127. New York: Museum for African Art.

Hess, Karen. 1992. *The Carolina Rice Kitchen: the African Connection.* Columbia: University of South Carolina Press.

Littlefield, Daniel C. 1981. *Rice and Slaves: Ethnicity and the Slave Trade in Colonial South Carolina.* Baton Rouge: Louisiana State University Press.

Mintz, Sidney. 2008 "Creolization and Hispanic Exceptionalism." *Review (Fernand Braudel Center).* (31) 3: 251–265.

Rosengarten, Dale. 2008a. "By the Rivers of Babylon: The Lowcountry; Basket in Slavery and Freedom." In *Grass Roots: African Origins of an American Art*, edited by Theodore Rosengarten, 104–121. New York: Museum for African Art.

Rosengarten, Dale. 2008b. "Missions and Markets: Sea Island Basketry and the Sweetgrass Revolution." In *Grass Roots: African Origins of an American Art*, edited by Theodore Rosengarten, 128–145. New York: Museum for African Art.

Rupert, Linda M. 2012. *Creolization and Contraband: Curaçao in the Early Modern Atlantic World.* Athens: University of Georgia Press.

Schildkrout, Enid and Dale Rosengarten. 2008. "African Origins: Ancestors and Analogues." In *Grass Roots: African Origins of an American Art*, edited by Theodore Rosengarten, 20–77. New York: Museum for African Art.

Van Andel, Tinde. "African Rice *Oryza Glaberrima*: Lost Crop of the Enslaved Africans Discovered in Suriname." *Economic Botany.* (64) 1: 1–10. DOI: 10.1007/s12231-010-9111-6

Washington Creel, Margaret. 1988. *"A Peculiar People": Slave Religion and Community-Culture among the Gullahs.* New York: New York University Press.

Wood, Peter. 1974. *Black Majority: Negroes in Colonial South Carolina.* New York: Alfred A Knopf Press.

Wood, Peter. 2008 "They Understand Their Business Well: West Africans in Early South Carolina." In *Grass Roots: African Origins of an American Art*, edited by Theodore Rosengarten, 78–93. New York: Museum for African Art.

6 "Wages of Empire"

American Inventions of Mixed-Race Identities and Natasha Trethewey's *Thrall* (2012)

Eloisa Valenzuela-Mendoza

> To live in the Borderlands means you
> are neither *hispana india negra española*
> *ni gabacha, eres mestiza, mulata,* half-breed
> caught in the crossfire between camps
> while carrying all five races on your back
> not knowing which side to turn to, run from …
>
> Gloria Anzaldúa[1]

Former US American poet laureate, Natasha Trethewey, notes that at the time of her birth and due to her biracial background: "laws against miscegenation rendered my parents' marriage illegal, my birth illegitimate …" (2010). Trethewey was born to a white father, who immigrated from Canada, and an African American mother one year before the federal landmark case, *Loving v. Virginia* (1967) that overturned anti-miscegenation laws throughout the United States. However, while the Supreme Court's decision declared interracial marriage legal, and by extension the offspring of these unions legitimate, the court could not legislate individual opinions. In the poem, "My Mother Dreams Another Country" (2006), Trethewey discusses the complexity of naming and racial categorization in the United States. Imagining her mother's life during her pregnancy, she writes: "Already the words are changing … / from *colored*, to *negro*, *black* still years ahead. / This is 1966 – she is married to a white man – / and there are more names for what grows inside her. / … words like *mongrel*…" (2006, 37). The terminology used to signify otherness is central to this poem. While a seemingly innocuous trajectory is traced from the word "colored" to "black," the potential violence of this type of naming is signified with the word "mongrel."

Trethewey's volume, *Thrall* (2012), centers on the *casta* paintings from eighteenth-century Mexico, and an ongoing desire – one that surpasses the imposition of borders and transcends time – to define and conquer the alterity of the Other. Her poetic vision establishes a kinship between the racial dynamics of eighteenth-century New Spain and the contested nature of contemporary race relations in U.S. America.[2] Within this work, Trethewey contemplates the enduring and rampant proclivity to define difference. For much of the eighteenth century, *casta* paintings – elaborate portraits of cross racial couples and their mixed-race offspring – were employed by the elite to establish a lexicon of difference wherein the Other would be constructed and categorized. This aspect of material culture gave privileged Spaniards the illusion of control over an increasingly complicated and diverse population. This is significant when considering the history of the Americas as a violent colonial space within which racially marginalized peoples were often regarded as the objects of empire, dehumanized within the rhetoric and slave economies of imperial rule.

DOI: 10.4324/9781003357117-7

Trethewey's engagement with these paintings presents an opportunity to consider societal classification of African, indigenous, and those of mixed heritage in connection to the often contradictory U.S. American legacy of freedom and inclusion, a legacy founded upon the violence of the Transatlantic Slave Trade. In fact, *Thrall* demonstrates the risk of aggression that categorization itself poses. Scholar, Linda Bolton, contends that the philosophy of Emmanuel Levinas helps us to understand that the question at the heart of systems of classification – "What is it?" – holds the potential threat of linguistic and physical violence.[3] Through the lens of Levinasian ethics, the Americas are understood as historically invested in defining and controlling the body of the Other as a way of shaping and re-shaping the power structures of white supremacy. Trethewey's ekphrastic poetics illuminate the racialized bodies upon which violent acts were committed by the empires of the Americas in order for their social, legal, and economic systems to flourish.

In *Thrall*, she argues that Enlightenment ideologies underline the global legacies of the Transatlantic Slave Trade as well as the propensity to define and contain the Other. Truly, the "scientific thought of the Enlightenment was a precondition for the growth of modern racism based on physical typology" (Fredrickson 2002, 56). The emphasis on the physical as a way of not simply acknowledging difference, but defining it, recalls an important concept from the ethical philosophy of Emmanuel Levinas. Within his work, *Totality and Infinity* (1969), Levinas offers a critique of Western philosophical thinking. He defines the hierarchical framework that seeks to create rational, ordered systems of the world and all that it contains as a "philosophy of power ... a philosophy of injustice" (1969, 46). Levinas views the systems produced by much of Western philosophical thought as unethical due to its propensity to exert power over the Other, defining and thus reducing the Other to what she is not, annihilating difference (44).[4] Adriaan Peperzak reasons that the danger in seeking to systematically generate definitions of otherness is that the "foreign being, instead of maintaining itself in the impregnable fortress of its singularity ... becomes a theme and an object" (1993, 97). The Other is effectively reduced to a quantifiable element within the demarcations of so-called rational thought.[5] Trethewey's work argues against this rationalizing through a poetic discussion of the detailed and elaborate *casta* paintings of New Spain.

However, art historian Ilona Katzew argues that the creation of the *casta* paintings began prior to the Enlightenment, "arising in classical and medieval times," and therefore, attributing their creation solely to the philosophies of the Age of Reason is inaccurate (2004, 7). Nonetheless, it is clear that their production throughout the eighteenth century was influenced by the scientific philosophies that were born of the Enlightenment era. Scientific classification of humans can be found in the seventeenth century, and these "ethnologists opened the way to a secular or scientific racism by considering human beings part of the animal kingdom" and the "efforts to demote Africans from human to ape or half-ape status ... revealed how a purely naturalistic chain of being could be employed to deny full humanity to non-Caucasians" (Fredrickson 2002, 57–58). The Enlightenment was not the only influence regarding the creation of racist caste systems in the Americas, but *Thrall* advances a strong correlation between the scientific philosophy of that era and the Creole culture of New Spain.

"Equations of Blood": Domesticating the *Castas* of New Spain

Interracial sex was common in New Spain throughout the sixteenth century, and interracial marriage in Mexico became customary by the middle of the seventeenth century (Katzew 2004). For the first half of the eighteenth century, these paintings revealed the pride of Spanish Creoles (those from Spain born or living in what is now Mexico) in the grandeur of the culture they had created as well as their ability to remain in control of an increasingly complex society (2004). The illusion of a legible mode of racial classification facilitated the imposition of a colonial political order in New Spain. This was demonstrated through the elaborate dress and accessories worn by the interracial families within many of the portraits as well as through the undeniable patriarchal position of the Spaniard as head of the family, and by extension, the state.

Many of the portraits that feature a Spanish patriarch with his African, Native, or mixed-blood wife and children rely upon ornate representations of the home as backdrops. Despite the tranquility of domestic life being depicted, and the legitimized (legalized church/state sanctioned) unions these images portray, they remain evidence of an emerging racist taxonomy within the Americas.[6] If anything, these portraits illustrate the ways in which the concept of race was far from stable, rather it was invented and reinvented within the private spaces of home-life and centered on control of the female body. Further, these interracial unions may give the impression of empowerment for some of the *castas* (African, Native, and mixed-race men and women), but the unequal power structure itself dismantles the possibility of equality. Further, the *casta* paintings obscure the fact that colonial power in New Spain – akin to the colonial power of the United States – was dependent on the slave labor of Africans and their descendants. The specter of the Atlantic slave trade underwrites these elaborate paintings. Moreover, these works primarily created and affirmed an increasingly racialized hierarchy with Spanish and Spanish Creoles functioning as the patriarchal heads of this system.

A change occurred around the middle of the eighteenth century with the production of *casta* paintings, one that did not reflect the pride of Spanish Creoles, but the growing concerns from reformers in Spain over what was perceived as an immoral, lax Mexican society. Certain post-1760s *casta* paintings were created with the purpose of instruction, highlighting the traits of a moral, productive society as hard working with strict adherence to caste positions. This change points to fear regarding the fact that phenotype, hair texture, and skin color, by the middle of the eighteenth century, were no longer reliable markers of race, and by extension, high or low status. Further, some of these paintings depicted that particular unions, namely between African and Native peoples or Spanish women with a *casta* of low *calidad* (caste or status), led to uncivilized domestic violence and a degenerate society (Katzew 2004, 114).

The Creole culture of New Spain was dependent on the domestication of men and women of difference. As David Spurr posits, "… the ultimate aim of colonial discourse is not to establish a radical opposition between colonizer and colonized. It seeks to dominate by inclusion and domestication rather than by a confrontation which recognizes the independent identity of the Other" (2004, 32). The domestication that Spurr discusses suggests a kinship between his scholarship and Levinasian philosophy. Levinas argues there is the threat of violence in believing it is possible to fully know the Other, for knowing entails a kind of mastery: "The achievement of knowledge consists of grasping the object. Its strangeness is then conquered. Its newness, the opening up of its otherness, is reduced to the 'same,' to what has already been seen, already known. In the ethical relation, the other man remains other to me. Despite our exchanges, he remains that which I … am not" (Robbins 2001, 191). Within the "ethical relation" the Other must, on some level, remain unknown, her alterity intact. The Levinasian concept of a totality – the reduction of the Other within the "same" – is premised on the destruction of difference. A totality will seek to make an object of the Other, an object that can be completely understood, "known." Historically, this has been demonstrated by plantation ledgers, the records that reduced human beings to (live)stock with dollar values. In essence, to believe the Other can be "mastered" through full intimate knowledge creates the possibility of destruction.

Within the context of New Spain, the violence of colonization and control, the mastery of the body politic, was aided through interracial unions. Historian María Elena Martínez argues, "early colonial sexual relations [were] acts of power" on the part of Spaniards over their so-called inferiors (2008, 8). The subjugation and enslavement of Africans as well as those indigenous to the Americas was achieved through various "acts of power" – including interracial marriage – designed to emphasize cultural and racialized differences, then domesticate, and ultimately control African, indigenous, and mixed-race peoples.

Spanish Creoles further asserted their privilege, authority, and control through segregation, complicating the multiculturalism the *casta* paintings portray. For example, within Mexico City there was strict segregation of living space that was dependent on one's *calidad*. However, the central Market Place of the city proved to be a subversive space where *castas* and Spaniards intermingled, selling, buying, and socializing. Nonetheless, racism gradually determined the legal and economic systems as well as the social customs of this diverse society. Laws were instituted that disqualified those of African descent (the *pardo* or free blacks) from military service and joining the guilds (associations of craftsmen or merchants). Certain spaces of Mexico City were entirely off-limits to the *pardo*. "Sumptuary laws" – laws that regulated the clothing *castas* were allowed to wear – were rampant throughout seventeenth- and eighteenth-century Mexico. One law in particular stated that Africans and "mulattos" were not allowed to wear gold, silk, lace, or pearls unless they were married to a recognized Spaniard (Katzew 2004; Carrera 2003; Earle 2001).

The main interest of the *casta* paintings was the variations in skin color of the mixed-race spouses and children produced from these unions as well as the terminology invented in order to categorize the *castas*. For example, the paintings rely on terms such as, *mestiso*, in reference to a person of Spanish and indigenous blood lines, while a *mulatto* was a mix of Spanish and African descent.[7] A *castizo* was the offspring of a union between a Spaniard and a *mestiza*, and a *morisca* was the offspring of a Spaniard with a *mulatta*. It would take three generations of interracial sex between mixed-bloods and Spaniards to produce a Spaniard; a Spaniard's alliance with a *castizo*, for instance, would then produce a person who would be classified a Spaniard. The *casta* paintings portray the attempt – at least on the part of the elite – to create a language that would classify and render legible the bodies of generations of *castas*. Katzew notes that while some of this complicated terminology took root in every-day Mexican society, many of these terms remained confined to the borders of the *casta* paintings (2004).

While these objects of material culture certainly illustrate a racially-mixed society of African, Native, and Spanish peoples, the underlying presumption throughout the century of their production was that Spaniards – that is, whiteness – were superior to all other racial designations and that eventually the *castas* themselves would become Spaniards or remain degraded low-caste laborers. For this reason the portraits – at times painted as sets, sometimes as many as sixteen depictions of different interracial families – were arranged hierarchically, with Spanish patriarchs and their families visually ranked higher than African, indigenous, and mixed-race patriarchs with their wives and children. Therefore, the "*sistema de castas* was invented to rank people according to their purported percentage of white, Indian, or black blood" and as such "it was a form of resistance of the nobility against encroachment on its privilege and source of wealth" (Katzew 2004, 201). At once a boast of prosperity and order, the *casta* paintings and the caste system they promoted attempted to mask the racial tensions of the time, and the strict cultural and racialized segregation of urban spaces – such as Mexico City – betraying, instead, a growing insecurity concerning the fluidity of racial categorization and its relation to the patriarchal power dynamics of New Spain.[8]

Within *Thrall*, Trethewey's engagement with *casta* paintings forcefully suggests a commonality between eighteenth-century Mexico's obsession with racialized categorization and the enduring thrall of defining and dehumanizing difference in the United States. For example, the sections within the poem, "Taxonomy," are each named for a painting from a *casta* series

"Wages of Empire": American Inventions of Mixed-Race Identities   109

Figure 6.1 Juan Rodriguez Juarez, *De español y de india produce mestizo* (1715), Oil on Canvas, 80.7 × 105.4, Breamore House, Hampshire, UK/Bridgeman Images.

created by Juan Rodriguez Juarez, around 1715. Of the first, "De Español y De India Produce Mestizo," (the Spaniard and Indian produce a Mestizo, Figure 6.1) Trethewey writes:

The canvas is a leaden sky

behind them, heavy
with words, gold letters inscribing
an equation of blood –

this plus this equals this – as if
a contract with nature or
a museum label,
ethnographic, precise …

(2012, 16)

Trethewey underscores the absurdity of treating the complexity of human identity as though it is an equation to be neatly and simplistically calculated. The ethnographic imperative to categorize and label is presented as suspect within the poet's interpretation of this particular painting.

In section three, "De Español y Mestiza Produce Castizo," (the Spaniard and Mestiza produce Castizo, Figure 6.2), Trethewey touches on the idea of "blood purity" supposedly contained within the Spanish patriarch as the representative of whiteness:

In the mother's arms, the child, hinged at her womb – dark cradle of mixed blood (call it *Mexico*) – turns toward the father reaching to him as if back to Spain, to the promise of blood …

(2012, 22–23)

110 *Eloisa Valenzuela-Mendoza*

Figure 6.2 Juan Rodriguez Juarez, *De español y de mestiza produce castizo* (1715), Oil on Canvas, 80.7 × 105.4, Breamore House, Hampshire, UK/Bridgeman Images.

Within this painting the child in the mother's arms – the "dark cradle" – is reaching out as if deliberately moving away from the "darkness" of her mother's African heritage toward the "whiteness" of her father. According to the poem, it is "three easy steps / to purity …" (2012, 23). Trethewey refers to the belief that three generations of mixed-blood cross racial sexual reproduction with Spaniards is needed in order to produce a Spaniard. She also suggests the child's actions allude to the notion of "limpieza de sangre" (blood purity) that Spaniards embraced, asking: "How not to see / in this gesture / the mind / of the colony?" (2012, 22) The child's outstretched arms signify not only the belief in the superiority of white blood but also a longing on the part of the colony for a "pure" Spanish "civilization." This poem highlights the primacy of white supremacy as an entrenched element within the *sistema de castas,* despite the increasing fluidity of caste and the common occurrence of interracial marriage. Therefore, at that time and place it was presumed that people of color were improved through intermarriage (and their offspring through cross racial sexual reproduction, regardless of marriage) to Spaniards, resulting in the "limpieza de sangre" already inherent within the white body.

However, "limpieza de sangre" predates Spanish America, and was used on the Iberian Peninsula to define Christians (i.e., Catholics) having "pure blood," as opposed to Jews or Muslims. In other words, it was not purely a racially-motivated concept, but one also based heavily on religious affiliations. Further, Martínez argues that "Despite the various transformations that the notion of limpieza de sangre underwent [in the Americas], it retained old layers of meaning" (2008, 249). Race is central for Trethewey's engagement with the *casta* paintings, but it is important to note that while the idea of "blood purity" was refashioned in colonial Mexico, religion remained part of the concept, particularly in opposition to the spirituality of non-Spaniards. Colonial Mexico was a deeply complex, contradictory society wherein caste, an increasingly fluid system, was premised as much on culture – religion, gender, wealth, family history, individual life-styles, and Spanish (white) superiority – as on invented racial categories. Nonetheless, it was the very fluidity of the caste system and the break-down of "limpieza de sangre" that inspired increasingly racist notions of Spanish identity dependent on the racialized bodies of the *castas*.[9]

As some of the *casta* paintings demonstrate, "evolution" of blood, as evidenced by skin color, was not always the result of interracial marriage. Children who were born with a darker skin-tone than their parents were regarded as "torna atras" (return-backwards). Trethewey engages with this concept of so-called evolution-in-reverse within the poem, "Torna Atras," named for the anonymously created painting "De Albina y Espanol, Nace Torna Atras" (from Albino and Spaniard, a Return-Backwards is born), circa 1785–1790.[10] Within this work the father is depicted as painting a portrait of his wife, with his dark-skinned son standing off to the side, and a servant working in the corner of the frame. Like the elegant clothing of the family and the other accoutrement of prosperity depicted within the home, the servant signifies this is a wealthy, high-caste interracial *familia*. However, the painting the father is creating of his wife (the "Albina") falls short in representing her beauty and affluent elegance.

Trethewey concedes the portrait depicted within the painting could act as a foil, illustrating the superior skill of the unknown artist when juxtaposed against the neophyte artistic attempts of the patriarch. However, the way in which the father "has rendered her / homely ..." (2012, 48) is troubling and he fails to include the crescent moon-shaped "chiqueador" above her right eye, which was, in eighteenth-century Mexico, a piece of velvet that was glued to a woman's face as an emblem of beauty (Katzew 2004). In Trethewey's rendering, the "chiqueador" as a mark of elegance is rewritten as a symbol of the continuing legacy of empire on colonial bodies:

> ... If you consider the century's mythology of the body – that a dark spot marked the genitals of anyone with African blood – you might see how the black moon on her white face recalls it: the *roseta* she passes to her child marking him *torna atrás*. If I tell you such terms were born in the Enlightenment's hallowed rooms, that the wages of empire is myopia, you might see the father's vision as desire embodied in paint, this rendering of his wife born of need to see himself as architect of Truth, benevolent patriarch, father of uplift ordering his domain. And you might see why, to understand my father, I look again and again at this painting: how it is that a man could love – and so diminish what he loves.
> (2012, 48–49)

The poem suggests that the father leaves out his wife's "chiqueador" because, rather than a mark of gentility and grace, it symbolizes the impurity of her blood, impurity that has bloomed within the dark skin-tone of their son. Trethewey's analysis of the patriarch's motivations, his need to be in control of the domestic space and the body of his wife, reflect the narrow, twisted vision of white supremacy – as part of the discourse of empire – that proves to diminish people of color as objects, plainly reduced, and vehemently controlled by their "white" betters. In this way, the father also reveals the insecurities of the elite regarding their power and wealth. Finally, if the privileged position of the Albina represents the permeability of the *sistema de castas*, her son represents the failures of Spanish blood – and specifically this patriarch as the would-be "father of uplift" – to improve on the bodies of the *castas*, depicting instead the inherent dangers in racial mixing, the "taint" lurking within the blood of non-whites when viewed through the myopic lens of empire.

The supposed improvement of the *castas* through mixing with Spaniards transcended concerns of skin color, and increasingly became a preoccupation with the minds and characters of racially-marginalized men and women. At this time, it was believed that positive characteristics (such as intelligence and mildness of temper) were concentrated within the bodies of the lighter skinned Spaniards. The domestication of the *castas* was then reliant on becoming more like their Spanish "superiors" in culture, mind, and body. Indigenous peoples of the Americas were considered malleable and able – to a certain extent and despite their supposed physical inferiority – to overcome their alleged debased blood lines and culture. But, those of African descent were, for the most part, considered lacking in moral fiber, their blood irrevocably "polluted" (Earle 2012; Martínez 2008; Carrera 2003).

Trethewey places her relationship with her father into the frame of this Mexican, eighteenth-century *casta* painting, a move which functions to re-center the questions within the text concerning race, empire, and exile as they relate to the twenty-first century. This poetic turn stresses the emotional entanglements of the familial relationship within the domestic space of the *casta* painting, entanglements previously undermined through Trethewey's ruthless analysis of the patriarch. This painting certainly functions as a symbol depicting "the wages of empire," yet, despite the ways in which he "diminishes" them, the patriarch loves his wife and child. Emphasizing this complexity, the end of the poem, "De Albina y Espanol, Nace Torna Atras," presents an unsettling twist – "… to understand / my father, I look again and again at this painting …" (2012, 49) – and suddenly the reader is flung out of the corridors of colonial Mexico and into twenty-first-century United States.

In an interview, Trethewey discusses the personal significance of the paintings: "The new book [*Thrall*] started with an investigation of Mexican casta paintings …I was, of course, drawn to them because they had the picture of the parents as well as the offspring and the taxonomy, the names created for those mixed-blood children. So it was like looking at portraits of my own family" (Brown 2012). Trethewey's familial ties provide a significant pivot wherein the focus of the poetry is able to shift from the *casta* paintings to larger issues of race within a U.S. context. In fact, increasingly, the text turns from the empire of Spain to that of U.S. America.

"The Iconography of Empire": The Racialized Bodies of U.S. America

Trethewey's previous poetry collections are firmly entrenched within U.S. historical and cultural contexts. Therefore, in certain respects *Thrall* is a departure from her other works. However, Trethewey emphasizes the themes and histories that continue to motivate her poetics, stating:

> My obsessions stay the same – historical memory and historical erasure. I am particularly interested in the Americas and a history that is rooted in colonialism, the language and iconography of empire, disenfranchisement, the enslavement of peoples, and the way that people were sectioned off because of blood.
>
> (Hall 2013, 107)

In the United States, blood quantum – particularly for African American and Native peoples – has been used as a legal and social justification for exclusion and violence. For African Americans, the "one drop rule" often determined their caste in the United States and their places within the segregated spaces of home, school, and work. Linguistically, a more fluid racial lexicon existed throughout the nineteenth century, but this began to change by the beginning of the twentieth, as demonstrated with the infamous New Orleans case of *Plessy v. Ferguson* (1896).

At the turn of the twentieth-century, the spectrum of racial terminology became limited to the simplistic binary of white or black. Terms like "quadroon" or "octoroon" were viewed as less effective – though no less dehumanizing – in protecting white privilege. This is significant

"Wages of Empire": American Inventions of Mixed-Race Identities

within the space of New Orleans considering its long history as demographically diverse with regards to the large population of free people of color. The landmark case of *Plessy v. Ferguson* (1896), posed a challenge to segregation that also symbolizes a turning point within the lexicon of race. Homer Plessy was part of the mixed-race population of New Orleans, the "creoles of color," a community "rooted in its prestige in ancestry and free forebears" (Landau 2013, 45). In 1892, he challenged Louisiana's recently passed Separate Car Act by sitting on a train car that was designated for white passengers. Since Plessy appeared, by all accounts, to be white (i.e., light skinned), he was arrested because he informed the conductor he was in fact, 7/8 Caucasian, meaning he was 1/8 black. In the parlance of the moment, Plessy was an "octoroon." However, in 1896, the U.S. Supreme Court ruled against Plessy, establishing the racist rule of "separate but equal" throughout the country.

This case illustrates the contradictory notions regarding race that proliferated at the turn of the twentieth century. In *Plessy v. Ferguson*, Homer Plessy's "personal history and community heritage were reduced to a crude racial designation: he was an "octoroon." At the end of the case, even that designation was rendered obsolete: "one drop" of "black blood" made him "colored." The only significant distinction, then, was between "white" and "black," and no longer between "light" and "dark" (Landau 2013, 46). This case marked a turning point in the systematic oppression of people of color, revealing the contradictory, changing landscape of racialized language and the proliferation of legalized racism within the U.S. American landscape.

Thrall introduces the reader to the iconography of the Spanish Empire within the Americas and then provides a turn toward the empire of the United States with the section titled "The Americans." This shift emphasizes a strident similarity between the dehumanizing of the *castas* as represented within the *casta* paintings, and the histories of racism and enslavement within the United States. There are three poems in this section; significantly, one of the poems takes as its subject matter George Fuller's painting *The Quadroon* (1880), and another considers one of Robert Frank's iconic photographs from his 1959 collection, *The Americans*.

The poem, "Blood," subtitled "After George Fuller's *The Quadroon*, 1880," begins:

It must be the gaze of a benevolent viewer
upon her, framed as she is in the painting's
romantic glow, her melancholic beauty
meant to show the pathos of her condition:
black blood – that she cannot transcend it.

(2012, 34)

The sorrow for this mixed-race woman is born of the fact that her light skin and beauty, the latter being perceived as a product of the former, does not make up for the "black blood" that courses through her veins (Figure 6.3). In nineteenth-century U.S. America, her lower caste status – born an enslaved mixed-race female – is irrevocable. Nonetheless, although the woman is the focus of the portrait, she is not entirely the point of the poem. There are Others silenced even more than the "Quadroon":

… How different she's rendered
from the dark kin working the fields behind her.
If not for the ray of light appearing as if from beyond
the canvas, we might miss them – three figures
in the near distance, small as afterthought.

(34)

Figure 6.3 George Fuller, *The Quadroon* (1880), Oil on Canvas, 50.5 × 40.5 inches, The Metropolitan Museum of Art, New York.

There is a romantic glow that surrounds the "Quadroon," a tragedy of birth that makes of her, at that time, a sympathetic and curious figure to white, particularly male, viewers. However, what sympathy existed for the darker-skinned, laboring figures in the background? Far off in the distance, they provide a hidden, unromantic subtext of enslavement and dehumanization. They may be an afterthought to the viewer, but they form the very foundation of the nation's culture, economy, and legal system.

Naming this short section after Robert Frank's collection is a signal to the reader regarding the intended nature of these poems as a provocative bridge to the racialized corridors of eighteenth-century New Spain. As Nancy Watson Barr argues, Robert Frank's *The Americans* "exposed the façade of 1950's America – questioning its implicit claim as the great land of democracy, prosperity, and freedom in his unforgiving black-and-white images" (2002, 63). Frank's photographs uncover the fissures and gaps within the ideology of American exceptionalism through depicting, in part, the U.S. American caste system. By invoking his work, *Thrall* suggests the racialized and dehumanizing language embedded within the *casta* paintings contains a similar intention to the ongoing discrimination found within U.S. sociopolitical and economic contexts.

Within the poem, "Help, 1968," subtitled "After a photograph from *The Americans* by Robert Frank," Trethewey illustrates the ironies of white supremacy. She writes:

> When I see Frank's photograph
> of a white infant in the dark arms
> of a woman who must be the maid,
> I think of my mother and the year
> we spent alone – my father at sea.
>
> (2012, 35)

Here Trethewey is referring to a photo taken in 1955 of an African American woman holding a white infant while standing on a sidewalk in Charleston, North Carolina. African Americans were not treated equally but, African American women were often entrusted with the care and upbringing of middle and upper-class white children. Fast forward to 1968, Trethewey is two years old and, due to her biracial background, was lighter in skin tone than her mother, Gwendolyn Ann Turnbough. Without her white father to accompany them, many people they encountered in public mistook Turnbough for Trethewey's maid:

> when my mother took me for walks
> she was mistaken again and again
> for my maid …
>
> she'd say I was her daughter, and each time
> strangers would stare in disbelief …
>
> (2012, 35)

It is only one year after the case, *Loving v. Virginia* and seventy-one years since *Plessy v. Ferguson*, and – as the poem demonstrates – there is a persistent inclination to categorize human beings based on the binary of white/black, the graduations of light and dark.

Once these strangers understand that Gwendolyn Turnbough is Trethewey's mother, not her maid, they respond by emptying "the change from their pockets … / …pressing coins into my hands …" (36). It is no coincidence that this poem directly follows "Blood," the poem about George Fuller's painting, "The Quadroon." The money these strangers thrust upon Trethewey, implies not only an assumption of poverty but also suggested that they pitied her. She is not unlike the tragic figure of Fuller's portrait. Trethewey, in this moment of family history, is painted as the perpetual outsider because she will never neatly fit the binary of white/black.

Trethewey ends the poem with a comparison of her mother and the woman in Frank's photograph:

> … How
> like the woman in the photograph
> she must have seemed, carrying me

each day – white in her arms – as if
she were a prop: a black backdrop,
the dark foil in this American story.

(2012, 36)

Trethewey's mother becomes nothing more than an object meant to highlight the light skin of her daughter. She is at once hyper-visible as a woman of color, but also diminished, her very humanity subsumed within the myopic gaze of onlookers. Just as Robert Frank's work exposed aspects of the U.S. American caste system (i.e., class inequities based on race and gender), so too does Trethewey's poem remind the reader of the ongoing dehumanization of difference that lies at the root of white privilege and the notion of whiteness in the United States. This is similar in meaning and execution to the caste system of New Spain which relied on marking difference in order to define racial, economic, and legal privilege for Spanish Creoles. Finally, the lines "… as if / she were a prop: a black backdrop, / the dark foil in this American story" (36), bring to mind the words of Zora Neale Hurston: "I feel most colored when I am thrown against a sharp white background" (1928). Connecting these texts only further emphasizes the need for whiteness to constantly shape and define itself against the Other. Hurston's words illustrate the hyper-visibility of African American men and women, while Trethewey's mother remains the undertone of a whiteness dependent on the racialized bodies of Others. In *Thrall*, Trethewey argues that these experiences remain a part of the legacy of the Enlightenment.

"White with Illumination": Enlightenment Legacies, Unwritten American Histories

When asked about the role of Western philosophy in society, Emmanual Levinas shares misgivings concerning the uses of philosophical thought: "… I express my reservations about a tradition that claims knowledge to be the supreme fulfillment of the human. I do not underestimate the importance of knowledge, but I do not consider it to be the ultimate axiological judgment …In the ethical relation, the other man remains other to me" (Robbins 2001, 191). Levinas expresses hesitation regarding the primacy of supposed knowledge over human beings and human experience. It is important to seek the truth, to attempt to understand the world and all that it contains. However, to place the "ultimate axiological judgment" on knowledge, meaning to bestow too high a value upon it, is to ignore that there are multiple dimensions of truth. The very methodology of Western knowledge-gathering is often premised on "conquering" the object or subject of study through the collection of facts and figures. This approach belies that the "other man remains other to me." An ethical approach to the Other demands acceptance that Others will never be fully *known*, and that any attempt to succinctly categorize them is unethical, holding within its very framework the threat of destruction.

The Enlightenment framed the *casta* paintings that are discussed within *Thrall* as works that symbolize precepts of categorization ascribed by that era and whose popularity for a 100 years can be attributed, in part, to Enlightenment scientific visions for the possibility of a fully known, neatly ordered world. In the previous poem, "Torna Atras," the Enlightenment is specifically connected to empire through the lexicon of difference highlighted within the *casta* paintings. Trethewey writes: "… such terms were born / in the Enlightenment's hallowed rooms…" (2012, 48) forcefully suggesting that the scientific ideology of Enlightenment thinkers provided a methodology that aided the empires of the Old World in constructing a framework of discrimination as they conquered and enslaved indigenous peoples throughout the globe. Toward the end of the volume, the Enlightenment is once again referenced, but in a different context. In one of the final poems, aptly titled "Enlightenment," Trethewey documents discussions between herself and her father concerning the life of Thomas Jefferson, his contradictory world-views and actions as well as his sexual "relationship" with his enslaved woman, Sally Hemings.

The poem begins with a contemplation about the portrait of Jefferson which hangs at Monticello, Jefferson's historically preserved home in Charlottesville, Virginia: "… he is rendered two-toned: / his forehead white with illumination – / … the rest of his face in shadow, / darkened as if the artist meant to contrast / his bright knowledge, its dark subtext" (2012, 68). Within this particular poem, Jefferson's portrait is a bridge allowing the reader to ideologically connect his imagery with the racialized depictions of the *castas* as part of the "dark subtext" to which Trethewey alludes. Regarding her own relationship with her father and their conversations about Jefferson, Trethewey writes:

> I did not know then the subtext
> of our story, that my father could imagine
> Jefferson's words made flesh in my flesh –
>
> *the improvement of the blacks in body*
> and mind, in the first instance of their mixture
> *with the whites* – or that my father could believe
>
> he'd *made* me *better* …
>
> (2012, 69–70)

The quote on the improvement of Africans with their "mixture with the whites," from Jefferson's *Notes on the State of Virginia* (1787), in combination with Jefferson's role as the problematic patriarch of his own interracial family, brings to mind colonial Mexico's "limpieza de sangre": the belief that white blood made mixed-race peoples more intelligent and more civilized even as it degraded Spanish "purity." This indicates that the heritage of the Enlightenment and empire, of *casta* paintings and "blood purity," form the undercurrent of a Jeffersonian legacy.

The poem ends with a joint visit to Monticello, and during a tour of the house, Trethewey highlights the history that connects and divides her and her father:

> *Imagine stepping back into the past,*
> our guide tells us then – and I can't resist
>
> whispering to my father: *This is where*
> *we split up. I'll head around to the back.*
> When he laughs, I know he's grateful
>
> I've made a joke of it, this history
> that links us – white father, black daughter –
> even as it renders us other to each other.
>
> (2012, 71)

The father-daughter relationship Trethewey traces throughout *Thrall* is one inescapably, heart-wrenchingly related to racist theories of humanity that have defined empires. The poetic voice proposes that dehumanizing racial philosophies are not neatly contained within eighteenth-century *casta* paintings of Mexico nor are they bound within the eighteenth-century writings of Thomas Jefferson. They continue to endure, to be part of contemporary twenty-first-century conceptions of race and the racially-marginalized body. Moreover, in the landscape of U.S. America, the enslavement of Africans and their descendants is, largely, a deliberately overlooked history. Yet, it is one that continues to shape lived experience – personal ties and socioeconomic status – upon the North American continent. As historian Saidiya Hartman argues, "I, too, live in the time of slavery, by which I mean I am living in the future created by it" (2007, 133). Far from a distant, ethereal past, the history of slavery, the dehumanization of men and women of color continues to hold "us captive, / its beautiful ruin etched on the mind's eye…" (Trethewey 2012, 70).

Part of Trethewey's work entails highlighting the lives and voices that have been disregarded. Within her poetics is a reclamation of people of color as much more than racialized objects to be feared and destroyed. Trethewey's poetry, when juxtaposed with the various lived experiences and contradictory histories of enslavement and racism in the Americas, connect these seemingly disparate elements as part of the future created by slavery and the "wages of empire." By bearing witness to this difficult history, Trethewey re-centers the complex humanity of men and women of difference. Demanding recognition for those who typically remain unseen, *Thrall* suggests that the story of the Americas remains unreconciled; until we learn to navigate the borderlands of these marginalized histories, the "rhetoric of empire" will continue as the white supremacist subtext that – however unacknowledged – controls the sociopolitical landscape of U.S. America.

Notes

1 Anzaldúa, Gloria. 1987. *Borderlands/La Frontera: The New Mestiza.* San Francisco: Aunt Lute Books.
2 Since the beginning of the nineteenth century, the word "America" has been used frequently and interchangeably with the title "United States." This continues despite the fact that the United States comprises only a portion of the American continents. The contested nature of the origins of the word – (Was it derived from Amerigo Vespucci or Richard Ameryk? Was it the Vikings or the Africans who coined this term? Or did the word derive from indigenous nations within the continent itself?) – creates an additional need for a mindful use of language. After all, language is powerful. Language is political. Language *is* culture, and for almost 200 years the use of "America" to signify the United States only proves to reinforce – however subconsciously – the idea that the U.S. is exceptional to the rest of the Americas. This false superiority is inescapably linked to white supremacy and the attending violence of colonial power through the enslavement and dehumanization of the racialized Other. Throughout my work, "U.S. America" is how I identify the United States in an attempt to remind myself, as well as my readers, that the U.S. is simply one among many nations within the American continents, existing historically and contemporaneously in relation to others. It is a less grandiose phrase than the "United States of America," and functions to disrupt methodologies of linguistic colonization.
3 I am indebted to Dr. Bolton's generosity, for the many times she shared her knowledge and interpretations of Levinasian ethics as work that not only questions basic assumptions of Western philosophy, but also re-envisions our relationship to the Other.
4 Non-Western philosophies have also invented Others with dehumanizing effect. However, when discussing the impact of Transatlantic Slavery, and the specifics of how subjugation of African peoples unfolded in the Americas, Western philosophical thought proves to form a large part of the foundation of the slave economy. The Enlightenment may have begun with an empowering concept of freedom, but Enlightenment thinkers – as Trethewey reminds us – also provided a framework for the persecution of the Other with the creation of a hierarchy of invented races. As Levinas discusses, this hierarchy is premised on the assumption of fully mastering the Other.
5 Levinasian ethics emphasizes that the violence of categorizing difference goes beyond the challenge of language itself to define or name alterity. Imposing rhetoric upon the Other in an attempt to answer the question – "what is it?" – is revealed as an exercise of power over the Other, rather than a benign limitation of language.

6 While many racially marginalized women certainly lived as sexual slaves and mistresses of elite Spaniards, legitimate marriage was – if not rampant – common enough to receive attention from the Church and the Crown. Within New Spain, for most of the eighteenth century, marriage was used as a tool of control and colonization of indigenous and African bodies through the sociopolitical power of the Catholic Church. In fact, the church actively sought to diminish "informal unions," compelling couples "to marry by threatening them with excommunication" (Martínez 2008, 238) at the end of the seventeenth and into the eighteenth century. The conversion of non-Spaniards was central to the Church's various campaigns to promote church-sanctioned marriage throughout New Spain; conversion was also another method of control and domestication of racially marginalized women to Spanish dominance. For a time, Spanish men were allowed – and encouraged – to marry women of indigenous or African descent, free or enslaved, particularly if they had already engaged in a sexual relationship. However, by the late eighteenth century, laws were passed that allowed parents and civil officials to forbid marriage between Spaniards and *castas*, particularly if the woman or man in question was of a lower *callidad* (Martínez 2008; Carrera 2003).

7 Within her work, *Borderlands/La Frontera: The New Mestiza* (1987), Gloria Anzaldúa refashions and reclaims the concept of the Mestiza and the connection to African, Native, and Spanish, blood lines as a positive, a complexity worthy of remembrance and exploration. Anzaldúa's notion of mestizaje views identity as a "crossroads," synthesizing the confluence of multiple histories and cultures. Her work is part of a twentieth-century shift within the discourse concerning Mexican, Mexican-American, Latina/o, Latin@ – and in the twenty-first century this includes Latinx – identities and histories.

8 While Katzew's work is extensive in discussing the changing sociopolitical and historical contexts of the *casta* painting genre, the time period and geographic focus is, most times, specific to eighteenth-century Mexico City, and the interactions between the elite of the city and the Spanish court. Magali M. Carrera's work, *Imagining Identity in New Spain: Race, Lineage, and the Colonial Body in Portraiture and Casta Paintings* (2003), examines the *casta* paintings through the lens of material culture, and while the majority of the text is focused on the eighteenth century, Carrera does discuss the end of the genre in the early nineteenth century. For a consideration of slavery and race in colonial Mexico, beyond Mexico City, please see Matthew Restall's study – covering approximately 1541–1821 – of the people he terms Afro-Yucatecans, in *The Black Middle: Africans, Mayas, and Spaniards in Colonial Yucatan* (2009).

9 For a study on medieval slavery, and the complexity of religion and race on the Iberian Peninsula, consider Debra Blumenthal's *Enemies and Familiars: Slavery and Mastery in Fifteenth-Century Valencia* (2009).

10 An albino or albina was believed to be the offspring of a morisca (Spanish and mulatto) with a Spaniard.

References

Anzaldúa, Gloria. 1987. *Borderlands/La Frontera: The New Mestiza*. San Francisco: Aunt Lute Books.

Barr, Nancy Watson. 2002. "Truth, Memory, and the American Working-Class City: Robert Frank in Detroit and at the Rouge." *Bulletin of the Detroit Institute of Arts* 76 (1/2): 62–74. http://www.jstor.org/stable/23183140.

Blumenthal, Deborah. 2009. *Enemies and Familiars: Slavery and Mastery in Fifteenth-Century Valencia*. Ithaca: Cornell University Press.

Brown, Jeffrey. 2012. "U.S. Poet Laureate Natasha Trethewey Talks about Her New Job and Fourth Book." *PBS Newshour Art Beat*. September 21. Accessed November 24, 2015, http://www.pbs.org/newshour/art/conversation-poet-laureate-natasha-trethewey/.

Carrera, Magali M. 2003. *Imagining Identity in New Spain: Race, Lineage, and the Colonial Body in Portraiture and Casta Paintings*. Austin: University of Texas.

Earle, Rebecca. 2001. "'Two Pairs of Pink Satin Shoes!!' Race, Clothing and Identity in the Americas (17th–19th Centuries)." *History Workshop Journal* 52: 175–195. http://www.jstor.org/stable/4289752.

Earle, Rebecca. 2012. *The Body of the Conquistador: Food, Race and the Colonial Experience in Spanish America, 1492–1700*. Cambridge: Cambridge University Press.

Fredrickson, George M. 2002. *Racism: A Short History*. Princeton: Princeton University Press.

Hartman, Saidiya. 2007. *Lose Your Mother: A Journey Along the Atlantic Slave Route*. New York: Farrar, Straus, and Giroux.
Hurston, Zora Neale. 2024, May 5. How it Feels To Be Colored Me. Project Gutenberg. Accessed September 17, 2024. https://www.gutenberg.org/cache/epub/73549/pg73549-images.html
Katzew, Ilona. 2004. *Casta Painting: Images of Race in Eighteenth-Century Mexico*. New Haven: Yale University Press.
Landau, Emily Epstein. 2013. *Spectacular Wickedness: Sex, Race, and Memory in Storyville, New Orleans*. Baton Rouge: Louisiana State University Press.
Levinas, Emmanuel. 1969. *Totality and Infinity: An Essay on Exteriority*. Translated by Alphonso Lingis. Pittsburgh: Duquesne University Press.
Levinas, Emmanuel. 2001. *Is It Righteous to Be? Interviews with Emmanuel Levinas*. Edited by Jill Robbins. Stanford: Stanford University Press.
Martínez, María Elena. 2008. *Genealogical Fictions: Limpieza De Sangre, Religion, and Gender in Colonial Mexico*. Stanford: Stanford University Press.
Mules and Men: Ways of Seeing ("How It Feels To Be Colored Me" by Zora Neale Hurston. Accessed April 2, 2016). http://xroads.virginia.edu/~ma01/grand-jean/hurston/chapters/how.html
Peperzak, Adriaan. 1993. *To the Other: An Introduction to the Philosophy of Emmanuel Levinas*. West Lafayette: Purdue University Press.
Restall, Matthew. 2009. *The Black Middle: Africans, Mayas, and Spaniards in Colonial Yucatan*. Stanford: Stanford University Press.
Spurr, David. 2004. *The Rhetoric of Empire: Colonial Discourse in Journalism, Travel Writing, and Imperial Administration*. 6th edition. Durham: Duke University Press.
Trethewey, Natasha. 2006. *Native Guard*. New York: Houghton Mifflin.
Trethewey, Natasha. 2010. "'Why I Write': Poetry, History, and Social Justice." Lecture at Emory University, Georgia, February 3.
Trethewey, Natasha. 2012. *Thrall*. New York: Houghton Mifflin Harcourt.
Trethewey, Natasha. 2013. *Conversations with Natasha Trethewey*. Edited by Joan Wylie Hall. Jackson: University Press of Mississippi.
Twinam, Ann. 1999. *Public Lives, Private Secrets: Gender, Honor, Sexuality, and Illegitimacy in Colonial Spanish America*. Stanford: Stanford University Press.

7 From Raw to Refined

Edouard Duval-Carrié's *Sugar Conventions* (2013)

Lesley A. Wolff

The nineteenth-century French gourmand Jean Anthelme Brillat-Savarin famously wrote, "Tell me what you eat, and I shall tell you what you are" (Brillat-Savarin 2009, 15).[1] *Sugar Conventions* (2013) (Figure 7.1), a mixed media work by the Haitian-born artist Edouard Duval-Carrié, heeds this call by laying bare the socio-political realities of one of modernity's most highly prized foodstuffs: sugar.[2] In this way, Duval-Carrié joins contemporary artists such as Kara Walker, Maria Magdalena Campos-Pons, Marc Latamie, and Vik Muniz, all of whom have used sugar as a means to critique the problematic encoding of race, gender, and class in the Americas. *Sugar Conventions*, however, stands apart from other works of and about sugar by exploring these relational dynamics through historical and Western canonical images of Caribbean culture. Of the nine images that comprise *Sugar Conventions*, none are unique to the work. Rather, Duval-Carrié has excerpted visual passages from images throughout Haitian history to produce an original work deliberately devoid of originality. In *Sugar Conventions*, Haiti's complex political past and present converge, raising questions about the ways in which colonial histories bleed into contemporary life and how diasporic identities may be negotiated within this contested cultural landscape. *Sugar Conventions*, therefore, embodies the vernacular dynamism that sociologist Michaeline A. Crichlow has ascribed to creolization itself.[3] By drawing upon established compositions rather than original images, Duval-Carrié paradoxically explores and critiques processes of creolization through the very forms and subjects by which it has been constructed and perpetuated. In so doing, *Sugar Conventions* implicates visuality as a critical aspect of Haitian socio-spatial production.

Materializing the Culture of Sugar

Duval-Carrié's mixed media work comprises nine gridded tiles (read left to right, top to bottom) whose overall form signifies the sacred geometry prevalent in Haitian Vodou practice. The grid functions as a source of both order and chaos, embodying regularity and structure, but also multiplicity and difference. In this way, the composition serves as a metaphor for the transcultural processes at stake in *Sugar Conventions*. Individually, each of *Sugar Conventions*' nine tiles appears self-contained and easily parsed, but together, the tiles compete with one another, the composition a cacophony of image, color, and form. Each tile addresses aspects of Caribbean society real and imagined, historical and contemporary. Collectively, the mixed-media panels—which include canonical reproductions of the Caribbean by Agostino Brunias and January Suchodolski and reimaginings of Duval-Carrié's past works—encompass a pastiche of Caribbean culture, foregrounding images of religion, politics, and history in a single, hyper-stimulating glance. Though the work's title, *Sugar Conventions*, betrays its conceptual ties to the refined foodstuff, images that directly pertain to sugar's role in the Caribbean

Figure 7.1 Edouard Duval-Carrié, *Sugar Conventions*, 2013, mixed media on backlit Plexiglas, 72 × 72 inches. Image courtesy of the Winthrop-King Institute for Contemporary French and Francophone Studies, Florida State University, Tallahassee, Florida. © 2020 Artists Rights Society (ARS), New York/ADAGP, Paris.

are scant.[4] Instead, sugar manifests materially within the work, the white crystals affixed to each of *Sugar Convention*'s tiles as Rococo-style ornament and framing that underscore the ominous colonial roots of Haitian economy and culture.

Sugar Conventions' nine tiles contain myriad materials, including glitter, sequins, glue, acrylic paint, paper, resin, and, of course, sugar, all affixed within three layers of Plexiglas. The Plexiglas proves more than mere canvas—this material participates in the visual and conceptual depth of the work, allowing the work's layered amalgam of material and color to reveal itself.

The translucency of the Plexiglas exposes the processes of the work's own construction. For each of the nine tiles, the bottommost layer of Plexiglas provides a colorful backing of mostly yellows and reds upon which glittered ornamentation has been glued. Nine lights, fastened into fixtures at the back of the work, gently shine through the painted layer, further intensifying the work's color and sheen and rendering an overall ethereal and fluid affect. A middle layer of clear Plexiglas further embellishes the composition through digital prints glued to its surface. These images duplicate passages from previous works by Duval-Carrié, historical photographs from Haiti (digitally manipulated by Duval-Carrié), and reproductions of works from the era of colonial Saint Domingue and early Haitian independence.[5] Affixed to the Plexiglas, these paper reprints appear thin and translucent, the backlighting betraying their duplicate nature—these are clearly not original oils on canvas.

Finally, the topmost layer of Plexiglas intensifies the composition through additional paint, glitter, and resin that frame the images in the layer below. Painted representations of sugarcane, Vodou insignias, and refined white sugar contribute complex symbolism to the topmost layer while also imposing compositional structure through materials and forms that invoke a uniquely Haitian heritage. The three layers of Plexiglas have been fastened together through a bolt in each corner of the nine tiles, lending the work an industrial, unfinished appearance. The layering of the three Plexiglas panes remains visible on all sides. No larger frame encases the work. In other words, Duval-Carrié has left the process of the work's construction available to the viewer. This layered progression—and its metaphorical and medial transparency—illuminates the visual stakes of creolization, whereby myriad images, subjects, and symbols compete and inform one another to produce a multivalent site unique in its expression of knowledge and the sedimentation of memory. *Sugar Conventions* is not merely a work to be seen, it embodies a process that informs, complicates, and reorients the individual components that it contains.

This chapter argues that, by juxtaposing Haiti's complex history of sugar production with a contingent European culture of sugar consumption, *Sugar Conventions* elucidates not only the means by which sugar functions as the vehicle and architect of coloniality but also the means by which sugar has historically dictated hegemonic power structures in the artistic canon.[6] Duval-Carrié utilizes sugar to draw attention to visual constructs, such as a Rococo "sweetness," around which imaginaries of the modern Caribbean have crystallized, while simultaneously reorganizing that aesthetic to reclaim agency and visibility for Haitian subjects emergent from the injustices wrought by sugar cultivation. In so doing, *Sugar Conventions* challenges established notions of Eurocentric visuality to locate creolization as a process entangled with, though historically veiled through, canonical Western image production. Medially and figuratively, *Sugar Conventions* subverts normative frameworks of Western and subaltern contexts—the very frameworks constituted by the power structures Duval-Carrié aims to critique—to elevate the instability, fluidity, and multivalence that underscore creolization. In this way, Duval-Carrié contests the privileged role of the Western imagination in Caribbean visuality. By formally and conceptually destabilizing Eurocentric standards such as artistic originality, purity, and "whiteness," *Sugar Conventions* navigates the consequences of sugar cultivation and its product, ultimately raising new questions about the complicity of images in the production and obfuscation of colonial dynamics.

A Layered Approach

Born and raised in Haiti, Edouard Duval-Carrié (b. 1954) fled the regime of "Papa Doc" Duvalier as a teenager, subsequently residing in locales as diverse as Puerto Rico, Montreal, Paris, and Miami. This cosmopolitan lifestyle shapes his artistic sensitivity toward the multifaceted identities that inform his native Haiti. Whether sculpture, painting, or multimedia installation, Duval-Carrié's work navigates the historically-rich and culturally-complex traditions that comprise a uniquely Haitian perspective.

Duval-Carrié's work has been featured in numerous exhibitions and monographs on the Haitian-born artist, most notably in the extensive volume edited by Edward J. Sullivan (2007), which explores the artist's work to date, and the more recent volume, edited by Anthony Bogues (2014a), which examines Duval-Carrié's use of landscape as a subversive tradition. This chapter builds upon the rich scholarship in these volumes, further exploring the manner in which Duval-Carrié's work functions through "*performances* and *texts*" (Sullivan 2007, 12). Duval-Carrié's *oeuvre* is one that strives for embodiment, theatricality, and, paradoxically, a studied quietude. In spite of his emergent prominence in Caribbean discourse, however, few art historians have attended to close readings of Duval-Carrié's individual works; rather, literary scholars and historians comprise the majority of authors engaging with the artist's corpus. While couching Duval-Carrié's work within Caribbean studies has helped to introduce the complexities of the region to a wider academic audience, close material study remains underemphasized in the scholarship. Further, while most scholars have taken interest in Duval-Carrié's use of the Haitian Revolution as the flash point of collective Caribbean memory, *Sugar Conventions* pivots attentions away from this rupture point and toward the persistent banality of evil that underscores both the culture of sugar and the production of colonial imagery. By closely examining how *Sugar Conventions* uses the artistic tools of iconography, materiality, and reception, this chapter explores how Duval-Carrié inventively entangles medium and message.

To approach a work as visually and conceptually rich as *Sugar Conventions*, I divide my argument into three discrete sections—background, middle ground, and foreground—that correspond to the three panes of Plexiglas comprising the work. While the visually demanding composition may initially make these three layers difficult to parse, close attention to the work's individual elements allows these layers to make themselves known to viewers. The organizational schema of this chapter is therefore a nod to the complexity of the artist's process as well as to the complex manner in which *Sugar Conventions* quietly builds upon itself to ultimately embody the conceptual tensions evident in each plane of the work.

To begin, I look to the background layer of *Sugar Conventions* to examine how expressions of migration, diaspora, and the slave trade materialize through the work's Francophone ornamentation. I suggest that Duval-Carrié invokes the problematic underpinnings of Caribbean culture through ornamental marginalia in order to highlight the critical and agentive role of visual representation in the rise of colonialism and modernity. Next, I address the work's middle layer, which comprises archival images, none original to the work. In this pictorial plane, specters of paintings, people, and heritage denote absence as much as presence, which I argue resonates with the veiled presence of Black bodies in the Caribbean and problems of diasporic agency in representation. Finally, I examine the foreground layer of *Sugar Conventions*, where sugar manifests both conceptually and materially. I briefly analyze the historical relationship between sugar and colonial perceptions of enslaved labor, and I then unpack how this hegemonic process collides with the Vodou iconography present in the work. By reframing the images and forms within *Sugar Conventions* as distinctly creolized symbols and processes, Duval-Carrié renders the work a literal embodiment, and critique, of the entangled cultures out of which Caribbean heritage emerged.

Background: Ornament as Transatlantic Bridge

In the background of *Sugar Conventions*, Rococo foliation delicately glistens. While these extravagant embellishments—composed of a thick, glitter paste that protrudes from the Plexiglas pane farthest from the viewer—exhibit unique forms in each of *Sugar Conventions*' nine tiles, they also evoke the formal opulence of Versailles and the hegemony of the seventeenth-century French monarchy (see Kimball 1943). The light sparkles as it strikes this ornamental background, lending an ephemeral and precious quality to the work. Though a minor aesthetic component within a busy pastiche, Duval-Carrié's reimagined Rococo extravagance couches *Sugar Conventions* within the artist's substantial body of works that challenge early modern globalization, colonialism, and enslavement by visually conflating Francophone ornamentation with historical figures and landscapes of France's most vital colony. In short, *Sugar Conventions*' foundational layer formally recalls the historical moment of human trafficking and forced migration out of which creolization emerged.[7]

A visual and conceptual precursor to *Sugar Conventions*, Duval-Carrié's *Mémoire sans histoire [Memory without History]* (2009) bookends scenes of transatlantic migration of the Vodou *lwa* with representations of Haitian land and politics (Bogues 2014a, 21). This work's multimedia panels bear a striking formal similarity to *Sugar Conventions*, as does its attention to the transatlantic (un)rootedness that undergirds Haitian identity. Blue *fleurs-de-lis* frame each of the six panels, though Duval-Carrié mottles the French heraldic symbol with navy and black discolorations, which lend the work an antique appearance, as though the panels had washed ashore, their vibrancy eroded by the sea. The ocean figures prominently in the work's iconography, with the sea looming large at the composition's center and boats carrying Vodou *lwa* making a perilous aquatic journey from one land to another. Signifying both the infamous Middle Passage and contemporary migrations of Haitian refugees to the U.S., the ocean represented in this work encodes the genesis and evolution of the diasporic self (see Gilroy 1993). Water at once separates and unites. Yet in its constant flow, it cannot contain any singular idea of nation or state. For Duval-Carrié, Haitian ties to the open seas thus stem not just from the waters that embrace its coastline, but also from the ocean's role as a vehicle of displacement. Though *Sugar Conventions* lacks the aquatic iconography prevalent in *Memoire sans histoire* and many of Duval-Carrié's other works, it nonetheless treats concerns of displacement, rupture, migration, and assimilation. *Sugar Conventions*' Rococo ornamentation provides a visually and conceptually Francophone foundation on top of which all subsequent symbols, images, and forms are layered, thereby giving visual life to the political ties between colonial powers and their transatlantic territories.

Time and again, Duval-Carrié's use of Francophone ornamentation invokes the processes of creolization that entangle Europe and Africa with the Americas. Duval-Carrié's *La vraie histoire des Ambaglos [The True History of the Underwater Spirits]* (2003) (Figure 7.2) presents a particularly amplified expression of this entanglement and, importantly, draws attention to the critical role of colonial visuality (Mirzoeff 2012).[8] Formally and conceptually, the questions, themes and tensions that Duval-Carrié exhibits in *La vraie histoire des Ambaglos* illuminate similar undercurrents in *Sugar Conventions*. In *La vraie histoire*, ancestral African figures (*Ambaglos*) float among vegetal forms on painted wood panels. Green leaves and vines, marked with sporadic and stylized daisies, fill the picture plane. The dense vegetal forms connect the floating, naked, black-skinned figures to one another and, ultimately, to Ginen, the ancestral and mythic Vodou homeland that may only be reached through undersea travel (Cosentino 2004, 48). These figures, their arms outstretched, clamor to connect with the world above the surface, yet their forms remain suppressed beneath the picture plane, just beyond the viewer's grasp. Like *Memoire sans histoire*, *La vraie histoire des Ambaglos* renders visible the multivalent condition of creolization in which the aquatic *Ambaglos* refuse to be stationary or static. The watery depths of Ginen link the Haitian soul to its African origins through the fluid, unrooted, and unfixed site of the sea. Though this work precedes *Sugar Conventions* by a decade, *La vraie histoire des*

Figure 7.2 Edouard Duval-Carrié, *La vraie histoire des Ambaglos [The True History of the Underwater Spirits]*, 2003, acrylic, sequins, collage, and resin on wood, 96 × 84 inches. On long-term loan to the Orlando Museum of Art from the collection of William D. and Norma Canelas Roth. Image courtesy of the Orlando Museum of Art. © 2020 Artists Rights Society (ARS), New York/ADAGP, Paris.

Ambaglos affirms Duval-Carrié's preoccupation with the strained ties among the Caribbean, Europe, and Africa.

Duval-Carrié further complicates the representation of transatlantic networks in *La vraie histoire des Ambaglos* by formally evoking the colonial era out of which Haitian Vodou emerged. Just as *Sugar Conventions*' glittering background draws upon aristocratic Rococo ornamentation, the vegetal ornament of *La vraie histoire des Ambaglos* conjures early Baroque grotesques that adorned colonial façades. Indeed, Duval-Carrié takes great interest in the ties between colonial commerce and the evolution of visual style, suggesting that sugar "created the Baroque, the Rococo" (Wolff 2014). The pronounced vegetal embellishment of Duval-Carrié's work, seemingly poached from colonial ornamentation, entangles the aesthetics of European imperialism with transcultural Haitian heritage. The yellow background, vegetal pattern, and contorted figures bear a striking resemblance to the sixteenth-century Spanish tile work of imperial edifices, such as that found on Seville's Casa de Contratación, an architectural complex devoted to the Crown's transatlantic commercial endeavors.[9]

In the colonial era, tile work promoted European ingenuity and innovation, allowing imperial visuality to be transported across the Atlantic and inscribed onto overseas territories (Frothingham 1969, 77; Ray 2000, 357). Historical reliance upon "visual avatars" for imperial sovereignty, such as tile work, rendered the Americas a site of simulacra in the eyes of the European powers that regulated the territories and the bodies within them (Bleichmar 2009). In short, people throughout the Americas became (forcibly) bonded to European powers, in part, through visual practices. The decorative vegetal forms rendered on tile work allowed motifs to be repeated, reappropriated, and disseminated organically and rapidly, thus proving a critical aid in the expansion and perpetuation of colonial empires (Ward-Jackson 1967, 59). Interestingly, these tiles typically adorned loggias and galleries, that is, liminal or transitional spaces, which expressed "movement and transference" (Hansen 2000, 252). The composition of *La vraie histoire des Ambaglos*, gridded, decentralized, and ornamental, draws upon this colonial practice that bridged the transatlantic gap and implicates creolization's embodiment of "movement" and displacement. By invoking the Vodou *Ambaglos*, Duval-Carrié subverts this ornamental Baroque practice, complicating the colonizer-colonized dynamic and triangulating transatlantic visuality among Europe, the Americas, and Africa.

I suggest that Duval-Carrié again explores creolization's relational aspect in the background pane of *Sugar Conventions*, where shimmering, Francophone ornamentation comes into contact, and conflict, with the distinctly Haitian and Vodou iconography present in the work's subsequent layers (discussed below). In the emergent global moment of sugar plantations and Rococo style, the saccharine pleasantries of ornamentation masked the laborious and oppressive institutions of the day.

The transatlantic, and therefore virtual, dynamic between colonizer and colonized meant that undesirable realities, such as the harsh treatment of enslaved laborers, were readily removed from the European visual field. Duval-Carrié thus utilizes the Francophone ornamentation of *Sugar Conventions* to historicize the extractive entanglements of global commerce. When prompted to discuss the ornamentation of *Sugar Conventions*, he asks, "Do people realize that refinement in Europe was based on this suffering?" Adding, "I'm just trying to make people remember" (Wolff 2014).

The background layer of *Sugar Conventions*, therefore, harnesses the visual weight of colonialism, whereby the very act of representation emboldens consumers while oppressing and suppressing producers. The Rococo ornament of *Sugar Conventions*—mere background, wallpaper—subtly couches the rest of this complex work within the persistent patterns of European luxury that emerged at the expense of enslaved labor. Duval-Carrié draws upon this Francophone elegance to demonstrate the banality of hegemony that belies the supposed freedom and Enlightenment of the day.[10]

Middle Ground: Mimesis and the Archival Impulse

In the middle ground of *Sugar Conventions*, Duval-Carrié affixes a prominent oval image on each of the work's nine tiles. Backlighting filters through the Plexiglas to the thin membrane of paper upon which these central images have been inscribed, producing an eerie glow that emanates from within the work itself. The lighting destabilizes any sense of rootedness, transforming these images on paper into radiant apparitions. The cropping of these images further enhances the ghostliness of the forms. Duval-Carrié deliberately conceals the entirety of the works he reproduces; rather, he excerpts elliptical passages from each original, denying the viewer unfettered access.

The images that comprise the middle ground—an amalgam of digital reprints—range from representations of the Vodou deity Dambalah to works by the eighteenth-century Italian painter Agostino Brunias to photographs of contemporary Haiti. Each image captures and contributes, through politics, sociability, and landscape, an element of Caribbean life.[11] Though each image is distinct, none are unique. Every middle ground image of *Sugar Conventions* copies or represents another version of its likeness. This interpretive pastiche elevates the representational problems of a place and people marginalized by the Francophone art historical canon. Duval-Carrié claims that the Caribbean "has always been subject to some sort of reinterpretation, always about enticing people to come" (Bogues 2014b, 39). For him, outsiders' perspectives on the Caribbean have been granted primacy in the visual (and cultural) record. Duval-Carrié complicates this center-periphery dynamic by shifting the signification of these images in *Sugar Conventions*. This reimagining, I suggest, breaks down the originality of the work, deliberately disrupting its aura of rootedness. The treatment subverts the Western gaze upon which the modern Caribbean was built and shifts the Black body from stable object to complex subject (Hall 1996, 442).

Regardless of the scene portrayed, Duval-Carrié has taken pains to unite these disparate images through their negation of originality. The digitally-manipulated photographs of the Haitian tombstone and post-earthquake ruins of the Haitian National Palace each resonate with a ghostly presence. In this work, corporeal absence reads as the specter of the deceased. Just as the photograph of the crumbling National Palace signifies the ghost of a structure that no longer stands, the image of the tomb likewise marks a loss of life, the transition of the soul from Haiti to the mythic homeland Ginen, and the irony that only in death do Haitian bodies return to Africa.

Duval-Carrié "opens" *Sugar Conventions* with the image of Dambalah la Flambeau, a *lwa* from the hot, *petwo* family, whose colors of red, orange, and purple (which have been mounted onto Plexiglas in yellow and red gradations) weave his vital, Vodou presence throughout the entire work (Stebich 1978, 76). Though Duval-Carrié insists upon his secular approach to Vodou iconography, he nonetheless describes Dambalah's presence in *Sugar Conventions* as an influential force of omnipotence: "Dambalah is the god, the opener, the sage, the one that knows. So it's almost like an act of faith, that this god should guide me through this project" (Wolff 2014). Duval-Carrié combines two identical reproductions from his previous work *Dambalah la Flambeau* (2000) and subtly skews their alignment to produce a dual-reflection of Dambalah's fiery pink head, rendering the *lwa* an uncanny replica. Although this panel is the only one in *Sugar Conventions* to explicitly attend to the *lwa*, this image nonetheless functions as the establishing frame, subtly crafting the lens of duality, instability, and mutability through which issues of Black Caribbean identity should be interpreted in the following panels.

The tensions among original and copy, hegemonic representation and Caribbean identity, converge in the central tiles of *Sugar Conventions,* where Duval-Carrié has inserted passages from two canonical paintings by Agostino Brunias.[12] In the late colonial era, these dulcet paintings circulated throughout Britain and France in printed form, thereby contributing to European perceptions of quaint Caribbean social and economic life. Although painted in the Ceded Islands,[13] British not French colonies, the global circulation of Brunias's work and its conceptual ties to Caribbean life writ large make it a poignant contribution to *Sugar Conventions* in terms of the complex dynamics of Caribbean visuality (Sullivan 2014, 17–18).

Though Brunias's paintings, such as *A West Indian Flower Girl and Two Other Free Women of Color* (c. 1769), seemingly exhibit a sensitivity to daily life and diversity on the islands, the reality of such works betrays their contrived and manipulative construction: "Brunias's painting and prints promote British West Indian colonies by visualizing plenitude while de-emphasizing the most profitable commodity produced there … sugar cane" (Kriz 2008, 38). In concept and form, this reproduction of Brunias' work further underscores the invisibility of plantation culture in the Western art historical canon. Through his paintings, Brunias sought to popularize an idyllic impression of the West Indies that would entice financial investment and European settlement. Kay Dian Kriz, whose work influenced Duval-Carrié during the creation of *Sugar Conventions*, suggests that Brunias tempted investors by foregrounding European civility in the West Indies: "In order to foster settlement, the islands' appeal as a potentially *civilized* space, as well as a profitable one, had to be emphasized"

(Kriz 2008, 37; Wolff 2014). Thus, Duval-Carrié's use of *A West Indian Flower Girl* becomes a strategy to foreground the absurdism of depicting the most benign of Caribbean commercial exchanges—a flower sale—while veiling the arduous and inhumane plantation labor that generated both the wealth drawing settlers to the island and supported the production of the commodities most beloved by Europeans. In other words, Brunias' tropes of Caribbean sociability inscribe European expectations onto the local landscape.

Portrayals of leisure, family, contentment, and prosperity populate Brunias' canvases while the backbreaking labor that funds this emergent bourgeoisie culture remains invisible to the viewer. To add insult to injury, this benevolent representation of colonial society was composed of standard types that Brunias utilized time and again to represent Caribbean diversity in his works. The reality present in these compositions merely reflects Anglophone expectations and desires. Thus, although Brunias' compositions feature a seemingly diverse array of Caribbean bodies and cultures, they are "also 'about' whiteness" (Kriz 2008, 55). Duval-Carrié underscores this racial hegemony by only drawing upon external, European artists, such as Brunias and Polish painter January Suchodolski, for the key reproductions within his work. Reproductions of works by influential Haitian artists such as André Pierre or Hector Hyppolite are notably absent from *Sugar Conventions*. This omission resonates as a poignant critique of the role outsiders have played in colonizing even the *image* of the Caribbean. Colonialism supplanted the reality of Caribbean social life with external visual negotiations of European desires.

Indeed, while Caribbean society was born of transcultural processes, the visuality of Caribbean bodies has been, to invoke Franz Fanon, a narrative of "black skin, white masks" (Fanon 2008, xviii). In other words, what Duval-Carrié seeks to unpack through these images is not just the internal struggle of the diasporic self but also the problem of Caribbean visibility. Fanon describes the difficulty of representing the Caribbean self as a problem of agency and artifice: "I am overdetermined from the outside. I am a slave not to the 'idea' others have of me, but to my appearance" (Fanon 2008, 94). Duval-Carrié's concerns with artifice and its entanglement with cultural production manifested in the exhibition *Edouard Duval-Carrié: Imagined Landscapes* (2014) at the Pérez Art Museum Miami. The works that comprised this exhibition (nearly all produced the same year as *Sugar Conventions*) build upon and subvert canonical imaginings of the Caribbean landscape with colors, images, and media that underscore the problematic recognition of the Western aesthetic as "neutral" (Mignolo 2011). In *After Bierstadt—The Landing of Columbus* (2013) (Figure 7.3), for instance, Duval-Carrié references Albert Bierstadt's serene painting *The Landing of Columbus* (1893) but challenges and supplants the pastel colors, serene landscape, and glorification of Christopher Columbus' initial arrival to the Bahamas in Bierstadt's canvas with dark, saturated colors, fictional characters such as Mr. Potato Head and Batman, and an overall sense of vitality in the landscape that is wholly absent from Bierstadt's idyllic portrayal of the Caribbean. In appropriating Bierstadt's depiction of a land that was not his own, Duval-Carrié attempts to break down these overdetermined Caribbean aesthetics in the very institutions (museums) responsible for solidifying such artifice in the Western imagination.

Sugar Conventions continues Duval-Carrié's efforts to challenge the normative whiteness that typically marks representations of Caribbean culture. In the tile at bottom center, just below Brunias' composition, sits a portrait of revolutionary leader Toussaint Louverture on horseback. Leaves of blue and red, the colors of the Haitian flag, frame Louverture. His likeness, a digital reprint framed by hand-painted and dense red and blue vegetation, references the historic struggle to eradicate "whiteness" from the young nation.[14] The literal and figurative removal of whiteness from the state underscores the continued socio-political and racial complexities in *Sugar Conventions*' panels. Yet, of course, this ideology yields an underlying and unavoidable friction against the essential desire for whiteness out of which plantation culture, and thus

Figure 7.3 Edouard Duval-Carrié, *After Bierstadt—The Landing of Columbus*, mixed media on aluminum, 96 × 144 inches. Image courtesy of the artist and Pan American Art Projects, Miami. © 2020 Artists Rights Society (ARS), New York/ADAGP, Paris.

Haitian statehood, ultimately emerged. A pulsating duality, a continued reminder of reproduction, and a sense of invisibility orbit the middle ground images of *Sugar Conventions* to remind the viewer of socio-political incongruities wrought by colonial institutions.

Throughout his career, Duval-Carrié employs Louverture's portrait to invoke the democratic potential of the Haitian Revolution—a historical moment that stands in stark contrast to the injustices that befell Haitians before and after statehood.[15] The repetitious nature of Louverture in Duval-Carrié's work converges with the reality of Louverture's personality and visage, both of which are "shrouded in mystery" (Bogues 2014c, 1). Louverture's true likeness remains unknown today, and thus this mythic Haitian hero exists in the visual record as a shadow of his true self (Geggus 2013). The myriad portraits of the leader that have circulated in print and paintings since the early 1800s are merely copies of copies—mechanical reproductions without an original. The struggle for Haitian autonomy embodied by the image of Louverture—his history as both an enslaved laborer and revolutionary leader render him at once less than a free and entitled human *and* a personification of the liberated state—likewise reaffirms the problematic visuality of Brunias' compositions, which prove more "typological classification" than portraiture (Sullivan 2014, 19).

The fundamental tension Duval-Carrié crafts between original and copy, colonized and colonizer, becomes further complicated through the work's archival composition. The middle ground images appear embedded within the Plexiglas panes as specimens enclosed within a slide, ready for microscopic scrutiny. These reproductions function as records of the Caribbean visual corpus, each one contributing, like a curio in a cabinet, to a distinctive aspect of the region's graphic history. The "archival impulse" within *Sugar Conventions*, a tendency that Duval-Carrié explicitly renders through the myriad copies of images neatly placed within an organized grid, foregrounds the agentive role of reproduction and imitation in the work.[16] The will of the archival work to connect disparate, and replicant, matter in the hopes of shifting the symbolic order "proposes new orders of affective association ... even as it also registers the difficulty, at times the absurdity, of doing so" (Foster 2004, 21). The act of compiling distinct images within a single work produces a palpable tension among the compositions that foregrounds visual and conceptual incongruities. In short, the archival nature of *Sugar Conventions*' use of reprints both represents and embodies the inherent contradictions of identity, heritage, and visibility in creolization. Individually, the images within *Sugar Conventions* portray concrete and specific histories; collectively, the images push and pull against one another, contesting each image's veracity and unveiling new layers of complexity. In this way, the archival impulse renders *Sugar Conventions* itself a work of creolization.

The friction embodied by *Sugar Conventions*' archival middle ground engages the viewer with the absurdities of the aesthetic norms that ultimately encompass Caribbean visuality. The reproductions within *Sugar Conventions* push back against their compositional aspiration to form *lieux de memoire* [sites of memory] (Nora 1989). These visual passages are each specters, ghosts of another and often-untraceable origin (Benjamin 2008). Indeed, Crichlow suggests that the politics of creolization encompass the struggle to find one's place, "or at least 'traces' of it" (Crichlow 2009, 21). Nora's *lieux de memoire* represents a Eurocentric consciousness that strives to galvanize imagined communities through monuments and memorials. Crichlow, however, highlights the problems of remembrance and erasure for the Black diasporic self, for whom "presence" embodies contested processes of upheaval, invisibility, and mimicry. Where creolization is concerned, authentic sites of memory struggle to emerge from under the shadow of the colonizer. The archival processes underscoring *Sugar Conventions*, therefore, pay homage to the problematic memory work and avowal of memory sites inherent to creolization.

The replicant quality of *Sugar Conventions* is not just befitting of an archival impulse but also of the problems of simulacra and mimesis emergent from the slave trade and plantation culture (Taussig 1993; Mintz 1996). As Duval-Carrié has integrated these discrete images into *Sugar Conventions*, they underscore and decolonize the rootlessness of the diasporic self (Mercer 2005, 10). These are images of absence—absence of bodies, absence of veracity, absence of originals—that were born out of the European thirst for conspicuous consumption, namely, the hunger for sugar.

Foreground: Visualizing Placelessness through Sugar

In spite of the many colors and forms stirring throughout *Sugar Conventions*, the asymmetrical white framing of the central panel brings that vignette into sharper focus than the surrounding tiles. The panel's contents—disembodied sugar cane, abstracted vegetal forms, and Brunias' *A West Indian Flower Girl*—seem to be drowning within a white substance that boldly, and amorphously, frames the work. Pushing against the front Plexiglas pane, this whiteness threatens to ooze out beyond the picture plane and into the viewer's space. The opaque substance swallows a partially obscured and glittering word at the tile's bottom, whose lettering can be made out to spell *SUCRE*—SUGAR. This reference to the most profitable French colonial plantation crop is further reinforced through the white matter that threatens to consume it. In other words, sugar is not merely a theoretical occurrence in this work. Instead, the refined white crystals have been affixed to each of *Sugar Convention*'s nine tiles in an experimental paste of paint, glue, and glitter. Though a seemingly invisible material in a medially complex work, the sugar's presence lends conceptual weight to the piece. Affixed to the tiles, these refined crystals become inedible, their use-value denied. The utilization of sugar in this work, then, resonates with the troubling politics of the colonial production of sugar through a rigid, but stealthy infrastructure from which the various Caribbean religious, political, and social lifeways depicted in *Sugar Conventions* evolved. This medial tension signifies the figurative tensions between subaltern bodies and dominant discourses in the creolization process.

The story of sugar production in the Caribbean is one of colonization and modernity.[17] Cuban anthropologist Fernando Ortiz once wrote, "Sugar comes into the world without a last name, like a slave" (Ortiz 2003, 42). Neither slavery nor sugar, in other words, is a natural entity; rather, both demand human construction and manufacture. Without the persistence of enslaved labor and dependence upon industrial machinery, sugar could not endure as a Caribbean commodity. As Sidney Mintz (1985) has shown, robust industrialization in Europe and rigorous colonial labor were not unidirectional—from these mutually constitutive systems, the financial and social hardships in the colonies produced and perpetuated financial and social liberties in Europe. To produce sugar from the cane, a laborious alchemical process transforms the essential substance of the raw sugar into something, ironically, "purer" than its harvested form. A "solid technical mastery," whereby the cane juice is extracted, boiled, skimmed, and reduced, is thus essential to the rendering of the finished product (Mintz 1985, 47). Through refinement, any flavor is chemically stripped from the juice; all that remains is blanket sweetness. Although a manipulative, arduous, and mechanized process, the alchemy of refinement has historically been framed as a means of returning the sugar to a *neutral* state—from one of brown contamination to white purity (Mintz 1985, 63).

Moreover, once refined, sugar becomes a placeless commodity (Merleaux 2015, 22). The refined crystals from one plantation become indistinguishable from the crystals of another: the process of refinement equates with the process of de-territorialization. Sugar thus embodies mechanization and purification, modernity and homogeneity. Importantly, this homogeny, rendered through processes of chemical purification, masks the enslaved labor that initially cultivates the raw sugar. At a fundamentally material level, any markers of locality become literally and metaphorically whitewashed by refinement: "The point of refining is, after all, to remove the last remnants of sweat and soil from the sugar so that its consumers are unaware of the product's natural and human history" (Merleaux 2015, 24). The shift, therefore, from natural product to industrial commodity also signifies the visual, gustatory, and conceptual veiling, if not erasure, of those who work the land. In short, just as sugar became naturalized in the Americas, so too did the racialization and enslavement of the bodies that cultivated it. Together, these rootless beings became commodified through a cycle of (seemingly) placeless production and conspicuous consumption. Thus, in *Sugar Conventions*, the presence of refined sugar brings to light both the Black body's condition of placelessness in the Western imagination and its conceptual origins.

Duval-Carrié demonstrates sensitivity toward this topic in his earlier work, *Confiserie Sucre Noir [Black Sugar Confectionary]* (1999), in which a black head appears, like a Byzantine saint, at once disembodied and imminently present. The figure's head floats atop a large, lacey ruffled collar, upon which the words *SUCRE NOIR [Black Sugar]*—a play on the origins of raw sugar—have been inscribed. The vague semblance of the figure's body is both distanced from the head and rendered into a stylized ocean, upon which militarized ships, doubling as fanciful shoulder pads, sail toward one another, destined for confrontation at the site of the disembodied Black head. This work thus situates the Black corporeal self as the very locus of confection and violence (Crichlow 2009, 22).

The nebulous nature of sugar and diaspora alike—bodies belonging to everywhere and nowhere—has, however, been refereed by the historic tendency to classify both sugar and Caribbean bodies by "purity." This history of categorization is marked in *Sugar Conventions* by the numbered system Duval-Carrié inscribes atop the figures in his reproduction of Brunias' painting *Free Women of Color with their Servants in a Landscape* (c. 1770–1796) at the far center right of the composition. The glittering, gold numerals assigned to each body correspond to the *Legende* below, which assigns a distinct caste to each number. By incorporating this grouping into Brunias' composition, Duval-Carrié further foregrounds the empty signification, lack of veracity, and dependency upon visual distinctions informing Western imaginings of the Caribbean. Duval-Carrié here references more than arbitrary musings on the agency of Caribbean bodies; his classificatory *Legende* portrays socio-economic classes derived from Moreau de Saint-Méry's *Description ... de la partie française de l'Isle Saint-Domingue* (1797; Dayan 1998, 229). This late eighteenth-century text sought to codify an exacting taxonomy for the population of colonial Saint Domingue based on skin color and blood purity—the observable and the invisible (Dayan 1998, 231).[18]

Together, these entangled institutions—early modern bloodlines and sugar refinement—demonstrate a deep and persistent desire to regulate, and ultimately purge, the perceived contagion of "color" from Western social life. The numbers inscribed on Duval-Carrié's reproduction of Brunias's *Free Women of Color* at once reference Moreau de Saint-Méry's nomenclature and the Dutch Color Standard, a taxonomic system used to distinguish raw from refined sugars. This numbered system, which placed sugar along a spectrum numbered eight to twenty-five, functioned solely based on appearance—the more brown in color, the higher the supposed molasses content, the less refined the sugar (Palmer 1909; Merleaux 2015, 23). In other words, the whiter the sugar, the more desirable and more lucrative the product. The Dutch Color Standard became the vehicle through which Europeans ensured that the sugar they consumed was sufficiently removed and purified from the Black bodies and plantation soil of which it was initially cultivated. By inscribing refined white sugar crystals onto the work, therefore, Duval-Carrié engages in an act of symbolic anthropophagy, threatening to collapse the colonial institutions upon which Haitian identity was built (Andrade 1928). The sugar dissolves into the work, invisible and non-functional, yet critical evidence, if not the embodiment, of the erasure of local labors that underpin and sustain global consumption.

The alchemy that the sugar trade necessitates—from raw to refined—situates it as a product exemplifying not just modern machinations, but also transformations, a fundamental prescription of Vodou belief. Indeed, Vodou elements emerge out of the foreground of *Sugar Conventions*, granting this uniquely Haitian practice primacy in the truest sense. Like the vegetation in *La vraie histoire des Ambaglos*, Vodou weaves itself throughout *Sugar Conventions*, becoming, along with sugar, the thread that knits these scenes together. While the visage of Dambalah is perhaps the most explicit Vodou image in *Sugar Conventions*, subtle references to the Haitian practice abound and situate the work within a Vodou aesthetic.[19] Donald Cosentino has remarked that Duval-Carrié "is more than mining the religion for imagery. He is meeting it on the common aesthetic ground of assemblage" (Cosentino 2004, 19). In *Sugar Conventions*, however, Duval-Carrié's interest in Vodou transcends aesthetics. He uses the practice and its associated iconography to deepen his critique of Caribbean visuality as a condition whose fluidity, non-fixity, and invisibility paradoxically emerged out of a Western desire to regulate, quantify, and define Caribbean bodies.

An examination of the foreground of the center-right panel containing Brunias' *Free Women of Color* reveals ties between Caribbean socio-political identity, the Western art historical canon, and Vodou iconography. A large, resin, flaming heart pierced by daggers looms over the passage

134 *Lesley A. Wolff*

from Brunias' work and protrudes outward from the very precipice of the panel. Stars cascade below the heart, framing the central image with seemingly ornamental forms. These disparate shapes, the pierced heart and star, symbolize the powerful presence of the *lwa* Ezili Dantó, a goddess from the hot *petwo* family who "is at once the mother figure and the quintessential combatant" (Beauvoir-Dominique 2007, 45). Like all aspects of *Sugar Conventions*, Ezili Dantó embodies multiple temperaments.

This is not the first time Duval-Carrié has called upon Ezili in his work. She manifests as a beautiful seductress disembarking from a militarized ship in *Le monde actual, ou Erzulie interceptée [The World at Present, or Ezili Intercepted]* (1996), again evoking themes of migration, displacement, and political threat. In *Sugar Conventions*, Ezili Dantó, summoned not as a personification but as her *veve* of stars and a pierced heart, reinforces the socio-political tensions resonant throughout the work and, importantly, does so on Haitian terms. Like so many references in *Sugar Conventions*, Ezili's origins emerge from the complications of transcultural processes. However, unlike many of the *lwa* who find their origins in Yoruba or Dahomey deities, Ezili is uniquely of Haiti. She was born in the Caribbean and embodies its violence and oppression largely through her ties to the impossible and painful condition of forbidden love. By symbolizing irreconcilable circumstances and a volatile spirit, this distinctly Haitian *lwa* frames the sweetness of Brunias' image with "a commentary on the harrowing reality of Saint-Domingue" (Dayan 1998, 59). Duval-Carrié thus supplants the Western visual rhetoric instilled in the art historical record by artists such as Brunias or Bierstadt with Vodou aesthetics and ideals that more accurately embody the complexities, tensions, and non-fixities of creolization.

In sum, *Sugar Conventions* lays bare a visual framework for creolization that both represents and embodies articulations of diaspora. *Sugar Conventions* builds upon itself, from background to foreground, rendering legible the multivalence that Western visuality has historically masked in Caribbean aesthetics. The transparencies prevalent in *Sugar Conventions* express a metaphorical and medial entanglement between local and global, dominance and subversion, Rococo and Vodou. The complexity of these transparencies—their layered, reproductive, and fluid presentations—connote the ways in which Eurocentric "sweetness" cannot be perceived without also bearing witness to the injustices and legacy of enslavement, and vice versa. Therefore, while *Sugar Conventions* participates in an ever-growing conversation about the complicity of products like sugar in racial, political, and economic imbalances, it uniquely does so through the very images upon which these colonial dynamics were built. *Sugar Conventions* looks back to the complex and sinister underpinnings of modernity and interrogates not just the oppressive origins of sugar production, but also the power of the *image* to erase, veil and reimagine its machinations. In so doing, *Sugar Conventions* works toward decolonial ends, bringing Brunias ever-closer to the hardships of plantation labor and uniting Vodou symbolism with both the culture of Versailles and the ancestral homeland of Ginen. *Sugar Conventions* thus bridges a transatlantic gap, rendering Haitian identity an amorphous site of memory, which can neither be contained by a singular meaning nor medium—an interminable process of creolization. As an amalgam itself, *Sugar Conventions* asks the viewer to acknowledge the pastiche that underscores the Western canon, to consider how Africa and Europe alike have informed the visuality of the Americas, and how Haiti has shaped the modern world.

Notes

1 This chapter has been adapted from an earlier article in *African and Black Diaspora: An International Journal* and was made possible thanks to the support of Drs. Michael Carrasco, Paul Niell, and Martin Munro at Florida State University. I am especially indebted to Edouard Duval-Carrié, who has so generously shared his time, knowledge, and artistic practice with me over the years.

From Raw to Refined 135

2 *Sugar Conventions* was originally commissioned by the Winthrop-King Institute for Contemporary French and Francophone Studies in celebration of the international conference "Haiti in a Globalized Frame," held at Florida State University, Tallahassee, Florida, 14–16 February, 2013.
3 Crichlow suggests that creolization is persistently constituted and reconstituted by vernacular, relational experiences, not broad, hybridic processes (Crichlow 2009, 16). In short, to understand creolization, one must acknowledge the local, lived environments that endlessly produce, perpetuate, and disrupt economies of power (Mignolo 2012).
4 Sugar's vital, and complex, role in the evolution of Haitian independence renders it an important material and conceptual product in Duval-Carrié's work. After Saint Domingue came under French control in 1697, sugar plantations began to populate the colony on larger scales than the island had previously known (Ferrer 2014). During the one hundred years in which French colonial rule dictated commerce in Saint Domingue, about eight hundred large-scale sugar plantations emerged, from which over one hundred forty one million pounds of sugar were exported annually (Henochsberg 2016, 15). This sugar was not intended for French consumption, but rather as a vehicle for French capitalist enterprise and the means by which the colonial empire accumulated vast sums of wealth in the eighteenth century. The proliferation of sugar plantations necessitated the importation of hundreds of thousands of enslaved laborers to Saint Domingue in the century prior to Haitian independence. The success of sugar as a trade good of the French Empire was thus directly tied to an increase in the enslaved population of Saint Domingue. On the eve of Haitian independence, the majority of people on the island were newly imported enslaved laborers—a demographic fact that would ultimately help the population claim the first successful slave rebellion in the Americas. In this manner, sugar and Haitian independence remain perversely entangled as vital aspects of the Haitian Revolution. Though Haitian sugar cultivation essentially flat lined after the revolution, the product remains a robust plantation crop in the Dominican Republic, where the contested migration of Haitian laborers today seeking work on sugar plantations has brought issues of national belonging, race, and coloniality to the forefront of modern-day island politics.
5 I reference Saint Domingue throughout this chapter to indicate the French-controlled colony on the west side of Hispaniola that subsequently became the independent nation of Haiti after 1804.
6 By "coloniality" I here mean, "a term that encompasses the transhistoric expansion of colonial domination and the perpetuation of its effects in contemporary times" (Moraña et al. 2008, 2). In his work on subaltern knowledges, Walter Mignolo (2011) has famously discussed how "coloniality" represents the "darker side" of modernity, thereby demonstrating the mutually constitutive natures of modernity and coloniality as two sides of the same coin that comprise our globalized world.
7 Historian Carlos Célius suggests that migration comprises the singular theme to which Duval-Carrié's *oeuvre* persistently attends (Célius 2014, 17). Indeed, Duval-Carrié's works encompass a materially diverse, but thematically cohesive body, which have centered on the convergence of Vodou, transoceanic migration, Haitian politics, and Francophone aesthetics. The background layer of *Sugar Conventions* represents yet another contribution to Duval-Carrié's expressions of movement and transatlantic dynamics, doing so through ornamentation, not figuration.
8 Duval-Carrié also produced a second version of this work entitled *La Triste et Malheureuse Histoire des Ambaglos [The Sad and Woeful History of the Ambaglos]* (2003). This version contains the same colors, vegetation, and figures as *La vraie histoire des Ambaglos*, but presented in a slightly different configuration. This mixed media work on Plexiglas has been affixed to a concrete wall, further evidencing its intentional evocation of an architectural façade.
9 The Casa de Contratación [House of Trade] was established in 1503. During the sixteenth century, all accounting, navigating, mapping, trading, or judiciary issues pertaining to the Spanish colonies were, by law, to be submitted to the Casa de Contratación. The Real Alcázar, the royal complex in which the Casa was located, as well as Seville itself, thus played a critical role in the political and economic management of the Spanish colonial agenda. The Salas de las Bóvedas of Seville's Real Alcázar contain elaborate ceramic wainscoting that adorns the halls. This ceramic décor, produced by Cristóbal de Augusta in the late 1570s, literally stages the visual backdrop to the Casa de Contratación. Any trade or business venture in the Spanish colonies, such as the production of sugar, had to be declared with the Casa de Contratación. Importantly, the building's ornamentation visually reinforced these commercial exploits. As early as 1509, Sevillian tile works were exported across the Atlantic to Santo Domingo, the Spanish-controlled colony on Hispaniola. The gridded (and thus infinitely expandable) form of the tile, its durable material, and new innovations in mass production all rendered the medium ideal as a visual means of imposing European iconography on American space.

10 In this way, Duval-Carrié follows in the footsteps of anthropologists like Fernando Ortiz and Sidney Mintz, whose work foregrounds the relationships between European sugar consumption, the rise of industrialization, the expansion of plantation culture, and the commercial trafficking of enslaved Africans in the colonies (Mintz 1985, 55; 1996, 19; Ortiz 2003). However, rather than looking exclusively to social dynamics, Duval-Carrié builds upon the work of Ortiz, Mintz and others to expose creolization's place within the visuality of colonialism.

11 A breakdown of the nine total images in the middle ground is as follows: three images reproduce previous works by Duval-Carrié; four images reproduce canonical, historical depictions of the Caribbean; and two images are photographs that have been appropriated by Duval-Carrié.

12 Brunias, an eighteenth-century Italian painter, followed Sir William Young on his voyage to the British West Indies in 1764. Brunias' tenure in the Caribbean proved an artistically fertile period for the artist; he remained in the region until his death in 1796, generating the largest body of work on the social life of people of color in the West Indies prior to the abolition of slavery (Kriz 2008, 37).

13 Brunias was invited to the Ceded Islands by Sir William Young, the Commissioner and Receiver for sale of lands in the islands of Dominica, St. Vincent, and Tobago. Young employed Brunias to make images that would attract white settlers (Kriz 2008, 37, 210, note # 5).

14 The mytho-historic narrative of Haiti's statehood tells of the heroic moment when General-in-Chief Jean-Jacques Dessalines ripped the white panel from the French tricolor flag, proclaiming only red and blue—symbols of mulatto and Black citizens—would comprise the new nation's banner (Dayan 1998, 52).

15 Duval-Carrié calls upon Louverture in works such as *The Fall of the Hero* (2000), *Le General Toussaint enfumé [General Toussaint Wreathed in Smoke]* (2003), *Five Flags for a Revolution* (2004), and in ten separate bust portraits of the General produced between 2006 and 2014.

16 Hal Foster claims that archival works, of which I here include *Sugar Conventions*, are typically composed of "passive" (i.e., duplicate) objects that strive to focus and engage the viewer through seemingly lifeless (i.e., replicant) media (Foster 2004, 6).

17 Sugar was first domesticated over two millennia ago in New Guinea, and it was only with Columbus' 1493 voyage to Hispaniola that the crop found its way to the Americas, where it quickly burgeoned (Mintz 1985, 19, 32). Mintz suggests that the prolific presence of sugar plantations and the enslaved labor it necessitated demonstrate "a depressingly enduring" institution, which began with the earliest enslaved Africans in the Americas, in 1503, and ended with the last enslaved Africans "smuggled" into Cuba in the late nineteenth century (Mintz 1996, 37; Smith 1992, 262). While sugar at first proved to be a luxury good for the aristocratic nobility, by the eighteenth century, it had been transformed into a product of British and French necessity (Mintz 1985, 78–96; Dayan 1998, 201). As the liberal, free subject prospered in Europe, enslaved labor increased in the Americas.

18 Duval-Carrié's reference to Moreau de Saint-Méry is not without absurdist undertones. While *Sugar Conventions* conveys six categories, Moreau de Saint-Méry's obsessive taxonomy contained no fewer than eleven categories of one hundred ten combinations ranking from absolute whiteness to absolute blackness—each of those composed of one hundred twenty-eight parts of white or black blood. The exhaustive nature of this system further underscores anxieties of blood purity in a society where "impure" bodies both outnumbered their white counterparts and were critical to the commercial success of the island.

19 By Vodou aesthetic, I here invoke the likeness of the individual images within each panel to Haitian calabash paintings; the work's formal reference to the glittering *drapó* (ritual flags); and the Rococo ornament that doubles as a *veve* (cosmogram) to call upon the *lwa*. In a discussion of the elaborate forms inscribed on Duval-Carrié's frames, Donald Cosentino (2004, 19) defines "the aesthetic of Vodou" as one of excess and overproduction. Importantly, the Vodou aesthetic also comprises non-figural forms. In his work, Duval-Carrié consistently plays with the overproduction and abstraction of Vodou imagery and its relationship to the excess and ornamentation that likewise marks the Rococo style, which was in vogue at the moment of French colonization of Saint Domingue. Duval-Carrié often references this European style as "sweet," thus connoting the many conceptual, temporal, and visual levels on which sugar, colonialism, Haitian independence, and contemporary Vodou practice converge. One might also consider the conceptual and visual relationship between Rococo, a derivative of the French word "rocaille" [shell], foliated forms that likewise comprise Vodou *veve*, and the forced transoceanic migrations of the slave trade. Duval-Carrié frequently references this nexus by literally inscribing images of Haitian political figures onto foliated Rococo cartouches, as he does in *Sugar Conventions*.

References

Andrade, Oswaldo de. 1928. "Manifesto antopofago." *Revista de Antropofagia* 1: 3–7.
Beauvoir-Dominique, Rachel. 2007. "Edouard Duval Carrié: The Vodou Pantheon." In *Continental Shifts: The Art of Edouard Duval-Carrié*, edited by Edward J. Sullivan, 41–50. Miami, FL: American Art Corporation.
Benjamin, Walter. 2008. *The Work of Art in the Age of Mechanical Reproduction*, translated from the German by J. A. Underwood. Revised edition. London: Penguin Books.
Bleichmar, Daniela. 2009. "Visible Empire: Scientific Expedition and Visual Culture in the Hispanic Enlightenment." *Postcolonial Studies* 12 (4): 441–466.
Bogues, Anthony. 2014a. "Reinventing the Caribbean: Edouard Duval-Carrié, History, Politics, and the Making of a Caribbean Aesthetic." In *From Revolution in the Tropics to Imagined Landscapes: The Art of Edouard Duval-Carrié*, edited by Edward J. Sullivan, 18–27. Miami, FL: American Art Corporation.
Bogues, Anthony. 2014b. "Art, History, and the Politics of the Imagination: An Interview with Edouard Duval-Carrié," In *From Revolution in the Tropics to Imagined Landscapes: The Art of Edouard Duval-Carrié*, edited by Edward J. Sullivan, 28–48. Miami, FL: American Art Corporation.
Bogues, Anthony. 2014c. "Curatorial Note." In *The Many Faces of Toussaint L'Ouverture and the Haitian Revolution, Featuring New Works by Renowned Artist Edouard Duval-Carrié*, 1–2. Providence, RI: Brown University Center for the Study of Slavery & Justice.
Brillat-Savarin, Jean Anthelme. 2009. *The Physiology of Taste or, Meditations on Transcendental Gastronomy*. Translated and edited by M.F.K. Fisher. Revised edition. New York: Everyman's Library.
Célius, Carlo A. 2014. "The Historical Art Traditions of Haiti." In *From Revolution in the Tropics to Imagined Landscapes: The Art of Edouard Duval-Carrié*, edited by Anthony Bogues, 10–17. Miami: Pérez Art Museum Miami.
Cosentino, Donald J. 2004. *Divine Revolution: The Art of Edouard Duval-Carrié*. Los Angeles, CA: UCLA Fowler Museum of Cultural History.
Crichlow, Michaeline A. 2009. *Globalization and the Post-Creole Imagination: Notes on Fleeing the Plantation*. Durham, NC and London: Duke University Press.
Dayan, Joan. 1998. *Haiti, History, and the Gods*. Berkeley and Los Angeles: University of California Press.
Fanon, Frantz. 2008. *Black Skin, White Masks*, translated from the French by Richard Philcox. Revised edition. New York: Grove Press.
Ferrer, Ada. 2014. *Freedom's Mirror: Cuba and Haiti in the Age of Revolution*. New York: Cambridge University Press.
Foster, Hal. 2004. "An Archival Impulse." *October* 110: 3–22.
Frothingham, Alice W. 1969. *Tile Panels of Spain, 1500–1650*. New York: The Hispanic Society of America.
Geggus, David. 2013. "Iconography." *The Changing Faces of Toussaint Louverture: Literary and Pictorial Depictions*. The John Carter Brown Library, Brown University Providence, Rhode Island. Accessed September 18, 2024. https://www.brown.edu/Facilities/John_Carter_Brown_Library/exhibitions/toussaint/pages/iconography.html
Gilroy, Paul. 1993. *The Black Atlantic: Modernity and Double Consciousness*. Cambridge, MA: Harvard University Press.
Hall, Stuart. 1996. "New Ethnicities." In *Stuart Hall: Critical Dialogues in Cultural Studies*, edited by David Morley and Kuan-Hsing Chen, 441–449. London and New York: Routledge.
Hansen, Maria Fabricius. 2000. "Maniera and the Grotesque." *Manier und Manierismus*. Tübingen: M. Niemeyer, 251–273.
Henochsberg, Simon. 2016. "Public Debt and Slavery: The Case of Haiti (1760–1915)." Thesis. Paris School of Economics.
Kimball, Fiske. 1943. *The Creation of the Rococo*. Philadelphia: Philadelphia Museum of Art.
Kriz, Kay Dian. 2008. *Slavery, Sugar, and the Culture of Refinement: Picturing the British West Indies, 1700–1840*. New Haven: Yale University Press.

Mercer, Kobena. 2005. "Introduction." In *Cosmopolitan Modernisms*, edited by Kobena Mercer, 6–23. London: Institute of International Visual Arts; Cambridge, MA: The MIT Press.

Merleaux, April. 2015. *Sugar and Civilization: American Empire and the Cultural Politics of Sweetness*. Chapel Hill: The University of North Carolina Press.

Mignolo, Walter. 2011. *The Darker Side of Western Modernity: Global Futures, Decolonial Options*. Durham, NC: Duke University Press.

Mignolo, Walter. 2012. *Local Histories/Global Designs: Coloniality, Subaltern Knowledges, and Border Thinking*. Princeton, NJ: Princeton University Press.

Mintz, Sidney. 1985. *Sweetness and Power: The Place of Sugar in Modern History*. New York: Penguin Books.

Mintz, Sidney. 1996. *Tasting Food, Tasting Freedom: Excursions into Eating, Culture, and the Past*. Boston: Beacon Press.

Mirzoeff, Nicholas. 2012. *The Right to Look: A Counterhistory of Visuality*. Durham, NC: Duke University Press.

Moraña, Mabel, Enrique Dussel, and Carlos A. Jáuregui. 2008. "Colonialism and Its Replicants." In *Coloniality at Large: Latin America and the Postcolonial Debate*, edited by Mabel Moraña, Enrique Dussel, and Carlos A. Jáuregui, 1–22. Durham, NC and London: Duke University Press.

Moreau de Saint-Méry, Médéric Louis Elie. 1797. *Description topographique, physique, civile, politique et historique de la partie française de l'isle Saint-Domingue*. Philadelphia. https://archive.org/details/descriptiontopog00more.

Nora, Pierre. 1989. "Between Memory and History: Les Lieux de Memoire." *Representations* 26: 7–24.

Ortiz, Fernando. 2003. *Cuban Counterpoint: Tobacco and Sugar*, translated from the Spanish by Harriet de Onís. Fourth Edition. New York: A.A. Knopf.

Palmer, Truman G. 1909. "The Dutch Standard of Color: Origin and Application." In *The American Sugar Industry and Beet Sugar Gazette* XI (1): 341–344.

Ray, Anthony. 2000. *Spanish Pottery 1248–1898: With a Catalogue of the Collection in the Victoria and Albert Museum*. London: V&A Publications.

Smith, Woodruff D. 1992. "Complications of the Commonplace: Tea, Sugar, and Imperialism." *The Journal of Interdisciplinary History* 23 (2): 259–278.

Stebich, Ute. 1978. *Haitian Art*. New York; The Brooklyn Museum; New York: Harry N. Abrams, Inc.

Sullivan, Edward J. 2007. "Continental Shifts: Edouard Duval Carrié and the Re- Invention of the New." In *Continental Shifts: The Art of Edouard Duval-Carrié*, edited by Edward J. Sullivan, 9–40. Miami, FL: American Art Corporation.

Sullivan, Edward J. 2014. *From San Juan to Paris and Back: Francisco Oller and Caribbean Art in the Era of Impressionism*. New Haven and London: Yale University Press.

Taussig, Michael. 1993. *Mimesis and Alterity: A Particular History of the Senses*. New York and London: Routledge.

Ward-Jackson, Peter. 1967. "Some Main Streams and Tributaries in European Ornament From 1500 to 1750: Part 1." *Victoria and Albert Museum Bulletin* III (2): 58–80.

Wolff, Lesley A. Personal interview. 14 May 2014.

Index

Note: **Bold** page numbers refer to tables; *italic* page numbers refer to figures and page numbers followed by "n" denote endnotes.

accents 55, 58, 64
adornment practices 2
African Americans 11, 40–42, 46, 63
Africa: culture 5, 6, 37, 61, 68; dress practices 1, 11; ethnicity 6, 58, 62, 68; musical cultures 10
African Canadian 63, 66, 67
Africultures 75, 80
After Bierstadt—The Landing of Columbus (2013) 129, *130*
Age of Reason 106
alkaline glazes 44
The Americans (Frank) 113–115
The Analysis of Beauty (Hogarth) 27, 29
Anderson, James *94*
Anglo-Caribbean 63
animosity 5
anonymous enslaver *2, 57, 65*
archival impulse 127–131
Arjona, Jamie 44, 46–48
art-making 15
Arts and Crafts movement 101
Auguste, Aïlo 74, 75, 82, 85
authorship 39
autonomy 97; Haitian 130; interventions 103; meaning and function 103

Bacon, Francis 25
Baldwin, Cinda K. 38, 49; *A Great and Noble Jar* 49
Barber, Francis 25
Barlet, Olivier 75
Baron, Robert 39, 43; *Creolization as Cultural Creativity* 39
baskets 90–103, *102;* coiled 90, 98; domestic 101; fanner 100; Gullah 98, 101; Lowcountry 99, 101, 102; naming 103; sewn 93, 95; sweetgrass 42, 98, 101; technologies 99; winnowing 100
Beaudry, Mary 34, 46, 47
Beckles, Hilary McD 11
Berlin, Ira 58, 68

Bible, James 42
Bickerstaff, Isaac: *The Padlock: A Comic Opera, in Two Acts* 61
Bierstadt, Albert 129, 134; *The Landing of Columbus* 129
Black Atlantic, Modernity and Double Consciousness (Gilroy) 80
Black Diaspora 12, 85
blackness 12, 19–31, 53; Britain's cultural fascination 19; as lines of beauty 24–31; London's visual signification 30
Black Rice: The African Origins of Rice Cultivation in the Americas (Carney) 92
black subjects 19, 30; and everyday life, London 20–24; proximity and visibility 28; visibility and movements of 20
Bogues, Anthony 124
Bolton, H. Carrington 49
Bolton, Linda 106
Bongie, Chris 86
Boumendil, Jacques 82, 83
Brathwaite, Kamau 75, 80
breeding 11
Brillat-Savarin, Jean Anthelme 121
British Caribbean 30
British Isles 25
British Jamaica 11, 14
British Quebec 8, 11, 55, 56
Brittian, James 62
broken English 1
Brooks, Tom 66
Brown, William 6, *7,* 8, 60, 62, 68
Brunias, Agostino 121, 127–129, 131, 133, 134; *Free Women of Color with their Servants in a Landscape* 133; *A West Indian Flower Girl and Two Other Free Women of Color* 128
Bunce Island 94
Burney, Frances: *A Busy Day* 61
A Busy Day (Burney) 61

Calfas, George 36, 37, 46
callouses of resistance 44
Campos-Pons, Maria Magdalena 121
Canada 1, 6, 8; African-ness 60; education 54; racial tolerance 53; slave minority context 63
Canadian Slavery 53, 54, 56
capital reproduction 95, 96
Cara, Ana C. 39, 43; *Creolization as Cultural Creativity* 39
Caribbean: culture 121, 124, 129; diversity 129; islands 4; visuality 123, 128, 131, 133
Caribbean Isles 25
Carney, Judith 90, 92, 93, 96, 97; *Black Rice: The African Origins of Rice Cultivation in the Americas* 92; *In the Shadow of Slavery: Africa's Botanical Legacy in the Atlantic World* 93
Carolina colony 93
Carter, Robert 58
casta paintings 14; eighteenth-century Mexico 105; Enlightenment 116; New Spain 105–112; racial terminology 14; skin color, variations 108
caste system 108, 115, 116
ceramics 44, 49
Césaire, Aimé 77
Chamoiseau, Patrick 74–78, 83–85
Chaney, Michael 38, 44, 48
Charleston 37, 41, 42
Charleston Evening Gazette 94
Chassot, Joanne 83
China 34; alkaline glazes 44; dragon kilns 13, 46
Chinien, Savrina Parevedee 76
Chonville, Claude 74, 77, 78, 83, 85
Civil War 54, 100
coiled baskets 99, 103
colonialism 19, 112, 124, 127, 129
Columbus, Christopher 129
commodity 96, 100, 132
commonness 3
The Complete Letter-Writer: or, Polite English Secretary (1778) 19
complexion 62–63
concatenation 34–50
Confiserie Sucre Noir 132
Congo Square 4–6, 8, 9; economic activity 15n5
congregation 6, 8
Cook, Lauren 34, 46, 47
Cosentino, Donald 133
creative cultural synthesis 92
Creoles 6, 9–11, 39, 62, 63, 90; enactments 43; formulations 43; inter-island slave trade 68; languages 4; poetics 40
creolization 20, 35, 74–86; concept of 1–15; creative synthesis of 91; cultural 91; definition of 4, 91; didacticism to 85–86; institutional transformation 91; linguistic 84, 91; material culture and 90–103; multilingualism 36; poetics of 44; slave burial 49; terrain of 8–12

Creolization as Cultural Creativity (Cara and Baron) 39
Crichlow, Michaeline A. 121, 131
cultural creolization 91
cultural funds of knowledge 93
culture 12; African musical 10; Euro-Canadian 8; European 8; Gullah peoples and 42; indigenous 10; material 90–103; memory 79; practices 5; preservation 5; slave 10; sugar 121–123
Curtius, Dominique 81

Dabydeen, David 20, 24–27, 29, 30; *Hogarth's Blacks* 29
Dalzell, L.B. 62
Dalzell, R.F. 62
Dambalah la Flambeau 128
Day, Greg *98*
De español y de india produce mestizo (1715) *109*
De español y de mestiza produce castizo (1715) *110*
De Groft, Aaron 39, 42; *Eloquent Vessels/Poetics of Power: The Heroic Stoneware of 'Dave the Potter'* 39
dehumanization 28, 55, 116, 118
Demerara 25–27, 30
Deslauriers, Guy 12–14, 74–86
de-territorialization 132
Diachronic Research Foundation 36
didacticism 85–86
discrimination 115, 116
docu-fiction 74; as *lieu de mémoire* 75–78; voice-over narration 86
domestic baskets 101
dragon kilns 13, 44, 46
Drake, Dave 12, 13; earthenware 34–50; inscriptions 44; *Jar* (1859) *45;* literacy 38; *Storage Jar* (1857, 1858) *41, 48*
Duchess of Queensberry 25
Dunlap, William 6, 7, 62
Dutch Color Standard 133
Duval-Carrié, Edouard 12, 14, 15, 121–134, *122, 126, 130*; *Sugar Conventions* 12, 14, 15, 121–134

earthenware 12, 34–50; Edgefield 13; mobility of 47; Pottersville 40
Eckstein, Lars 85
Eco, Umberto 36
Edgefield 12, 13, 44, 49; alkaline recipes 44; Asian kilns 36; Black population 37; pottery production 34, 38; remainder of the untranslatable 35; slave burial 49; syncretism of 50; white population 37
Edgefield Advertiser 38
Edgefield Hive 38
Edouard Duval-Carrié: Imagined Landscapes (2014) 129

eighteenth-century Anglophone Atlantic world 19–31
eighteenth-century Quebec 53–68
Eloquent Vessels/Poetics of Power: The Heroic Stoneware of 'Dave the Potter' (De Groft) 39
English (language) 1, 8, 11, 43
Enlightenment 106, 116–118
enslavement 37, 49, 56, 108, 113, 118, 132
equations of blood 106–112
ethnicities 5, 6, **67**; African origins and 58; birth origin and 64–67; complexion and 62–63
ethnic specificity 5, 68
Euro-Canadians 53
European Americans 11
European: and African musical legacies 84; clothing 2; imperialism 4, 126; powers 126
extraordinary heterogeneity 11
Ezili Dantó 134

fanner baskets 100
Fanon, Franz 129
Faulkner, William: *Go Down, Moses* 49
Fennell, Christopher 38
Ferguson, Leland G. 43
Finlay Sr., James 60
Francophone ornamentation 127
Frank, Robert 113–116; *The Americans* 113–115
Fraser, Simon 64
Free Women of Color with their Servants in a Landscape (Brunias) 133
French (language) 1, 8, 11
French West Indies 76
Fryer, Peter 19
fugitive slave advertisements 6, 8, 53–68; Canadian 13, 55; ethnicity and birth origin 64–67; excavation of 12; naming 56–62; print culture of 12; slave ethnicity and birth 13; slave sale and 1
Fuller, George: *The Quadroon* 113, *114*

Gaillard, Theodore *94*
Gainsborough, Thomas 19, 24
Gangas community 5
Gatto, Robin 76
Geechee 42, 91
Gehenna 83
gender 93, 96; labor and rice-knowledge 95; roles and relations 96
genesis 83
Georgia 61
Gerzina, Gretchen 19
Gilliland, William 60
Gill, William 64
Gilmore, Thomas 6, 8, 62
Gilroy, Paul 75, 80, 81; *Black Atlantic, Modernity and Double Consciousness* 80
Glissant, Édouard 13, 36, 37, 39, 40, 43, 44, 46, 47, 50, 75, 77, 78, 80, 82, 83, 86; *Poetics of Relation* 13, 36, 39, 43; *Poétique de la relation* 80, 83
Go Down, Moses (Faulkner) 49
Goldberg, Arthur 50
Gray, Edw. Wm *3*
A Great and Noble Jar (Baldwin) 49
Gregory, John 60
Gullah 35, 42, 91; baskets 42, 98, 101
Guthrie, Robt. M. *53*

Haiti 121; economy and culture 122; heritage 123; National Palace 128; sugar production 123; Vodou practice 121, 126
Haitian Revolution 130
Halifax Gazette 61, 63
Hall, Stuart 90
hand milling 96
Harris, Leslie M. 58
Hartman, Saidiya 118
HBO Television 74
Hemings, Sally 117
Heriot, George 9, *9,* 10; *Travels through the Canadas* 9
heterogeneity: African descent, enslaved people of 53–68; extraordinary 11, 13
Hirsch, Marianne 78
Historica Canada 54
Hogarth's Blacks (Dabydeen) 29
Hogarth, William 20, *23,* 24–30, *28*; *The Analysis of Beauty* 27, 29; *A Taste of the High Life* 23
Hounsou, Djimon 76
Huang, Kristina 12
hucksteering 11
hulling process 93
Hurston, Zora Neale 116
Hyppolite, Hector 129

iconography of empire 112–116
illicit marketplace economy 42
indigenous clothing 2
indigenous language 1, 11
indigenous peoples 1, 4, 8, 112, 116
institutional transformation 91
instrument-making 5
interconnectedness 31
inter-island slave trade 11, 68
interracial sex 106
interracial unions 107
In the Shadow of Slavery: Africa's Botanical Legacy in the Atlantic World (Carney) 93
intra-community creolization 10

Jackson, Mary 101, 102, *102*
Jamaica 58, 61–63
Jarratt, Devereux 3
Jefferson, Thomas: *Notes on the State of Virginia* 117
Jekyll, Joseph 20

Joe, in Quebec City 6–8
Johnson, Samuel 19, 25
Johnson's Dictionary 20, 24–26, 28–30
Johnston, James 57, *57*
Joseph, J.W. 40–43
Journal of American Folklore 49
Juarez, Juan Rodriguez *109, 110*
Judaism 83

Katzew, Ilona 106, 108
Klein, Rach 12–14
Klopper, Sandra 99
Knepper, Wendy 85
Kotto, Maka 76
Kozloff, Sarah 75
Kriz, Kay Dian 128
Kuhn, Jacob 1, 3, *3*

labour economy 41
Laforce, René Hippolyte 65
The Landing of Columbus (Bierstadt) 129
Landrum pottery production 38
Landrumsville *see* Pottersville
languages 4, 5, 30, 44; aesthetics and 25; skills 8
Lasser, Ethan 44, 50
Latamie, Marc 121
Latrobe, Benjamin 4, 5
La vraie histoire des Ambaglos 125–127, *126,* 133
Lawson, John 94, 96
Le discours antillais 80
Leonean, Sierra 99
Le passage du milieu 13, 74–86, *79, 81, 82*
Les anneaux de la mémoire 76
Les statues meurent aussi (1953) 77
Letters of the late Ignatius Sancho, An African (Sancho) 22
Letters of the Late Rev. Mr. Laurence Sterne to his Most Intimate Friends (Sterne) 19
Levinas, Emmanuel 106, 107, 116; *Totality and Infinity* 106
Levy, Eleazar 66
Liberia 90
lieu de mémoire 75–78, 131
Lindsay, R.W. *94*
lines of beauty, blackness and 19–31
linguistic creolization 84, 91
A List of Negroes on Hope Plantation in St. Andrews (1788) 58, *59,* 61
Littlefield, Daniel 92
London 28; blackness, visual signification of 30; black subjects 20–24; Caribbean colonies 24; cultural landscape 19; everyday life 20–24; kinetic energy of 20; marginal masses 24; sexual favors 29; social space of 20, 28
Louverture, Toussaint 129, 130
Loving v. Virginia (1967) 105, 115
Lowcountry 42, 90–103; baskets 99; culture and agriculture 92; material culture 98; rice economy 94

Mackey, Frank 55, 56, 60
Maharaj, Sarat 34
Manigault, Arthur *98*
Manigault, Mary Jane *98*
marginal masses 21, 24, 25
Marker, Chris 77
Maroon rice culture 97
Martínez, María Elena 107
Martin, Michael T. 85, 86
Martin, Sam 76
material culture 90–103, 105, 108
Mauger, Joshua 63
McCord, John 60, 66
McCusker, Maeve 78
McKittrick, Katherine 24, 28
Meheux, John 22, 23
Mémoire sans histoire 125
memorialization 75–78
Mexico 106, 118
The Middle Passage 12–14, *79;* as Afro-diasporic discourse 74–86; slave ship 80–82, *81, 82;* as visual discourse 74–75
Mi'kmaq 1, 11, 15n1, 67
Miles, Lewis 40, 42
milling: hand 96, 97; mechanical 96; mortars and pestles 93, 94, 97; rice 92, 94; technologies 96
mimesis 127–131
miniature Othello 24
Mintz, Sidney 1, 4, 5, 8, 11, 12, 14, 36, 91, 95, 96, 102, 132
Minuets of the Canadians (1807) 9, *9*
"Missions and Markets: Sea Island basketry and the Sweetgrass Revolution" (Rosengarten) 101
mixed-race identities 105–118
Molineux, Catherine 19, 21
Montreal Gazette 53, *53*
Morgan, Philip D. 61
Mosley, Walter 76
Mrozowski, Stephen A. 34, 46, 47
mulattos 108
Mulira, Sanya Ruth 44, 49
multiculturalism 53, 108
multifariousness 75
multilingualism 36
Muniz, Vik 121
"My Mother Dreams Another Country" (Trethewey) 105

Naipaul, V.S. 74
namelessness 57
naming: basket 103; complexity of 105; power of 56–62; practices 62–63
Negroes 1, 61–63

New-England 53–68
New Spain: casta paintings of 106–112; caste system of 116; colonial power 107; creole culture of 107; interracial sex 106
Niculescu, Tatiana 44, 45
Nora, Pierre 78, 131
Notes on the State of Virginia (Jefferson) 117
Nova Scotia 1, 15n1, 58; black populations 63; racial discourse 62; slave sale 63
Nova-Scotia Advertiser 63

Opala, Joseph 99
ornament, as Transatlantic bridge 124–127, *126*
Oryza glaberrima 92, 94, 97
Oryza sativa 92
Osborne, Anne 21

The Padlock: A Comic Opera, in Two Acts (Bickerstaff) 61
Palcy, Euzhan 77
peculiar institution 14
Peperzak, Adriaan 106
permissiveness, New Orleans 5
Petley, Christer 61
Pierre, André 129
placelessness, sugar 131–134
plantation 19–20, 24, 27, 39, 62, 101; Caribbean 21; colonies 90, 91; economy 96, 103; enslaver households and 5; local and regional 13; Lowcountry 91; Pottersville 37; thrust 4; tropical 4, 8
plantocracy 20
Plessy v. Ferguson (1896) 112, 113, 115
Plexiglas 122–124, 127
poetic axiom 50
Poetics of Relation (Glissant) 13, 36, 39, 43
Poétique de la relation (Glissant) 80, 83
Polinacci, Yannis 76
"The Port Royal Experiment" 100
Pottersville 12, 34, 36; enslaved laborers 46; excavation (2011) 46; plantation owners 37; potter working 46
Potts, Alex 47
power 10, 13; colonial 107, 125; cultural ideals and 20; European 126; fugitive slave advertisement 60; of naming 56–62; violence and 27
preferred styling 2
Pretchard, Azariah 1, *2,* 61, 66, 67
print technology 53
proto-creolization 14, 81, 83, 84
pug mill 38
Puro, Pascal 66
Purss, John 57, *57*

The Quadroon (Fuller) 113, *114*
Quebec 13; African-born people in 6; black populations 63; eighteenth-century 53–68; enslaved people 9; ethnicity and birth origin 64–67; fugitive slave advertisements 6, 13; racial discourse 62
Quebec Gazette 6, *7,* 55, *56, 57, 57,* 60, 62, *65*
Quebec Slavery 1, 10

racial bias 93
racialization 132
racial tolerance 53
racism 20, 113
Rediker, Marcus 13
regional origins **67**
relational meaning 99
renaming process 58
Resnais, Alain 77
rice: commodity 96; cultivation 93, 94; culture 14, 90, 93; domesticated species 92; economy 94; knowledge system 92, 94; material culture 95; milling 93, 94; religious communication 97; slavery and 92; storage and transportation 100; winnowing *98*
Rice Coast 90, 92–96
Ritchie, Hugh 66
Roger, Creole 61
Rosengarten, Dale 98–101; "Missions and Markets: Sea Island basketry and the Sweetgrass Revolution" 101
Royal Gazette 63
Rue Cases-Nègres 77
runaway slave advertisement 53, *53,* 55
Rupert, Linda M. 4, 11, 103

Saint-Just, Sophie 12–14
Samuel Augustus, Mitchell *35*
Sancho, Ignatius 12, 13, 19–25, *22,* 30; *Letters of the late Ignatius Sancho, An African* 22
Santamarin, Xiomara 42
scarification 1, 62
Schildkrout, Enid 99
"The Sea is History" (Walcott) 79, 80
self-actualization 48
self-care 2
Senegal 90
Separate Car Act 113
Service Municipal d'Action Culturelle (SERMAC) 77
sewn baskets 90, 93, 98
Shepherd, James 6
Shlensky, Lincoln Z. 40
simulacra 126, 131
skill sets 46
slave: advertisements 6, 8; burial 49; ethnicity 13; majority demographics 41; port 37; sale 58, 63
slavery 3, 4, 10, 34, 76, 84; British abolition of 55; British Quebec 55; Canadian national imagination 54; rice and 92; United States of America 54

slave ships 11, 20, 36, 74, 79, 85; as cultural "patrimony" 81; as trope 80–82, *81, 82*
slave trade 78; British abolition (1807) 62; colonialism and 19
social institutions 96, 97, 101
social justification 112
Soubise, Julius 25
South Carolina 41, 49; African Americans 42; ceramic glazes 44; clay gathering 34; Gullah 35, 42; labor cost 46; Lowcountry 90–103
Southern United States 37
Spanish creoles 107, 108, 116
Spencer, William 1
Spurr, David 107
Stadler, J.C. *9*
The Star-Apple Kingdom (Walcott) 80
Steen, Carl 44
Sterne, Laurence: *Letters of the Late Rev. Mr. Laurence Sterne to his Most Intimate Friends* 19
subjugation 108
Suchodolski, January 121, 129
sugar: Caribbean 132, 133; cultivation 123; nebulous nature 133; production 132; refinement 133; trade necessitates 133
Sugar Conventions (Duval-Carrié) 12, 14, 15, 121–134, *122;* background of 124–127, *126;* foreground 131–134; layered approach 123–124; middle ground of 127–131, *130*
Sullivan, Edward J. 124
Sumptuary laws 108
Sundance Film Festival 76
sweetgrass baskets 42, 98, 101, 103
syncretism 34–50

tambourine 10
task system 95–97
A Taste of the High Life (Hogarth) *23*
Taylor, Simon 61
Téno, Jean-Marie 76
Thompson, Robert Farris 49
Thrall (Trethewey) 14, 105–118
"The Times of the Day, Noon" (1738) 28–30
Tobin, Beth Fowkes 61
toombah/tabor *see* tambourine
Totality and Infinity (Levinas) 106
Transatlantic Slavery 4, 38, 42, 53, 54
Transatlantic Slave Trade 74, 81, 106
transcultural Haitian heritage 126

Travels through the Canadas (Heriot) 9
Trethewey, Natasha 14, 105–118; "My Mother Dreams Another Country" 105; *Thrall* 14, 105–118
Trouillot, Michel-Rolph 20
Turnbough, Gwendolyn Ann 115
Turner, John 55, *56*
Turner, Matti 14
typological classification 130

Underground Railroad (1991) 54
United States of America (USA): caste system 115, 116; Civil War 54; naming and racial categorization 105; racialized bodies of 112–116; slavery 54
"The Unity is Submarine" 80
urban enslavement 8

Valenzuela-Mendoza, Eloisa 14
Van Andel, Tinde 97
violence 107; dehumanization and 28; domestic 107; exclusion and 112; linguistic and physical 106; oppression and 134; power and 27
visual memory 78–80
Vlach, John Michael 34
voice-over narration 75, 76, 83, 85

wages of empire 105–118
Walcott, Derek 36, 75, 79; "The Sea is History" 79, 80; *The Star-Apple Kingdom* 80
Waldstreicher, David 1, 3, 55
Walker, Kara 121
Washington, George 62
Werden, Isaac 58
West Africa 90–103; coiled baskets 99; material culture 93; *Oryza glaberrima* 92; Rice Coast 92; rice milling 96
A West Indian Flower Girl and Two Other Free Women of Color (Brunias) 128
White, Graham 62
whiteness 129; hierarchization of 54
White, Shane 62
white with illumination 116–118
wig-wearing 2, 3, 11
Will, Creole 61
Williams, Francis 25
Wolff, Lesley A. 12, 14
Wood, Marcus 55
Wood, Peter 92, 103
Wynter, Sylvia 21, 24, 28